Praise for *From Reopen to Reinvent*

"Michael has been at the forefront of reimagining education for over 15 years. His work has inspired me and continues to be a beacon toward which we seek to design our solutions and transform learning worldwide. This book continues that tradition by pointing in a clear direction that all schools should strive to unleash the talents of each and every learner."

—**Sal Khan**, founder of Khan Academy

"*From Reopen to Reinvent* offers a blueprint both for what schools should be and a set of steps to help educators start moving in that direction to better support each and every student. At a time when districts could easily freeze in the face of challenges from all directions, the wisdom in the book is in helping them carve out pathways to move forward and prioritize the success of each child and family."

—**Arne Duncan**, former U.S. Secretary of Education

"The pandemic exposed serious, long-term problems in K–12 education and identified significant educational achievement gaps across this country. If ever there was a time to hold ourselves accountable for student performance and consider new strategies, it is now. As Michael Horn's book, *From Reopen to Reinvent: (Re)Creating School for Every Child*, reveals, our education system must consider new strategies that ensure that every child has the opportunity to achieve their full potential and is prepared for both work and life in the twenty-first century."

—**Margaret Spellings**, former U.S. secretary of education under President George W. Bush and president and CEO of Texas 2036

"In this book, Michael Horn has beautifully articulated a profound, insightful examination of the future of learning and a call to action for us all. He truly raises the bar of what education should look like in a post-pandemic world. Bravo!"

—**Phyllis Lockett**, CEO, LEAP Innovations

"In *From Reopen to Reinvent*, Michael Horn presents a carefully reasoned case for moving from time-denominated public education to a system of student-centered mastery. Reinforced with ample evidence, his insightful articulation of the operation and impacts of our current design is clear-eyed and pragmatic, showing that improvement is not only needed but mandatory. He offers clear and sensible ideas for building support and practice to move to a mastery system. Wide-ranging examples of schools, districts, and communities where successful adoption of mastery-based education already has been achieved provide compelling proof that we can do far better for our students, educators, and the nation."

—**Macke Raymond**, director of CREDO
at Stanford University

"The challenges facing our K–12 schools are unprecedented. In this book, Michael Horn gives a concise, compelling outline of a way forward that holds the promise of excellent education for every child."

—**Jane Swift**, president of LearnLaunch Institute and
former Massachusetts governor

"For those of us who work in education, are impacted by its outcomes, or are passionate about its possibilities, *From Reopen to Reinvent* belongs in the small, dog-eared stack of resources we keep close to hand. Michael Horn asks not for immediate, radical overhaul; rather he artfully combines research-based vision with pragmatic solution-seeking to paint a picture of achievable progress. Rich with examples, *From Reopen to Reinvent* calls for us to be curious about how schooling can benefit from the new knowledge, new tools, and new opportunities in front of us, and to let that curiosity lead us to shed old assumptions and reinvent for the sake of today's students and all we aspire for them."

—**Vicki Phillips**, CEO, National Center on Education and the Economy, and former director of education, College Ready at the Bill & Melinda Gates Foundation

"Michael Horn does not shy away from presenting bold ideas and frameworks to make learning more equitable and empowering for every student, with care and attention to how critical parent involvement and understanding are as we seek to unlock each child's potential. This book is packed with research alongside concrete strategies for implementing the ideas presented; the storytelling and examples woven throughout make it particularly compelling and powerful. At a time when being an educator feels challenging, this book is filled with a hopeful vision of what is possible and methods educators and administrators should consider as we seek to improve the education system."

—**Stacey Roshan**, math teacher and director of innovation and educational technology at Bullis School and author of *Tech with Heart: Leveraging Technology to Empower Student Voice, Ease Anxiety, & Create Compassionate Classrooms*

"Michael Horn's new book is a must-read for all true champions of public schools. COVID-19 shone a light on the many learning and equity problems that students were facing prior to the pandemic. In *From Reopen to Reinvent*, Michael shows the path forward to future success for public schools and the millions of students they educate. Through all the challenges in this tough time, Michael explores the great opportunities that exist to better educate students in a learning environment that is personalized, mastery based, and focused on the most important goal—individual student success. This book lays out how teachers, school board members, school leaders, parents, and others interested in education can come together, move forward, and embrace the opportunities available in a tough time. This is the right book at the right moment that lays out the future of learning leading to the success of our students and the nation."

—**Chip Slaven**, former executive director and CEO, National School Boards Association

"While some wring their hands about the disruption of school as we knew it, Michael Horn asks us to seize this moment to design the learning environments and experiences our children have needed and deserved all along . . . and then offers a practical guide on how to begin. Let's go!"

—**Jim Shelton**, chief impact and investment officer, Blue Meridian Partners and former deputy secretary, U.S. Department of Education

"Michael Horn's call to recreate schools so that they work for every child is particularly timely and important for our nation. Horn provides a clear pathway and action plan for school leaders, teachers, and parents to envision a different future—one that really honors and enables the individual talents and dreams of each child. A thought-provoking read with great real-life examples, this book should be essential reading for school leaders, teachers, parents, policymakers, and others who want to step up and create more opportunities for students and schools to thrive."

—**Kevin Hall**, CEO of the Charter School Growth Fund

FROM

REOPEN

TO

REINVENT

MICHAEL B. HORN

FROM

REOPEN

TO

REINVENT

(RE)CREATING SCHOOL FOR EVERY CHILD

JB JOSSEY-BASS™
A Wiley Brand

Jossey-Bass
A Wiley Imprint
111 River St, Hoboken, NJ 07030
www.josseybass.com

Jossey-Bass books and products are available through most bookstores. To contact Jossey-Bass directly, call our Customer Care Department within the U.S. at 800–956–7739, outside the U.S. at +1 317 572 3986, or fax +1 317 572 4002.

Wiley also publishes its books in a variety of electronic formats and by print-on-demand. Some material included with standard print versions of this book may not be included in e-books or in print-on-demand. If this book refers to media such as a CD or DVD that is not included in the version you purchased, you may download this material at **http://booksupport.wiley.com.** For more information about Wiley products, visit **www.wiley.com.**

Library of Congress Cataloging-in-Publication Data:

Names: Horn, Michael B., author.
Title: From reopen to reinvent : (re)creating school for every child / Michael B. Horn.
Description: Hoboken, NJ : Jossey-Bass, [2022] | Includes index.
Identifiers: LCCN 2022010314 (print) | LCCN 2022010315 (ebook) | ISBN 9781119863021 (cloth) | ISBN 9781119863496 (adobe pdf) | ISBN 9781119863502 (epub)
Subjects: LCSH: School management and organization. | Educational technology.
Classification: LCC LB2805 .H678 2022 (print) | LCC LB2805 (ebook) | DDC 371.2—dc23/eng/20220425
LC record available at https://lccn.loc.gov/2022010314
LC ebook record available at https://lccn.loc.gov/2022010315

COVER ART & DESIGN: PAUL MCCARTHY

FIRST EDITION

SKY10034026_052422

*To Madison and Kayla and the educators
who support them.*

Contents

Acknowledgments

Every book has its origin story. This book came about because of the work Diane Tavenner and I started in May of 2020 with the launch of our *Class Disrupted* podcast.

With the COVID-19 pandemic disrupting every facet of schooling, parents and educators had big questions about why our schooling system works the way it does. The podcast was a place where we could provide answers.

Diane and I had been pursuing transformational changes in education for years—me from a position of thought leadership and her from a position of starting, running, and growing an inspiring network of innovative schools. The pandemic lifted the lid on education in America—and opened many to the idea that school can work differently from how it has over the past many decades. We wanted to seize that opportunity for reinvention to benefit all students.

Three school years later, Diane and I never imagined we would still be doing our podcast, but we are. Each episode, I learn from and enjoy the time with Diane. Her imprint—in her ideas and wisdom—is on the text and structure of this book. I owe her a debt of gratitude for her insights, balance in a world of extremes, grace, empathy, and curiosity.

Steve Chaggaris, Jenna Free, Emmeline Zhao, and the rest of the team at The 74, an education news site that has hosted and distributed the podcast, played a valuable role in bringing Diane and my musings to life.

The teachings of Clayton Christensen have continued to give me a set of lenses through which I see the world. I remain not only indebted to him, but also to the Clayton Christensen Institute we cofounded. My colleagues—Julia Freeland Fisher, Ann Christensen, John Riley, Everett Poisson, Bob Moesta, Efosa Ojomo, Ruth Hartt, and many others—have all played a role in helping this book come together. I also want to single out Thomas Arnett for his help. He not only read through the manuscript and provided valuable edits and feedback, but he also allowed me to call and email him several times to continue to test new ideas and drafts.

Susan Patrick, Tom Vander Ark, Razan Roberts, Jane Swift, and the ever-formidable Gisele Huff also provided valuable input, edits, and pushback.

Many individuals provided encouragement and support as well, including Jeff Selingo, Lucy Greenslade, Jen Holleran, Biff Maier, Sarah Jamison, and Maxwell Bigman, along with the inspiring team at Guild Education, including CJ Jackson, Andrew LaCasse, Rachel Romer Carlson, Paul Freedman, Sam Olivieri, Christy Stanford, and Sveta Dawant.

Guests on our *Class Disrupted* podcast, including Evan Marwell, Larry Berger, Sal Khan, Angela Duckworth, Todd Rose, Jeff Wetzler, and Aylon Samouha, played a significant role in the shaping of the book, as did guests on my YouTube channel, including Annette Anderson, Mark Van Ryzin, Cory Henwood, Gina Meinertz, Hattie Sanness, Brigid Moriarty-Guerrero, Pete Driscoll, Macke Raymond, David Miyashiro, Ed Hidalgo, Jonathan Haber, Elizabeth Chu, Matt Bowman, Andrew Frishman, Izzy Fitzgerald, Dayvon W., Amy Anderson, Joel Rose, Amir Nathoo, Scott Ellis, Julie Young, Doug Curtin, and more.

I also want to thank my literary agents Danny Stern and Kristen Karp, as well as Paige Russell at Stern Speakers. They have been there every step of the way for me, as usual.

It's been wonderful to once again work with the team at Jossey-Bass Wiley. Thank you to Amy Fandrei, Pete Gaughan, Mary Beth Rosswurm, Ajith Kumar, Kim Wimpsett, Philo Antonie Mahendran, and Cape Cod Compositors for their help in shaping this work.

My parents were, as usual, instrumental in the book-writing process. Although I'm sure I haven't fully followed my mom's wisdom to shorten and simplify, their dedication, edits, and pushback to their son are always appreciated. I promise. My brother and bestselling author Jonathan Horn's wisdom on the publishing process was helpful as usual, as was Steven Horn's love and unflagging support.

Finally, a thank you and love to my family that, given the pandemic, has often seen me during almost every waking minute. Madison and Kayla were thrilled to provide some edits for this book—and were understanding that there were fewer pictures than in my previous one. And my wife, Tracy Kim Horn, not only once again provided valuable feedback on the manuscript, but she also heroically gave me the time and support to finish this labor of love as she worked through her own challenges. We remain fortunate with more blessings than I can count.

About the Author

Michael B. Horn strives to create a world in which all individuals can build their passions and fulfill their potential through his writing, speaking, and work with a portfolio of education organizations. He is the author of many books, including the award-winning *Disrupting Class: How Disruptive Innovation Will Change the Way the World Learns*; *Blended: Using Disruptive Innovation to Improve Schools*; *Choosing College: How to Make Better Learning Decisions Throughout Your Life*; and *Goodnight Box*, a children's story.

Michael is the cofounder of and a distinguished fellow at the Clayton Christensen Institute, a nonprofit think tank. He cohosts the popular education podcasts *Class Disrupted* and *Future U*. He also serves as an executive editor at *Education Next*.

Michael was selected as a 2014 Eisenhower Fellow to study innovation in education in Vietnam and Korea, and *Tech & Learning* magazine named him to its list of the 100 most important people in the creation and advancement of the use of technology in education. He holds a BA in history from Yale University and an MBA from the Harvard Business School.

Foreword

Fine. The word I most often hear people use to describe how their child is doing in school is "fine." And these are the people whose children are doing best in school. I believe our children, our communities, and our country need better than fine. I think most people agree. The challenge is, how do we transform schools that are "fine" for some to places that are preparing all for a good life?

I met Michael sometime around 2011, when we discovered in a public dialogue that we share a vision for what American schools can be and a disappointment in what they are. As it turned out, we also share a commitment to doing everything in our power to help schools realize a much more compelling vision.

In late March of 2020, a few weeks after working around the clock to convert all of our schools from in-person to virtual in response to the global pandemic, I had two realizations. First, closing our school buildings was the easy part. Getting back into the buildings was going to be a long and difficult process, and there would be real costs for the students. And second, given that toll, we could not waste this unprecedented opportunity to truly redesign schools to serve every student and society, which even our "best" schools simply aren't doing. The next thing I did was call Michael.

My pitch was simple. The pandemic might be a once-in-a-lifetime opportunity to transform schools (he agreed). Parents are seeing first-hand some of the significantly flawed structures and elements of schools that need changing (he really agreed as a parent). Redesigning during a crisis would be extraordinarily challenging and we should try to make it as easy as possible (he was in). As a first step, we decided to create the podcast *Class Disrupted* to surface real questions from families stemming from the pandemic chaos, ask "experts" to illuminate design principles and design advice, and then engage in real talk about what is required for schools to change.

Michael then took this joint project a step further. In this book he captures the best of those discussions and our dialogue over the past two years and combines them with additional research and insights. He has the incredible ability to take nuanced ideas and make them clear and, most importantly, implementable. His curiosity leads him to pursue understanding to a depth that is imperative for those of us who are doing the work. Over a decade ago, the book he coauthored with Clay Christensen, *Disrupting Class*, played a profound role in how we at Summit thought about redesigning our school model.

Leading and operating schools during these pandemic years is by far the most demanding and least rewarding experience I've had in my 25 years as an educator. On many days, simply keeping schools open takes every minute and all of the energy. Finding the mental space to step back and up to seize this moment, which is begging us to change, most often feels untenable, and yet imperative. It is my hope that this new book is as faithful and helpful a companion to educators, parents, and policymakers alike as Michael's previous works and weekly conversations have been for me.

Diane Tavenner
Cofounder and CEO of Summit Public Schools
Cohost of the podcast *Class Disrupted*
Author of *Prepared: What Kids Need for a Fulfilled Life*

The Story of Jeremy and Julia

Jeremy and Julia are two of the 600 students at Spruce Park Elementary School in California.

As the bus rolled in to the school parking lot at 8:30 a.m., Jeremy trudged down the stairs and outside. He yawned.

After pausing for a moment, he noticed his fellow fifth-grade classmate Julia and a couple of her friends skipping up the hill to school. Walkers, he thought. A moment of envy flashed through his mind and then passed. He waved to Julia, who smiled and waved back.

Then his stomach grumbled. He turned to walk toward the school cafeteria to grab a quick bite before the bell rang. His mom had been so tired from working the late shift at the convenience store that she hadn't had time to scrounge some breakfast together. Again.

Jeremy couldn't sort through what was worse: when his mom was laid off when the pandemic started and she moped around the house all day while he was stuck inside away from his friends, school, and reliable food, or now when she had finally decided to work again and barely saw him—but at least he could see his friends at school and eat the cafeteria food. Maybe his teacher, Mrs. Alvarez, would ask him to write about it again. He sighed.

While Jeremy scarfed down food in the cafeteria, Julia happily skipped rope with her friends as they waited for the bell to ring. She loved these precious moments with her friends before they were told to sit silently during class and before the cascade of after-school activities that greeted her each day after dismissal. She loved gymnastics, piano, soccer, and robotics, but she sometimes longed for parts of the early days of the pandemic when the whole neighborhood was outside playing games of socially distant hopscotch under the California sun.

The principal, Dr. Kathleen Ball, watched all the students arrive—bussers and walkers alike. Her gaze was pleasant as she greeted each child by name. But her mind was elsewhere, as she wondered what was worse—the chaos and confusion of the early days of the pandemic or the tormented and unsettled nature of the current school year with so many students having so many different needs and so many parents frustrated that their child's needs still weren't being met.

Things were hard at the outset of COVID—so many decisions to make, so much uncertainty, so little time.

Ball had been so proud of how her teachers banded together and came up with creative solutions. They weren't perfect. But what they put together and the speed with which they did so was better than the alternative.

The parents were so kind, understanding, and appreciative back then. They understood the stress under which she and all her teachers were operating—even as they dealt with so much at home as well.

Things were different now. Different pockets of parents had different priorities and opinions. On everything.

That had always been true, of course. But now there was less trust. Needs had gone unmet and become more severe. Parents held higher expectations that these needs would be—no, should be—met. Many displayed a lack of common courtesy.

Now in the fourth school year impacted by the pandemic, her teachers and team just didn't have the same reserves to deal with the heightened expectations. They were all just exhausted—physically *and mentally. They were overworked, and the school still struggled with staffing shortages.*

Why couldn't parent emotions be focused on something else other than being angry at teachers, Ball wondered. If she were principal of a high school, maybe she could have at least rallied parent emotions around something else, like the opposing players on other schools' sports teams. She knew that sounded better only in theory compared to her current day-to-day reality.

Introduction

In the wake of the COVID-19 pandemic shattering the routines and lives of students, parents, and educators, schools have been through so much.

In the *Boston Globe*, Sarah Carr told the story of 10-year-old "Daniel"—his middle name to protect his identity. A struggling reader who is dyslexic, Daniel had finally gotten the support he needed from his school district after six years of effort by his parents.

Yet when schools shut down in March 2020, the support stopped—the tutoring, small-group classes, and specific teaching interventions.

Daniel's heartbreaking story was far from unusual, as COVID-19 interrupted schools' operations across the world.

But schools were struggling before the pandemic as well.

Most of these challenges weren't of any one person's making, nor were they the fault of the people who work in schools today. Many of the challenges were the result of structures and processes that were designed long ago for a different age. These structures have become stuck in our world as "the grammar of schooling" or "just the way school is."

That students start kindergarten fascinated by schooling and end up bored isn't a coincidence. It's the logical outgrowth of how our schools are built. For decades, it was a successful design.

But in today's knowledge economy that prizes intellectual capital—where we need all individuals to build passions and develop their full human potential—it no longer suffices.

Amid the disaster since the pandemic's assault on society and schools over multiple school years, there is opportunity to rebuild better by altering the fundamental assumptions undergirding our present-day schooling model.

Despite my background, this isn't a book about disruptive innovation.

Nor is it a book about the devastation and disruption that the pandemic caused.

It's about what we build out of this devastation. What we choose to create.

It starts with educators.

Although there are many obstacles over which educators have little control, this is a book for administrators, teachers, and those communities involved in schools—parents and school boards—to help them reconceive what they are trying to accomplish and create a more supportive model that allows them to better serve each child. For parents frustrated with the challenges their children have faced at schools, the book presents a path forward from the pandemic.

It's also a book for policymakers and voters to help them rethink what is standing in the way of building better learning opportunities for all individuals.

The idea of this book is to shift us from seeing the pandemic as a giant threat to also viewing it as an opportunity. An opportunity to overthrow an education system that's not working as well as it could for anyone—certainly not for low-income students. Certainly not for far too many boys and girls who are judged by the color of their skin rather than for their vast potential. Nor is it working for wealthy and privileged children in our society, despite popular perception.

THE SCHOOL SYSTEM ISN'T OPTIMIZED FOR ANYONE

In a podcast called *Class Disrupted* that I started during the pandemic with Diane Tavenner, the founder of Summit Public Schools, a network of 11 schools in California and Washington State, we told two stories of fictional students to illuminate a flawed education system that treats students not as individuals but as parts of a group.

The first student we called Jeremy, an only child of a single mom who works multiple minimum-wage jobs, which leaves Jeremy home alone at many points during the day. The other student we called Julia, a student from an upper-middle-class home with lots of parental support.

In the podcast, we talked about why and how the school system doesn't work well for students like Jeremy along three dimensions: resources, curriculum, and sorting.

Resources

Today's school system assumes that children like Jeremy will have tools, resources, and opportunities—when in fact they aren't readily accessible to them.

Families with means can buy enrichment and advancement opportunities or, at the minimum, childcare. But families without these resources just have to make do—whether that means hours in front of the TV and video games, or worse. Jeremy has no access to summer camp or other chances to expand his horizons and imagine life outside of his home and immediate neighborhood. In normal years, when Jeremy returns to school in the fall, his classmates have done everything from coding to sports to arts camps. Or they've taken advanced math classes so they can get an edge when they go back to school. Jeremy has none of that.

The system also assumes that Jeremy has access to things like computers and the Internet—or even books at home to build his background knowledge across an array of subjects, which will give him the foundation to learn what his school teaches. But as we've learned during the pandemic, many families can't afford these tools and services. Even after roughly a year of trying to get all children connectivity, somewhere between 9 and 12 million students still didn't have adequate Internet at home.[1]

It's not like Jeremy's mom consciously realized she couldn't afford all these products and services. No one sent her a list. Families with means talk and network to find these opportunities. Families without struggle.

Curriculum

In life, success isn't just about the academic knowledge one masters or one's "intelligence." Those are important, but other skills and habits are also critical. After achieving a baseline of academic preparedness, many studies suggest that these other skills and habits, along with access to social networks, rise in importance.

Jeremy misses building these skills and habits because his school's curriculum doesn't adequately address them.

In many schools, things like working on projects, teaching habits of success, providing actionable feedback, and connecting students to new networks of people aren't integrated into the curriculum—or are offered only as a dessert to the traditional main meal.

By not receiving these opportunities, Jeremy misses out on many experiences that could change his life. Take habits of success, which include mindsets and behaviors like self-direction, agency, growth mindset, and executive functions,[2] to illustrate why.

Jeremy, like most of us, didn't come out of the womb as an organized human being. He hasn't learned explicit habits in the context of his academics to help him excel. Not having support to learn self-direction or executive function skills means that it may be hard for Jeremy to complete and turn in his homework each day. Unlike many of his peers, he doesn't have an adult there to remind him. That lowers his self-efficacy.

It's one thing to preach about growth mindset or grit to children, but it's a different thing to model it. Our education system does the opposite of modeling it, instead affixing labels to students, sorting them into static groups, and signaling that their effort doesn't matter.

This is because in today's system, time is held as a constant and each student's learning is variable.

Students move from concept to concept after spending a fixed number of days, weeks, or months on the subject. Educators teach, sometimes administer a test, and move students on to the next unit or body of material regardless of their results, effort, and understanding of the topic. Students typically receive feedback and results much later and only after they have progressed.

The system signals to students that it doesn't matter if you stick with something, because you'll move on either way. This approach undermines the value of perseverance and curiosity, as it does not reward students for spending more time on a topic. It also demotivates students, as many become bored when they don't have to work at topics that come easily to them or fall behind when they don't understand a building-block concept. Yet the class continues to progress, and students develop holes in their learning. This fixed-time, variable-learning system fails students.

Contrast this with a mastery-based—or competency-based[3]—learning model in which time becomes the variable and learning becomes guaranteed. Students only move fully from a concept once they demonstrate mastery of the knowledge and skills at hand. If they fail, that's fine. Failure is an integral part of the learning process. Students stay at a task, learn from the failures, and work until they demonstrate mastery. Success is guaranteed.

Mastery-based learning systematically embeds perseverance into its design. It showcases having a growth mindset, because students can improve their performance and master academic knowledge, skills, and habits of success.

Even if Jeremy's teachers talk about the importance of perseverance and growth mindset, today's system in which he's stuck doesn't reward it. It undermines it.

Similarly, by not providing timely feedback that is actionable, schools demotivate learners. Research shows that when a student receives feedback but cannot improve their performance with that feedback, it has a negative influence on student learning. Conversely, when the student *can* use the feedback, it positively impacts learning.[4] It also opens the door to more positive and personalized interactions with teachers to build trust.

Most schools also don't make a point of offering students access to new networks that help them discover new opportunities and endeavors beyond those of their immediate family and friends. Connecting students to new individuals can be life-altering. It brings students together with people who can open doors and allows them to build passions in areas about which they would never otherwise know. Introducing students to successful individuals, particularly those with whom they share commonalities, can inspire them. In life, success is often not about what you know, but who you know. There's a mountain of research to back that up.

But children like Jeremy struggle because they don't get these sorts of opportunities in school. And all too often they don't have the offerings in their own lives to compensate.

Sorting

As if this weren't bad enough, the current education system was built to rank and sort students *out* of the system at various intervals. It makes judgments about the capacity of students before they have had a fair chance to prove themselves.

The traditional grading system doesn't exist to convey what a student knows and can do. The grades are there to rank students—and sort them out of certain life paths. This didn't cripple an individual when the economy offered well-paying jobs for those who hadn't succeeded in school. But that no longer describes today's economy.

When Jeremy doesn't turn in his homework because he doesn't have a structure at home conducive to reminding him—and his school hasn't explicitly helped him develop his own self-direction and executive function skills—his grade is docked. And he can't change that because the grade is designed to label him so that schools know in which classes he should and shouldn't be enrolled.

Summative and standardized tests similarly aren't used to help students and teachers figure out how to make progress. They're used to help sort students into different pathways.

Tests aren't inherently bad. They are critical to learning. But when they are used as an autopsy on a student, as opposed to an actionable moment, they become counterproductive. If Jeremy developed a misconception in an earlier grade because he lacked the background knowledge to make sense of a concept that is critical to a new lesson he's tackling in the fifth grade, his lack of understanding will show up on a test. The implications will haunt him.

These structures of our schools are built from a historical legacy of sorting students into different careers, from factory-line workers to managers to leaders. They stem from a scarcity mentality—that there are only a few select opportunities such that we must select the few students who will benefit from them.

This zero-sum mindset—that for every winner there must be a loser—means that by age 18, before people have lived most of their lives, we have labeled the vast majority of students and signaled to many that they aren't good enough for certain pathways or that they are "below" others.

Although this might be easier administratively than the alternative, it is devastating. This overlooks talent that could be developed. And it ignores that so much of our society—like capitalism, when it works properly—is built on a positive-sum mindset. Schooling and its scarcity mindset are anomalies today.

As Todd Rose, author of *The End of Average*, told us on our *Class Disrupted* podcast, the opposite of a zero-sum game is a positive-sum one in which the pie grows larger as individuals achieve success. One of Adam Smith's central insights in the 1700s, Rose said, is that "the mercantilist idea of zero-sum economies was just fatally wrong" and that society should instead create the correct conditions in which self-interest could create positive-sum outcomes. A big benefit from moving to a positive-sum system is that instead of competing to be the best—as in a zero-sum game—you compete to be unique.

"The last thing you want to do is be competing with some other people on the exact same thing. It limits you. It limits your value," Rose said. "[Our research shows that trying to be unique] translates into much higher life satisfaction."

That's the opposite of those who compete to be their best, "in which even higher levels of achievement do not correlate with higher life satisfaction or happiness. So there's something about understanding how to compete, to be unique and achieving on that uniqueness. That matters both for personal fulfillment and the life I want to live, but also ultimately my greatest contribution to society."[5]

Competition can be good. Social comparisons can help an individual realize certain things are possible that they never otherwise would have imagined. But when we narrow the definition of life success and only rank and value people on a uniform and narrow dimension, competition is problematic. Competition is also a problem when we declare prematurely that the game is over.

That's because people don't learn in a linear way all on the same path and at the same pace. People develop at different rates. They have different strengths and weaknesses, which means they have what some call "jagged profiles." That's because students have different working memory and cognitive capacities, background knowledge, social and emotional learning states, and contexts.[6] Customizing is critical to meet this reality and help every child fulfill their human potential. It's vital that we do not sort students out of a pathway too soon.

An anecdote that played out in California several years ago shows just how flawed this system is—and how the Jeremys of the world could benefit if we would just change the assumptions.

At Santa Rita Elementary School in the Los Altos School District in California, a suburban school in an affluent area of California, a scene unfolded in 2010 not too different from scenes in schools around the country. A fifth-grade student, "Jack" (his name has been changed to protect his identity), started the year at the bottom of his class in math. He struggled to keep up and considered himself one of those kids who would just never quite "get it." In a typical school, he would have been tracked and placed in the bottom math group—because the system is built to sort, not support, students. That would have meant that he would not have taken algebra until high school, which would have negatively impacted his college and career choices.

But Jack's story took a less familiar turn. His school transformed his class into a blended-learning environment in which students not only learned in person but also used some online learning. After 70 days of using Khan Academy's online math tutorials and exercises for a portion of his math three to four days a week, Jack's learning started accelerating. He went from a student who was well below grade level to one who was working on material well above grade level.

Of importance wasn't just the use of technology to personalize Jack's learning, but that his class rejected a fundamental and implicit assumption in today's schooling model: that just because Jack started the year behind his peers, the school should judge him as a slow learner and place him in a group out of which he couldn't move. Fixed grouping of children by perceived ability as measured by point-in-time tests and grades narrows opportunities.

What blended learning looked like in Santa Rita:
https://www.youtube.com/watch?v=q7lttowsC0Y
What Santa Rita looks like today:
https://www.youtube.com/watch?v=gU6KRKHndJI

It's Not Just Bad for the Jeremys of the World

People's typical perception is that the schooling system won't change because those who come from well-off families benefit from it. Although there's some truth to that, the system doesn't work well for students from privileged backgrounds either.

For students like Julia, who has lots of resources outside of school, we leave a lot to chance. How is an elementary school student with busy parents to know what digital resources to trust or which ones are reliable or safe? Social media and search engines expose individuals to lots of questionable information.

A long summer break probably doesn't work for Julia. She crams a bunch of her interests into the break instead of spreading them throughout the year. Why is this negative? Instead of modeling a balanced lifestyle, it pits academics, athletics, arts, and other areas of passion against each other.

It also doesn't work for her busy parents as they figure out in which camps to enroll Julia and how to make the schedules work with their demanding jobs—to say nothing of the expenses and stress they incur as they try to make sure Julia won't "miss out" on any opportunity. It will also force Julia to load up on what she's doing during the school year, which creates significant stress.[7] Creating a more flexible, balanced, year-round calendar wouldn't take anything away from Julia. She and her parents could ideally still take breaks when it made sense for them. But it could improve her baseline.

That speaks to the second bucket. Although it's likely that given Julia's family background and her resources she will perform well enough in school, that doesn't mean that she finds school engaging. She's likely bored. She may be stressed soon, too. Odds are her focus will be all around "getting by," but it's unlikely she finds that school speaks to her or how she learns. Witness the numbers of second-semester seniors in high school who stop trying once they figure out which college they will be attending. It's also likely that Julia will graduate without a real sense of what she cares about or different pathways she could carve out for herself after high school ends. Even worse, many Julias graduate high school burned out and feeling like a failure after being rejected by the dozens of selective colleges to which they apply. One student we spoke to for my book *Choosing College* said he felt like he had "had a midlife crisis" after his dream school rejected him. He was 18 at the time.

This speaks to the final set of reasons why today's schooling system doesn't work for the Julias of the world. Spending her weekends doing test prep or extra math classes in the afternoons just to stay ahead in the rat race of rankings is exhausting. And it sends the unambiguous signal that schooling is a game to be won—not a pathway to help individuals prepare themselves for life. Although Julia might have the tools to play the game well, that doesn't mean it's a game worth playing. It's likely that once she enters middle school what she's really learning to do is constantly compare herself to others along a narrow set of measures. Nor is it likely that she's learning critical organizational or collaboration skills, let alone agency, self-efficacy, and self-direction. These are critical skills not to get *in* to college, but to *successfully navigate* college, the professional world, and her life. School is setting her up for a "real" midlife crisis.

A BETTER WAY FORWARD

Too often the debates around improving schooling get stuck in a zero-sum framing where for every winner there must be a loser. But the reality is that there are many more losers in our current education system than winners. By moving to a positive-sum system and a mindset of abundance rather than scarcity, we can transform that system into one that benefits both the Jeremys and the Julias of the world.

In that world, as children grow up, schools will help them discover and build their passions, understand what it takes to pursue what they want, learn how they can contribute value to society, and fulfill their human potential. Although many people are scared of change because of what they might lose, everyone has much to gain.

As schools have struggled over the past three academic years and the media has fretted about learning loss, education experts have recommended everything from summer school for all to redshirting every student. What these ideas share in common is that all students should just have more of the same type of schooling experience they've always had—a schooling experience that wasn't working.

In the years ahead, students will need personalization to meet them where they are—not just academically, but emotionally and socially as well. They will need support and help building strong relationships and networks. They will need to develop strong habits of success. We will need to think comprehensively and expansively, because if the goal is to help all students succeed in today's complex society, going back to the way things were is not an option.

That's what this book is designed to do. In the chapters ahead, we revisit many of the themes and ideas presented here in the Introduction. Unpacking them offers a way forward so that all members of society can benefit from a better, more enjoyable, and more positive schooling experience.

- Chapter 1 explains how to reframe the predicament in which educators find themselves as an opportunity, not a threat.

- Chapter 2 encourages educators to start with the end in mind—what's the purpose of schooling?

- Once the goal is defined, it's easier to work backward to make sure students develop what they need to be successful. Chapter 3 walks through a theory to help schools define their proper scope so that they can successfully fulfill their purpose.

- Against that backdrop, Chapter 4 describes what students are really trying to accomplish—and where traditional schools fall short. It asks all of us to move past the notion of learning loss.

- Chapter 5 outlines what the student experience should look like to help students accomplish their priorities. It shows why we need a system that guarantees mastery for each student.

- Chapter 6 reimagines the teaching experience with an emphasis on helping educators think about the "T" in teachers standing for "teams."

- Chapter 7 speaks to the parent experience and how to design schools and new solutions to fit into the progress that parents desire.

- Chapter 8 talks about the technology imperative in today's world and offers some tips for choosing educational software.

- Chapter 9 discusses the importance of the right culture and how to create it.

- Chapter 10 helps educators create a mindset of testing, learning, and iterating. It proposes that rather than creating a "plan" and following it blindly, educators shift to thinking about "planning" as a verb—a perpetual cycle that allows people to learn and improve.

- All of these changes described in the preceding chapters will be hard. Stakeholders will have varying levels of agreement. To bring the different strands together, Chapter 11 offers a framework to help leaders manage change when key stakeholders have varying views on the goals of schools or how to realize those outcomes.

With the havoc that COVID has caused and the challenges educators, students, and parents face, the appetite for new solutions that work for everyone will be larger than before.

* * *

To seize the moment, we will follow the fictional stories of Jeremy and Julia set in an elementary school in California at the beginning of each chapter.

KEY TAKEAWAYS

- Today's school system doesn't work well for anyone given the complex demands of today's world.

- The system assumes all students have resources that they don't; it neglects teaching them certain key skills and dispositions and connecting them to other networks of people; and it sorts them prematurely.

- Moving from a time-based system to a mastery-based one is imperative.

- Shifting from a zero-sum mindset to a positive-sum one is overdue.

- There's a way forward that can customize for different student needs and help all individuals build their passions and fulfill their human potential.

NOTES

1. Mark Lieberman, "Most Students Now Have Home Internet Access. But What About The Ones Who Don't?" *Education Week*, April 20, 2021, https://www.edweek.org/technology/most-students-now-have-home-internet-access-but-what-about-the-ones-who-dont/2021/04#:~:text=School%20districts%20are%20aware%20much%20more%20work%20needs%20to%20be%20done&text=Still%2C%20the%20report%20estimates%20between,at%20home%20for%20remote%20learning.

2. According to Prepared Parents, habits of success encompass a range of mindsets and behaviors, including attachment, stress management, self-regulation, self-awareness, empathy/relationship skills, executive functions, growth mindset, self-efficacy, sense of belonging, believing in the relevance of education, resilience, agency, academic tenacity, self-direction, curiosity, and purpose. Self-direction refers to students being able to drive forward the actions needed to achieve goals, with or without help. Agency refers to the ability of an individual to make their own decisions and act on them. Growth mindset means believing that one can become smarter; they aren't born with a fixed level of smarts. And executive function refers to the ability to concentrate, stay organized, juggle lots of things happening at once, and plan for the future. "Focus on Habits Instead of Test Scores," Prepared Parents, https://preparedparents.org/editorial/focus-on-16-habits-of-success-not-test-scores/ (accessed November 4, 2021).

3. CompetencyWorks, an initiative of the Aurora Institute, has developed an updated definition, as of 2019, of competency-based learning. Their original definition started with a question of what does "high-quality" competency-based learning, not just competency-based learning, look like? The current definition, while dropping

the "high-quality" moniker in the report, has retained that emphasis on what good practice of competency-based learning looks like. It has seven parts, which are abbreviated here:

1. Students are empowered daily to make importance decisions about their learning;
2. Assessment is meaningful and yields timely, actionable evidence;
3. Students receive timely, differentiated feedback based on their needs;
4. Students progress based on mastery, not seat time;
5. Students learn actively using different pathways and varied pacing;
6. Strategies to ensure equity for all students are embedded;
7. Rigorous, common expectations for learning (knowledge, skills, and dispositions) are explicit, transparent, measurable, and transferable.

See Eliot Levine and Susan Patrick, "What Is Competency-Based Education? An Updated Definition," Aurora Institute, 2019, https://aurora-institute.org/wp-content/uploads/what-is-competency-based-education-an-updated-definition-web.pdf.

4. Barbara Gaddy Carrio, Richard A. DeLorenzo, Wendy J. Battino, and Rick M. Schreiber, *Delivering on the Promise: The Education Revolution* (Bloomington, IN: Solution Tree Press, 2009), Kindle Locations, pp. 1624–1630.

5. "LISTEN—Class Disrupted Podcast Episode 6: Help! My Child and I Are Overwhelmed!," The 74, June 22, 2020, https://www.the74million.org/article/listen-class-disrupted-podcast-episode-6-help-my-child-and-i-are-overwhelmed/.

6. Barbara Pape, "Learner Variability Is the Rule, Not the Exception," Digital Promise Global, June 2018, https://digitalpromise.org/wp-content/uploads/2018/06/Learner-Variability-Is-The-Rule.pdf.

7. This stress is something that has been well documented and is the flip side of the challenges faced by marginalized students and families. See, for example, Alexandra Robbins, *The Overachievers: The Secret Lives of Driven Kids* (New York: Hyperion, 2007).

Chapter 1

From Threat to Opportunity

Dr. Ball slumped down at her desk after the bell rang. She couldn't help but feel like that's what the school was in: a slump.

How had it happened, though?

The summer after the pandemic started, she and the other school principals in the district, along with the central office staff, had hunkered down. They worked tirelessly to get remote learning in place and improve it in accordance with the state's mandate.

Then they worked to develop a reopening plan that would keep students and teachers safe and healthy—and able to learn—once the state started allowing people back into the buildings, which didn't happen until the spring. The team developed in-person options with rotating schedules for the students to reduce building density. They created mask rules. New air filtration systems were installed. They partnered with other districts to continue to offer a full-time virtual option for those whose parents for, whatever reason, didn't feel comfortable sending their children back in person at all. They built testing protocols, and they prioritized the most essential learning standards.

And then they detailed all their efforts in a comprehensive 70-page reopening plan that they circulated to the community. The plan had sections on everything from health, safety, and well-being to facilities and from equity and student engagement to technology. There was a section detailing plans on school personnel and staffing, professional development, and family partnerships and supports. They held several feedback sessions and iterated more.

The principals and central office staff even included a section on reimagining teaching and learning. In truth, however, Ball had always felt that that hadn't been the most urgent and immediate of their concerns—and the writing reflected that. There were a lot of buzz phrases about differentiation and equity but nothing concrete on how they would fulfill those aspirations.

The whole effort, though, had been nothing short of Herculean. To get back to normal. Whatever that was.

"Normal is good. Discuss," she muttered.

Her phone buzzed. It was a calendar alert, but it prompted a different thought. In the months after the start of the pandemic, Ball remembered how hard it had been to get in touch with some families. It had actually always been tough, if she was being honest.

But then she remembered the day in early May when she and her team stopped trying to send long emails to every parent and guardian and instead she sent a couple short text messages to the parents. She remembered how Jeremy's mom, who had never come to any school events, had texted her back within minutes.

Ball found the conversation. "Thank you," Jeremy's mom had texted her in June. "It was so nice to have heard from the school."

But then when the district sent out the 70-page plan in the fall, Ball heard nothing from Jeremy's mom. Crickets.

Why was that? Ball felt like they had been building a rapport.

She struggled to think back. Her team had been so busy. No one had any time to reach out. And then the fights with parents began. Arguments over everything, and it was all hands on deck.

But never a peep from Jeremy's mom. Jeremy didn't return to in-person school until the year after that, sometime in November. What had happened all that time?

Ball decided to text Jeremy's mom, when, seemingly out of nowhere, Julia's parents startled her by knocking on her office door.

Now here were two parents from whom she had heard plenty. She blinked her eyes, straightened her jacket, and popped up from her desk wearing her biggest smile.

How was that for a transition?, she thought. The text would have to wait.

"Mr. and Mrs. Owens. It's so nice to see you again!"

* * *

In the wake of COVID-19 shattering the traditional routines and plans of so many schools nationwide, many understandably felt a great sense of loss. Their ways of life were under assault. The threat was clear.

In response, schools' priority was safety. District and school leaders—a group that I often shorten to "schools" or "school leaders" throughout the book for brevity and simplicity—focused on how to reopen schools by digging deep into the logistics and operations to figure out how to create safe, hygienic environments for students, teachers, and staff. Schools focused on how to offer a hybrid arrangement of schooling—with a mix of in-person and online, remote opportunities. They debated whether students should rotate by attending two days a week or every other week. Could there be Saturday schooling so students could attend three days a week? They pored through the data and politics around mask wearing; would they require students to wear them? What was the latest from the CDC? What about when they were indoors versus outdoors? Could they do more schooling outdoors? What was the maximum number of students allowed inside a classroom anyway? Were there other ways to decrease the density of classrooms? Did they have to upgrade their air filtration and ventilation systems or leave the windows open all the time? And what about busing and sports?

This work was important, but it was also insufficient.

What much of the conversation missed was what should *learning* look like? That is, regardless of where students learn, how can schools innovate to move past an instructional model designed to standardize the way we teach and test that worked well for the industrial era but is a misfit for today's world?

In too many cases, schools have sought to replicate the traditional classroom in a new format. A striking 42 percent of teachers, for example, reported in a nationwide survey by the Clayton Christensen Institute that they replicated their typical day in a remote format during the pandemic.[1] Schools alternatively offered a subpar learning experience in which students, like Daniel whose story I told in the Introduction, didn't receive the supports they needed.[2]

Why have schools remained stuck? How could they move beyond just focusing on logistics to asking deeper questions about the model of learning itself?

THREAT RIGIDITY

Balancing multiple concerns amid limited resources, restrictive policies, and work contracts that often limit educators' responses helps explain some of the struggles to innovate. Research by Clark Gilbert, previously the president of Brigham Young University Pathway Worldwide and BYU-Idaho, suggests another important set of factors—as well as a pathway forward.

In Gilbert's research, he found that when there was a "discontinuous" change—an abrupt event in the environment—if an organization framed it as a threat, then it was able to marshal far more resources to meet the challenge than if it framed something as an opportunity. That means that saying that the COVID-caused disruption is an opportunity to reinvent schooling is unlikely to gain traction. This echoes the findings of Nobel Prize winners Daniel Kahneman and Amos Tversky that individuals are typically more willing to commit financial resources to something when they perceive it would otherwise result in a loss rather than a gain.

But there's a further insight.

Although framing something as a threat caused an organization to marshal the resources to tackle a challenge, it also caused organizations to respond with something called "routine rigidity," or "threat rigidity." When this happens, an organization doubles down on its existing processes or routines. That results in more top-down control; reduced experimentation—at precisely the time that an organization needs to be experimenting a lot, given the new circumstances; and a focus on an organization's existing resources, rather than questioning what else it might use to respond to the threat. When Gilbert studied this in the newspaper industry, he found that organizations that saw the Internet as a threat marshaled resources to invest in the Internet, but "most sites simply reproduced the newspaper" online.[3]

Sound familiar?

This is, in many ways, what schools did during the pandemic. Amid a flurry of headlines and studies around the learning loss of their students and questions about how schools would deliver learning online or, better yet in most cases, be able to get students back in the classroom, there was no question that schools would see the moment as a threat. Many marshaled resources to meet that threat. Most schools battened down the hatches and just sought to get things running without asking more fundamental questions around what the teaching and learning experiences should look like. They typically replicated the existing assumptions around the classroom, teaching processes, educator roles, the curriculum, content, and so forth—and merely modified them for the circumstance and modality, meaning whether they were online, in person, or in a hybrid format.

In other words, framing the pandemic as a threat has been important to marshal resources. Gilbert's research suggests that framing concerns around learning loss have been important to galvanize the unprecedented levels of federal investment into schools.

But leaving it in that threat framing created an inflexible response that was bound to traditional processes, rather than imagining what schooling could be. This isn't all that different from research that shows that it's difficult for individuals to feel curious while feeling threatened.[4]

Chapter 4 delves deeper into why a shift away from the initial framing of learning loss is important and what that should look like within schools. But Gilbert's work suggests a more generalizable, structural way to escape threat rigidity.

After defining something as a threat to muster the required resources, it's then important to shift responsibility to a new independent group that can reframe the threat as an opportunity. In this case, that opportunity is to reimagine the schooling experience. As Gilbert noted, having both a threat and opportunity framing was "hard to maintain in an environment in which operating responsibilities for the [existing organization] predominated."[5]

Another way to think of it is that if there isn't at least one person in the organization whose full-time job is to focus on the opportunity at hand and innovate, then it's no one's job. That's because the day-to-day priorities of the organization will drain energy away from any efforts to create something new and different. In other words, the urgent and immediate tasks in front of someone—even if they aren't important in the long run—will almost always drown out the important but less urgent work of long-term transformation.[6]

AUTONOMY

Exactly how independent must a group be for it to be able to reframe a threat as an opportunity, escape the gravitational pull of the existing organization, and innovate successfully? Gilbert's research highlights the benefits of an organization creating a separate entity that has ties back to the parent group for the sharing of certain resources. To calibrate more precisely what this might look like, here is a framework to help guide school leaders.

Every organization has resources, processes, and priorities.

Think of resources as being things like teachers, curriculum, classrooms, technology, books, and so forth.

Processes are ways of working together to address recurrent tasks in a consistent way. They cover everything from how teachers take attendance to how they lesson plan and teach to how the school creates its master schedule and conducts professional development.

Priorities are what an organization must accomplish.[7]

Once you understand an organization's resources, processes, and priorities, you can see what it is capable of doing—but also what it is incapable of doing. Any innovation that fits into an organization's resources, processes, and priorities will be readily adopted, but any innovation that doesn't fit neatly into all three will either be twisted and morphed to fit the organization's existing capabilities or ignored and rejected.

What's key when trying to reframe a threat as an opportunity is to create a new organization that has enough freedom to rethink a parent organization's resources, processes, and priorities. This doesn't mean that it will discard all of those things. It may very well borrow things from the parent organization, particularly resources, which are the easiest of the three to share without ruining an independent group's chances of creating something wholly new.

If total transformation is the goal, then the rule of thumb is that a leader must not allow the parent organization the ability to impose its existing resources, processes, and priorities on the autonomous group. The independent team must have the freedom to make the decisions as to what it will and won't take from the parent.[8] The more freedom it has to rethink the parent organization's processes and priorities, the greater the level of innovation possible.

That means that the leader's job is twofold: to make sure the existing entity recognizes its critical role of continuing to execute on its priorities while the new group innovates and to protect the independent team.

THE TOYOTA PRIUS

The story of how Toyota created the Prius, the first commercially successful hybrid car, shows how to bring together a group of individuals with functional expertise in a new team with the flexibility and freedom to rethink the resources and processes for building cars.[9]

Amid a flurry of interest in boosting the fuel efficiency of automobiles in the 1990s, Toyota became interested in building a hybrid automobile that would use both gas and electricity. When Toyota developed its Prius hybrid car, however, it could not use its existing functional teams and hierarchical rules of production because the hybrid constituted a completely different architecture.

Toyota had to develop new components that interfaced with each other in novel ways. The internal combustion engine had to share responsibility for powering the car with an electric motor, and each had to hand off that responsibility to the other in different circumstances. The brakes didn't just slow the car; they also needed to generate electricity. This, in turn, completely changed the role the battery played in the system. With the components performing nontraditional functions, the engineers needed to find alternative ways of integrating them into a coherent whole.

To solve these problems, Toyota pulled key people from each department and put them together as a separate team in a completely different location. Although these people brought their functional expertise to the team, their role was not to represent the interests or needs of their respective departments. Rather, their role was to use their expertise to help generate a completely different architecture for the automobile.

This separation and clarity of mission—and sense that they were creating something for the future rather than guarding against a threat of higher fuel standards—gave them the ability to trade the interests of one group against another's: to add costs in one place so they could improve performance or save cost in another; to combine certain components, eliminate others entirely, invent new ones, and so on. This team structure facilitated the creation of an elegant machine.

In contrast, most of Toyota's competitors designed their hybrid cars using their existing departmental structures and hierarchies. Their cars did not perform as well as the Prius, which had superior performance and much higher sales than did the other hybrid offerings.

Toyota kept its team intact for the second-generation Prius to refine the architecture and ensure that it knew how the pieces of the system worked with each other. As its engineers learned clearly how the system worked, they began to codify exactly how to make each component, and how each component had to interface with all other affected components. By doing so, in the next generation the engineers could design the Prius back in a new departmental structure that they could then use for other new automobiles they would create.

SOUTHERN NEW HAMPSHIRE UNIVERSITY

The logic of forming an independent team to solve a pressing problem hasn't just been borne out in industries outside education. Southern New Hampshire University has used it extensively in designing its own responses to what at first were seen as deep threats before it turned them into opportunities.

If you haven't heard of Southern New Hampshire University (SNHU), today it's one of the largest, most successful universities in the world, with over 160,000 students enrolled. But it wasn't always this way. When its current president, Paul LeBlanc, joined SNHU in 2003, it was a threatened institution. Its enrollment was declining. Its finances put the university on the brink of survival.

One interesting asset the University did have was an online offering, but it was small and not growing. With its survival at stake, it wasn't hard to make the case that investing in online learning was critical. But it was LeBlanc's move to separate the online division and create a governance structure different from the one that oversaw the brick-and-mortar campus of the University that proved critical.

With a separate organization in place, the University was able to change everything about its online division. The team first noticed that the students who were enrolling in the online programs were different from those coming to the on-ground ones. In the latter case, they were typically high school graduates looking to take the next logical step in their educational journey. In contrast, the students coming to the online programs were typically adults in the working world looking to step it up in their careers. They had had all the life experience they could handle, as LeBlanc said, and what they wanted was the most efficient pathway to gain new skills. To serve both groups well necessitated very different sets of processes.

For example, for the 18-year-old students it served, SNHU would inform them about general, basic financial aid information during their junior year of high school. Not having specifics for at least a year worked fine for both the student and the University. Any student inquiry would take weeks to resolve because there was no urgency on either side.

But for older students who had an urgency in their lives to step it up, they needed answers on financial aid right away. Their time to act was now or never. Waiting hours, let alone weeks, to respond was too late.

What had to change at SNHU? "Pretty much everything," LeBlanc told the authors of the book *Competing Against Luck*.[10] He gave the online team the ability to rethink not just SNHU's resources and processes, as in the Toyota example, but also the organization's priorities, which resulted in innovations that dramatically departed from the status quo at SNHU.

Prospective students needed quick responses to inquiries about financial aid. They also needed to know within days whether previous college courses would count as credit toward an SNHU degree. And they needed to know quickly after applying whether they were admitted—otherwise they would look somewhere else. The months-long admissions process that was routine for high school students wouldn't work online.

SNHU realized that it was not enough just to enroll students; it had to support them to and through graduation. That meant focusing on the emotional and social dimensions around a student's journey. SNHU's online school began assigning students a personal advisor, for example, who would stay in constant contact with students and pick up on red flags, in many cases even before students would.

This also changed how SNHU measured success at each step of the student journey. For example, SNHU would have formerly measured how it responded to student inquiries in terms of how many packages were mailed out. It would then wait for the interested students to call. But now SNHU Online's goal was to call a prospective student back in under 10 minutes.

The move to give the online division autonomy allowed it to see online learning not just as something to try and stave off an existential threat, but as a great opportunity for SNHU to serve the millions of working adults from around the world who need more education to improve their lives.

The team seized that opportunity. From serving roughly 500 online students in 2010, SNHU grew to serve roughly 17,000 students in 2012, 35,000 students by 2014, 60,000 in 2016, and over 130,000 by 2018. What's more, the success also helped the brick-and-mortar campus grow from roughly 2,500 students in 2010 to 3,913 students in 2018.[11]

When COVID hit, LeBlanc decided to seize the pandemic as both a threat and an opportunity. The threat to traditional brick-and-mortar campuses was clear. LeBlanc intended to use that threat as an opportunity to reinvent the collegiate brick-and-mortar experience, which in his view had been flailing for years and was increasingly out of reach and unsustainable from a financial perspective for both students and the colleges themselves.

The team at SNHU had long been convinced that there must be a way to reinvent the campus experience. The goal was still to allow students to enjoy the coming-of-age experiences that college is so good at providing, but also to leverage online, competency-based learning—in which, as explained in the Introduction, students would progress based on mastery of the material, not seat time—to create a more robust learning experience. In so doing, LeBlanc also wanted to dramatically lower the sticker price of college, a stop sign for so many who question whether college is right for them.[12] COVID allowed SNHU to accelerate and inject urgency into planning that had been underway for some time.

In April 2020, SNHU announced that all of its incoming freshmen would receive a one-time "Innovation Scholarship" that would cover their full first-year tuition. In turn, the freshmen would take all their courses online while living on campus (assuming it was open during COVID) and participating in college activities.

After the first year, SNHU's plan was to relaunch its brick-and-mortar program with a $10,000 per year price tag—a 61 percent reduction from its previous rate of $31,000 per year—and offer a program that mixed in-person with online, competency-based learning. The free first year would give faculty the opportunity to develop and test the program before relaunching the brick-and-mortar campus experience. It reopened ultimately with programs offered at two price points: one at $10,000 per year with a significant component of project-based learning and a second price point of $15,000 per year that would offer more traditional in-person instruction.[13]

To accomplish this, LeBlanc said that they pulled people from their day jobs and assigned them to the campus transformation team. The team was led by one of their deans, who was released on an interim basis from his previous responsibilities. SNHU also took its dean of students and placed her on the team full-time—and replaced her role on an interim basis. From there, SNHU added three project managers. All the roles were full-time so that the individuals could concentrate completely on the new experience, although LeBlanc recognized that some members of the team might transition ultimately back to their old jobs or to new assignments once SNHU entered full implementation mode.

The autonomy was critical so that the individuals would have the time, space, and freedom to design the new offerings—and not be weighed down with simultaneously balancing the demands of their prior jobs, which would always present themselves as more urgent and pressing given the day-to-day needs of existing students, faculty, and staff.

The pattern is straightforward. A threat galvanizes resources, but a leader must not stay in that framing. Creating an independent team to take on the threat enables the organization to reframe it as an opportunity. That allows the organization to escape a top-down, command-and-control response and reinvent the experience.

Southern New Hampshire University:
https://www.youtube.com/watch?v=MxYZgmoeluM

WHAT THIS COULD LOOK LIKE IN K–12 SCHOOLS

When talking to K–12 education leaders, this framework can feel overwhelming and even impossible. How could administrators possibly grant the required autonomy short of forming a wholly new school? That's what the Hawken School, a prestigious private school near Cleveland, did, for example, to pioneer mastery-based learning. It created a school called the Mastery School of Hawken. And it's what another prestigious private school, Lakeside School in Seattle, did to launch a new microschool, the Downtown School, at a significantly lower price point.

Is this strategy out of reach then for public schools?

No.

In K–12 schools, an autonomous team could take many forms. A superintendent could free a group of educators in a district from their day-to-day roles and task them with reimagining what they might offer. This group might function as a separate team within a school and pioneer either a new classroom model or a novel way of offering a particular subject or grade. The independent group could also exist as a school within a school, a microschool, or a learning pod. It could also create a new school entirely.

The charge might be to design a more compelling experience that focuses less on the time students are taught and more on helping each child develop character and habits of success, like agency and executive function skills; ensuring each child has a strong social, emotional, and health foundation with a reservoir of social capital; and rather than simply focusing on the teaching of academic knowledge and skills, making sure each child learns and masters those that are critical and allows them to build passions and develop their unique potential. The traditional hierarchy in a district could continue to focus on operating schools as we've known them, while this group focuses on implementing different innovations designed to give teachers and students more support.

This model suggests a new way for districts to engage with microschools and learning pods. Many districts have viewed these emergent schools as threats to the way they have always operated or things that will create inequity. But the threat–opportunity perspective helps us see that districts could reframe microschools and learning pods as something they themselves could operate to make sure that all children have deep and healthy social relationships. They could envision them as part of a mosaic of offerings so that they are able to provide an array of options that fit the different circumstances of all students and families. And they could see them as ways to offer personalized learning experiences for children's particular needs so that children don't fall behind in learning to read or doing math or in the exploration of coherent bodies of knowledge.

The key is to escape threat rigidity by arming a relatively independent team of educators absolved from their existing responsibilities. However it's done, the autonomy and focus is critical.

As Jeff Wetzler, cofounder of Transcend Education, a school design consultancy, said, "[The work is] time consuming. We have yet to find a way for this to work without some protected time and space. If you just try to jam it into the existing schedule, it just doesn't happen."

Or as Tavenner said, "School doesn't stop. Usually educators think 'I get one week to do my master visioning' in the summer and that's it."[14] That's not enough time to rethink the possibilities for an already-antiquated schooling model and view it as a true greenfield opportunity.

We dig deeper throughout the book on how to rethink schooling, but there's one final observation in Gilbert's findings worth highlighting.

In his research, an outside party wielded significant influence with each of the newspapers that moved successfully from seeing the Internet as a threat to viewing it as an opportunity and tasking an independent group to chase it. A board member, associate, or someone new to the organization would say that the newspaper must question its fundamental assumptions around what their online site and the supporting structure should look like rather than simply replicating what they already had—just online. As Gilbert wrote, "Involving outside influence when deciding how to respond to discontinuous change will increase the likelihood that managers will structurally differentiate a new venture from its parent organization."[15]

In schools, that implies that school boards and the broader community have a critical role to play in giving permission to or pushing school and district leadership to create relatively independent entities that pioneer new ways of schooling—whether those arrangements are new schools, schools within schools, microschools, or learning pods. As Gilbert wrote, "Outside influence, structural differentiation, and opportunity framing [that] combine to relax routine rigidity in a new venture" were consistently critical in times of discontinuous change.[16] Examples from real districts help show what that arrangement and sequencing can look like.

Mastery School of Hawken:
https://www.youtube.com/watch?v=LZ2Pk6TcQCU

Kettle Moraine

About 30 minutes outside Milwaukee sits the Kettle Moraine School District. A suburban school district with 11 schools that serve just under 4,000 students who hail mostly from middle- and upper-income families, the district was considered relatively high-performing, with over 80 percent of graduates enrolling in postsecondary education and training each year.

Beneath the positive results, however, there were opportunities to improve. Only 45 percent of students were completing their postsecondary programs—below the national average. With a threat identified, the district marshaled resources to address the challenge.

The district didn't maintain the threat framing. Once it had galvanized resources, it moved to create a variety of independent environments in which to personalize learning through microschools—schools within schools in this case—of no more than 180 students. Each had its own unique spin. Kettle Moraine authorized three charter schools on its high school campus and one at one of its elementary schools to help implement a mastery-based model that personalizes learning, along with seven "houses" in its middle school.

Within each learning environment, educators implemented comprehensive, data-rich learner profiles and customized learning paths for each student in which students' progress is contingent upon their performance. Its elementary micro charter school, for example, centers around projects. Students use the projects to demonstrate mastery of the required competencies. Another microschool at the high school level allows students to earn nursing and emergency medical technician certifications.

With a high degree of accountability in place, the innovations appear to be working.[17] Results on the PISA exam, the OECD's Test for Schools, would rank the district among the top countries in the world. According to *Education Week*, the students in the district's traditional high school performed as well as students in Canada, Finland, and other European countries, while its students in its charter school performed in the same ballpark as that of Singapore—the second-highest-ranking country at the time—with very high engagement in the learning.[18]

Kettle Moraine School District:
https://www.youtube.com/watch?v=GhuTgnAz6fQ

Microschool Movement

Many school districts looked upon the rapid growth of micro-schools and learning pods during the pandemic as something akin to students signing up for the Russian School of Mathematics outside of school hours. They thought it was something certain families were doing to give their children a leg up on the other students around them. They wished these new schools would disappear.

But some districts took a different perspective.

As Eric Gordon, the CEO of the Cleveland Municipal School District, said, "Suburban communities were forming pods on their own. Why shouldn't my kids have those benefits?"[19]

The district leveraged new resources by working with a variety of community organizations—the Cleveland Foundation, MyCom, Say Yes Cleveland, and United Way of Cleveland—to open 24 pods during the pandemic and serve 808 of Cleveland's most vulnerable students.[20]

Cleveland was among the 11 percent of school districts, according to a national survey by the Clayton Christensen Institute, that operated "learning hubs" in the Spring of 2021. According to the survey, 5 percent of districts intend to continue operating pods postpandemic.[21]

The Center for Reinventing Public Education worked with TNTP, a nonprofit education consultancy, to create more in-depth partnerships with six school districts that would lead to something more lasting and transformational out of the pod movement.[22]

The DeKalb County School District in Georgia, for example, is using pods to reinvent alternative schools, which serve students who have dropped out or transferred from traditional schools. Given that many alternative schools have traditionally struggled, it's a place where the district thinks pods can help make a difference.

Edgecombe County Public Schools in North Carolina launched learning hubs during the pandemic to help students connect to online classes and receive in-person support. District leaders discovered that families valued increased flexibility around where and when learning happened, so they worked with students and teachers to design a "spoke-and-hub model." Long-term, the district hopes this model will offer a new approach to school that builds stronger connections between school and community. In this more hybrid future of schooling, students would enroll in a brick-and-mortar or virtual school for the "hub" of their experience, and then elementary and middle school students would join "spokes"—or interest-based groups—for the other time. High school students would receive tutor-like support and work at paid positions or internships.

Guildford County Public Schools, which is also in North Carolina, is looking to craft school days in which high school students learn for three hours in person and then have more flexible time out of school to engage in a variety of activities, including completing assignments, working, or receiving tutoring or other enrichment opportunities. The district envisions this as part of a greater overhaul of their high schools that weren't serving many students effectively, even before COVID.[23]

Cleveland Learning Pods:
https://www.facebook.com/watch/?v=826632394829967

What If a District Doesn't Have Enough Internal Capacity?

Given scarce resources, overtaxed educators, and constrained work arrangements, many districts will not have the internal capacity to do what Kettle Moraine did.

But just because a given school or district doesn't have the time or resources itself to do this work, it doesn't mean it can't execute on these ideas—nor is it necessary to build from scratch. There are countless schools around the world that have already put in place many innovative ideas from which schools can borrow and adapt. To build the capacity to execute, schools can look to outside groups—be those unpaid community members, parents, consultants, or seasoned service providers—who can fully dedicate time to innovate.

For starters, districts can leverage the significant infusion of federal dollars from the CARES Act. Many have expressed concerns that these dollars may be used to add roles or services that are not sustainable after the funding dries up. But using the money to temporarily stand up an autonomous team like SNHU and Toyota did in order to create a lasting innovation that can roll back into and transform traditional schools is a great use of these recovery dollars.

Wetzler suggested that schools look to things like release time for teachers, after school and summers for intense design sprints, and the use of outside support that can do everything from facilitating design sessions, synthesizing research, or operating as a project manager.

As his cofounder at Transcend Education, Aylon Samouha, said:

> In other industries it's worth remembering that that protected time and space for R&D is often not put on the practitioners themselves while they do their jobs. Doctors who were on the front lines of the COVID pandemic were not charged with coming up with the vaccine.

To bring capacity to the table, one approach, according to Samouha, is for an outside group to help a team from a school or district brainstorm for an hour. Even if the team doesn't have the ability to devote hours to the follow-on work, if an outside consultant can do 15 hours of work after the session, then a district starts to get the kind of capacity it needs to fully seize these design efforts as opportunities, rather than remain frozen in place by the threat of what it could otherwise represent.[24]

Spring Grove Public Schools, a small school district of about 370 students in southeast Minnesota in a town of about 1,200 people, has just one school for all of its K–12 students. Yet it was able to execute significant innovations during the pandemic. One key to its success has been having outside support in the form of a consulting firm, Longview Education, that was there to do everything from compiling research around different design options to helping connect strands of work across the school into something larger and more transformational.

Similarly, microschool providers like MyTechHigh and Prenda Learning partner with districts and schooling systems to help them quickly stand up learning pods with curriculum and teacher support. Prenda Learning, for example, creates groups of five to 10 students in grades K–8. Its enrollments quadrupled during the first year of the pandemic. MyTechHigh, which partners with public schools to offer a full curriculum for K–12 learners at no cost to families, experienced similar rapid growth. As of September 2021, it served more than 18,000 students across seven states—Utah, Colorado, Idaho, Arizona, Wyoming, Indiana, and Tennessee. Some of its more robust partnerships range from the Tooele County School District in Utah to the Vilas School District in Colorado and from the Oneida School District in Idaho to Putnam County Schools in Tennessee and Cloverdale Community Schools in Indiana.

Likewise, there are a multitude of providers that can help stand up full-time virtual schools—or hybrid variations—like Arizona

State University Prep Digital, Stride, or Connections Education—or individual courses with teachers, like those just mentioned plus Outschool, Florida Virtual School, Edmentum, New Hampshire Virtual Learning Academy Charter School, and others.

Spring Grove Public Schools:
https://www.youtube.com/watch?v=E6A_Is6JuCU

MyTechHigh:
https://www.youtube.com/watch?v=u9iYz4njgdE

Prenda Learning:
https://www.youtube.com/watch?v=hZPWw0wojlw

---

* * *

The threat of COVID is no longer new. Early on, schools and policymakers did a good job of marshalling resources. Without the initial threat framing, the massive infusion of federal and local resources and attention would have been impossible. COVID aside, there are many discontinuous changes that educators can frame as threats to seek greater resources, from a specific challenging situation to a new education innovation that has appeared in schools or a changing reality in society or the region.

But framing something as a threat is insufficient. If the goal is to better serve all students, then schools must create an independent team that can shift from seeing the situation as a threat to viewing it as an opportunity. Then this autonomous group will be able to rethink the resources, processes, and priorities of schooling to chase that opportunity. What schools should bear in mind as they do so is where our tale takes us next.

KEY TAKEAWAYS

- When something occurs that will negatively impact schools, framing it as a threat is critical to marshal resources and tackle the threat.

- Leaving it in that threat framing, however, leads to "threat rigidity" and a "top-down, command-and-control" response, rather than innovation.

- To reframe the threat as an opportunity to innovate and reinvent, it's necessary to create an independent group. The key measures of independence revolve around resources, processes, and priorities. Team members must not be weighed down by the responsibilities of their prior job.

- Schools and districts can set up an independent group by establishing a school within a school, a separate classroom model or band of teachers, a microschool or learning pod, or a new school.

- Even if a district or school doesn't have enough internal capacity to execute on this set of ideas, there are other strategies that leverage external resources.

NOTES

1. Thomas Arnett, "Breaking the Mold: How a Global Pandemic Unlocks Innovation in K–12 Instruction," Clayton Christensen Institute, January 2021, https://www.christenseninstitute.org/wp-content/uploads/2021/01/BL-Survey-1.07.21.pdf.

2. Sarah Carr, "For Schoolchildren Struggling to Read, COVID-19 Has Been a Wrecking Ball," *Boston Globe*, January 19, 2021, https://www.bostonglobe.com/2021/01/19/magazine/schoolchildren-struggling-read-covid-19-has-been-wrecking-ball/?p1=StaffPage.

3. Clark Gilbert, "Unbundling the Structure of Inertia: Resource versus Routine Rigidity," *Academy of Management Journal* 48, no. 5 (October 1, 2005), https://journals.aom.org/doi/10.5465/amj.2005.18803920.

4. Amanda Ripley, "Complicating the Narratives," *Solutions Journalism*, June 27, 2018, https://thewholestory.solutionsjournalism.org/complicating-the-narratives-b91ea06ddf63 (updated January 11, 2019).

5. Gilbert, "Unbundling the Structure of Inertia."

6. Stephen Covey, *The 7 Habits of Highly Effective People* (Miami, FL: Mango, 2017), p. 206.

7. A more complete rendering of this idea showcases that organizations have four components that make up their core operating model–their value proposition, resources, processes, and revenue formula—how they bring in dollars to support their resources and processes, which allow them to deliver on their value proposition. Although it would be ideal for educators to also be able to revisit their revenue formula and focus on models that don't just allocate money based on the number of students who enroll and/or show up to class in the form of average daily attendance or other such measures of seat time and instead paid some portion for the actual learning progress students made, the ability to directly create these models is not one most public schools possess. There are experiments along these lines—like New Hampshire's Virtual Learning Academy Charter School (VLACS)—but it is largely the exception that proves the rule.

8. Scott D. Anthony, Clark Gilbert, and Mark W. Johnson, *Dual Transformation: How to Reposition Today's Business While Creating the Future* (Boston, MA: Harvard Business Review Press, 2017). In Chapter 4, the authors describe the concept of a "capabilities link," which connects the efforts of the autonomous group to the parent. The link should contain three things: capabilities that will help the new, transformational effort but not burden it; a way to manage interferences through clear decision rules; and a leader there to protect the new group and arbitrate disagreements.

9. To be clear, the team designing the Prius didn't have the freedom to rethink Toyota's priorities, so the result was still a car for which they were able to charge higher prices than their traditional automobiles. In other research, we call this a heavyweight team.

10. Clayton M. Christensen, Taddy Hall, Karen Dillon, and David S. Duncan, *Competing Against Luck: The Story of Innovation and Customer Choice* (New York: HarperCollins, 2016), pp. 50–56, 156.

11. Bob Moesta with Greg Engle, *Demand-Side Sales 101* (Carson City, NV: Lioncrest, 2020), p. 54.

12. According to the National Center for Education Statistics, college enrollment rates rise for those who believe their family can afford college. "College Affordability Views and College Enrollment," U.S. Department of Education National Center for Education Statistics, January 2022, https://nces.ed.gov/pubs2022/2022057/index.asp? utm_medium=email&_hsmi=200841088&_hsenc=p2ANqtz-8XW SHcWPCXwpBBo6TQE0JP60FrQYbAtC07jTTOoPniZbEUOL8J YNMtnwcJpk8rD5Pj6rFgsDuJrDs82eeZQutd-XDr6g&utm _content=200841088&utm_source=hs_email.

13. Natalie Schwartz, "Southern New Hampshire Sets Annual Tuition at $10K and $15K for In-Person Degrees," Higher Ed Dive, December 16, 2020, https://www.highereddive.com/news/southern- new-hampshire-sets-annual-tuition-at-10k-and-15k-for-in- person-d/592310/.

14. "Transcending Today's Schools through Design," *Class Disrupted*, Season 2, Episode 16, April 6, 2021, https://classdisrupted.word- press.com/2021/04/06/season-2-episode-16-transcending-todays- schools-through-design/.

15. Gilbert, "Unbundling the Structure of Inertia: Resource versus Routine Rigidity."

16. Ibid.

17. Across the schools, Kettle Moraine has embraced interdisciplinary learning and a focus on developing students' ability to drive their learning, communicate, collaborate, think creatively and critically as they work through academic content, engage actively as a citi- zen, and be resilient.

18. Kettle Moraine School District, GreatSchools.org, https://www .greatschools.org/wisconsin/wales/kettle-moraine-school-district/ #students, accessed August 9, 2021. Learning Without Boundaries, Kettle Moraine School District, https://www.kmsd.edu/domain/479, Accessed August 5, 2021. Chris Sturgis, "Kettle Moraine: How They Got Here and Where They Are Going," *CompetencyWorks* blog, December 4, 2017, https://aurora-institute.org/cw_post/kettle- moraine-how-they-got-here-and-where-they-are-going/. Michele Molnar, "Personalized Learning in Practice: How a Risk-Taker Tailored Learning in Her District," *Education Week*, February 22,

2017. https://www.edweek.org/leaders/2017/personalized-learning-in-practice-how-a-risk-taker-tailored-learning-in-her-district.

19. Michael B. Horn, "Schools Squandered Virtual Learning," *Education Next* 21, no. 3 (Spring 2021).

20. Michael B. Horn, "Some Pods Will Outlast the Pandemic," *Education Next* 21, no. 4 (Fall 2021), https://www.educationnext .org/some-pods-will-outlast-pandemic-students-parents-appreciate-support/.

21. Thomas Arnett, "Carpe Diem: Convert Pandemic Struggles into Student-Centered Learning," Clayton Christensen Institute, August 2021.

22. "We Will Never Return Back to the Old Normal: District- and Community-Driven Learning Pods," Center for Reinventing Public Education, https://www.crpe.org/current-research/community-of-practice (accessed November 13, 2021).

23. Horn, "Some Pods Will Outlast the Pandemic."

24. "Transcending Today's Schools through Design," *Class Disrupted*.

Chapter 2

Begin with the End: What's the Purpose of Schooling?

Julia's parents didn't match Dr. Ball's smile. From the looks of it, they were in no mood for pleasantries.

Par for the course, Ball thought.

Mrs. Owens started talking first. "Hi, Dr. Ball. Thanks for seeing us on such short notice."

"Of course," Ball said. "Have a seat. What's on your mind?"

"It's been a year since Julia got vaccinated. You think normal would have returned by now, but we're still hearing stories of fights on the playground from Julia. She's scared sometimes to go outside after lunch. That's not normal," Mrs. Owens said.

Ball nodded. Mrs. Owens wasn't wrong. The return from the time at home had created a lot of challenges that schools hadn't been prepared to meet. She chose not to say anything or defend the school. Five years in the job had trained her to listen and affirm.

Meanwhile, Mr. Owens twisted in his seat. His lips were pursed. Then he unloaded.

"How are you going to ever get the kids back on track, Dr. Ball? I'm hearing stories from my colleagues whose children go to Bradley Mountain Elementary. Their kids are already doing work light years ahead of where Julia is in her classes. I'm thinking of starting Julia on some educational software again in the evenings, but I can't even figure out what you all are trying to prepare Julia for here. Things feel all over the map."

"And what about helping the children be kind and stop all this fighting?" Mrs. Owens chimed in.

"It's a good question. I can barely make sure all the children are fed properly and have the right glasses to read books clearly. And some young scholars clearly have extra energy they need a way to channel," Ball said.

She instantly regretted speaking. Her jumbled thoughts of self-pity did her no favors.

Mrs. Owens glared at her. Mr. Owens' mouth hung open. They both folded their arms. Then Mrs. Owens broke the silence.

"I have no idea how these things are our problems. But I do know that Julia seems really interested in robotics these days. Maybe she could do that during recess?"

"Or you could at least get the basics right so she doesn't fall so far behind the kids in the other schools," Mr. Owens said. "She's just gotta keep up or else it'll come back to bite her in middle school."

Julia's parents kept throwing a torrent of ideas and conflicting thoughts at Ball. It was hard to make sense of them all, but it did prompt a question in her mind: What were Ball's hopes and dreams for the children at Spruce Peak? Did her teachers agree? What about the parents? Heck, did she even agree with herself? It seemed the Owens weren't on the same page as each other.

* * *

What's the purpose of schooling?

Even though it may seem like a straightforward question, once you scratch the surface, it's anything but. There are countless views on the topic.

Lists of things schools should do—or have historically done, for better or worse—grow long. Things like convey knowledge; ensure learning; sort students; build citizens; prepare learners for employment; focus on skills; teach children to interact with others and socialize; educate the whole child; help students become independent thinkers; and many more.

Clarifying priorities is challenging. Making trade-offs is tough.

Different communities and pockets of parents hold different opinions, points of emphasis, and priorities based on their specific circumstances.[1] Chapter 7 explores what parents want from schools, but, suffice to say, parents don't always agree with what educators think—nor do educators always agree with each other. Policymakers have their own sets of views that often clash.

Many schools struggle because there is a lack of coherence amid competing priorities. Chapter 11 offers a framework to help leaders understand which tools will help them when there isn't agreement on the goals of a school, which is a common occurrence and thus a critical topic.

But schools also often suffer because there is a lack of clarity about what they are trying to accomplish. There are unspoken assumptions about what schools are trying to do. Unstated goals lie embedded implicitly in policies, regulations, structures, and practices formed long ago.

Addressing the purpose of school in each community is critical.

A BRIEF HISTORY OF THE PURPOSE OF SCHOOLING

The primary policy rationale for public schools' purpose has changed over time.[2] In *Disrupting Class*, Clayton Christensen,

Curtis Johnson, and I offered an overview of these shifts.[3] Here's a brief summary.

Through much of the 1800s, a kind reading of history would say that the central role of public schools was to preserve the American democracy and inculcate democratic values.[4]

In the 1890s and early 1900s, competition with a fast-rising industrial Germany constituted a mini-crisis. The country shifted by creating a new role for public schools: to prepare everyone for vocations. That meant providing something for everyone, with a flourishing of tracks and courses and increased enrollment in high school, which in 1905 just one-third of children who enrolled in first grade ever attended.

Another purpose was added to America's schools in the late 1970s and early 1980s: keeping the country competitive. Although this one had echoes of the prior purpose, it was different, as the nation became consumed by how students were doing in school as measured through average test scores. The vast choices that students had in a "cafeteria style curriculum," the landmark report "A Nation at Risk" noted, was one "in which the appetizers and desserts can easily be mistaken for the main courses."[5] Having something for everyone, in other words, was no longer a virtue. It was a vice.

Just 20 years later, the primary purpose shifted again. This time society asked schools to eliminate poverty by not just focusing on schools' average test scores, but instead to make sure that children in every demographic reached a basic measure of proficiency in core subjects. The theory of action was that academic achievement unlocked opportunity.

As that consensus has eroded in recent years, there has been some drift in the primary purpose of schooling from a political perspective. Given that erosion, clarifying an individual school's purpose is perhaps now an even more vital conversation to have to build a coherent school model.

THE IMPORTANCE OF BEGINNING WITH THE END

Without clarity around purpose, educators are often caught in what famed author Stephen Covey called "the activity trap"— working harder at the things schools do just because they are the things they do, not because they are the most important things.

In one of the best-selling nonfiction books of all time, *The 7 Habits of Highly Effective People,* Covey wrote how beginning with the end in mind is critical. Without a clear understanding of your destination, you won't know if the steps you're taking are headed in the right direction. "People often find themselves achieving victories that are empty, successes that have come at the expense of things they suddenly realize were far more valuable," Covey said.

Covey's basic argument is that "all things are created twice." The first step is to create something in the mind. Then there's the physical act of creating something to make it real. If you haven't thought through what you want a school to do up-front, then it's easy to let past habits and inertia shape what schools accomplish by default.

If famed leadership and management scholars Peter Drucker and Warren Bennis are correct that "management is doing things right; leadership is doing the right things," then management is all about executing, but leadership is about clarifying purpose and priorities, Covey argued in his book. To be clear, this can and should be an iterative and emergent process based on putting something into action, learning, and adjusting course. We talk a bit more about that in Chapter 10. But not deliberating about the end reduces educators to "straightening deck chairs on the *Titanic*," but not ensuring that the ship isn't simply headed down.[6]

As Grant Wiggins and Jay McTighe wrote in the context of education in *Understanding by Design,*[7] good teachers start with the goals and how they would know if students have met them. They then backward map all the things they need to provide to get to those outcomes. The same is true for good schools.

AN OPPORTUNITY TO CLARIFY PURPOSE

In line with the previous chapter, the pandemic isn't just a threat. It has created an opportunity to have a conversation within individual communities to clarify the purpose of schooling. Many communities are ready for and having this conversation.

Starting in March of 2020, phrases that were considered educational jargon became mainstream in the public conversation about schools. Things like remote learning, virtual learning, online learning, learning loss, hybrid learning, asynchronous and synchronous learning, microschools, and learning pods, as well as questions around what gets taught—like Critical Race Theory—entered the popular verbiage (see Figure 2.1).

Many of the educators with whom I speak aren't thrilled that many of these phrases have become central. They wish we were having conversations about things like social-emotional learning, active learning, mastery-based learning, habits of success, personalizing learning, relationships, agency, skills, supporting the whole child, knowledge, character, lifelong learning, civics, and more.

Figure 2.1 Today's educational jargon

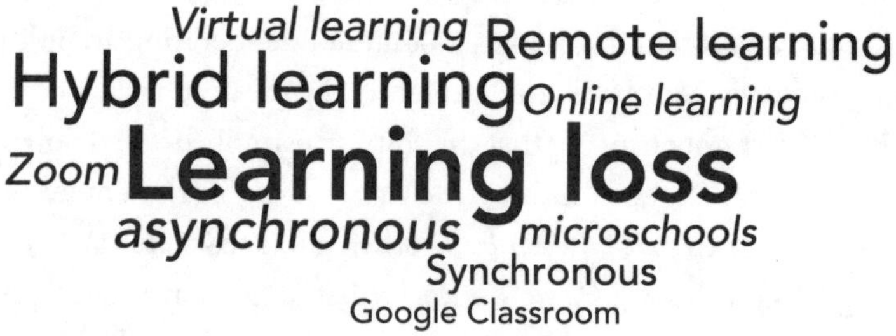

But by making education front and center in many parents' minds and creating radical transparency into what their children were doing every day, the pandemic has created broader and deeper interest in a conversation for which many educators have been clamoring: the purpose of school and how to prepare all students to achieve lifelong success.

That's an opportunity to seize because where there are questions, there is space for answers and solutions.

Without having a conversation to make the purpose explicit—and be clear about people's real differences—it's likely that many schools will return to how they operated prior to the pandemic when they didn't serve large swaths of the population well.

Although there may be a high-level consensus across communities on the purpose of school, there may also be differences—some small and nuanced and others dramatic. That's okay as long as the differences don't result in reduced expectations for certain students just because of their zip code or background. Having different purposes is part of a robust pluralism underlying our democracy that values the fact that students sit in different circumstances and have different needs. Clarity in each schooling community, however, is critical.

A STARTING POINT FOR THE PURPOSE CONVERSATION

Schools can tackle this work in different ways. The "tools of cooperation" framework that Chapter 11 explores shows that when a school community doesn't have alignment around what it wants or how to get there, public school leaders are limited in the tools they can use to create forward progress and change. If leaders can help stakeholders rally around a shared vision for the purpose of schooling, then they will have more tools from which they can draw.

One way to create a shared vision is to engage in the common exercise of constructing a portrait of a graduate.[8] The idea is to sketch what an individual entering the world in some number of years would need to be prepared to lead a choice-filled and civically engaged life.

When I have mentioned the importance of doing this sort of work, some have pushed back. They have said that starting with a blank slate when so many educators and school communities have already done great work on the portrait of a graduate exercise seems like reinventing the wheel—often in the name of a purposeless local control. This can be true. Yet going through the process is valuable. It can create consensus and clarify genuine differences in viewpoints.

Although the headlines from such an exercise may be roughly the same, the nuances and what it will specifically take to fulfill a school's purpose will differ. That's why it's critical to not just make high-level statements about a school's purpose, but also to make clear how you would know if your school was successful in this pursuit. What are the goals and how would you measure them? Yes, government agencies require that public schools measure certain outcomes, but schools should also figure out what's important to them and then identify specific metrics to indicate whether they are on the right track. Specificity and clarity are important.

To this point, this is a conversation that shouldn't just happen at the individual school level. It's one that should happen at all different levels, from states to districts and from charter management organizations to individual schools. Public educators are quick to point out that their autonomy is limited because of regulations that mandate they teach certain subjects, standards, and courses. Even in states that have created pathways for mastery-based, or competency-based, learning, they still often require that students take certain numbers of course credits in different subjects, for example. In many cases, portraits of a graduate at a state level are more aspirational than actionable. Still, the conversation is an important start to clarifying the destination.

Utah

Many states are undertaking these conversations. Utah, for example, approved its "Portrait of a Graduate" model almost a year before the pandemic in May of 2019. The resulting Utah Talent MAP, which stands for "Mastery, Autonomy, Purpose," identifies the "ideal characteristics of a Utah graduate after going through the K–12 system."[9]

In the category of mastery, the characteristics cover academic mastery; wellness—or the development of self-awareness and knowledge to maintain a healthy lifestyle physically, mentally, socially, and emotionally; civic, financial, and economic literacy; and digital literacy.

Autonomy, which refers to having the "self-confidence and motivation to think and act independently," includes the skill areas of communication, critical thinking and problem solving, creativity and innovation, and collaboration and teamwork.

The last category is purpose. It's about helping individuals guide their life decisions, craft goals, shape their direction, and create meaning. The characteristics include honesty, integrity and responsibility, hard work and resilience, lifelong learning and personal growth, service, and respect.

Utah isn't telling individual schools and districts to just adopt its portrait of a graduate.[10] The state is instead encouraging schools and districts to use its model as a jumping-off point to develop their own portraits,[11] much as Juab School District in Utah did to craft its own portrait, which revolves around the knowledge, skills, and dispositions students should have to be able to successfully navigate the world after graduation.[12] You can check out many other portraits of a graduate that states, districts, and schools have constructed at portraitofagraduate.org.

Grosse Pointe Academy

The Grosse Pointe Academy in Michigan undertook this work during the pandemic and arrived at the purpose illustrated in Figure 2.2. You'll see some familiar themes—objectives around

Figure 2.2 Purpose

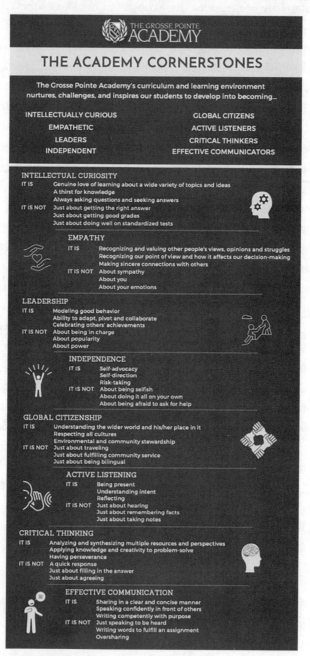

THE GROSSE POINTE
ACADEMY

THE ACADEMY CORNERSTONES

The Grosse Pointe Academy's curriculum and learning environment
nurtures, challenges, and inspires our students to develop into becoming...

INTELLECTUALLY CURIOUS	GLOBAL CITIZENS
EMPATHETIC	ACTIVE LISTENERS
LEADERS	CRITICAL THINKERS
INDEPENDENT	EFFECTIVE COMMUNICATORS

INTELLECTUAL CURIOSITY
IT IS — Genuine love of learning about a wide variety of topics and ideas
A thirst for knowledge
Always asking questions and seeking answers
IT IS NOT — Just about getting the right answer
Just about getting good grades
Just about doing well on standardized tests

EMPATHY
IT IS — Recognizing and valuing other people's views, opinions and struggles
Recognizing our point of view and how it affects our decision-making
Making sincere connections with others
IT IS NOT — About sympathy
About you
About your emotions

LEADERSHIP
IT IS — Modeling good behavior
Ability to adapt, pivot and collaborate
Celebrating others' achievements
IT IS NOT — About being in charge
About popularity
About power

INDEPENDENCE
IT IS — Self-advocacy
Self-direction
Risk-taking
IT IS NOT — About being selfish
About doing it all on your own
About being afraid to ask for help

GLOBAL CITIZENSHIP
IT IS — Understanding the wider world and his/her place in it
Respecting all cultures
Environmental and community stewardship
IT IS NOT — Just about traveling
Just about fulfilling community service
Just about being bilingual

ACTIVE LISTENING
IT IS — Being present
Understanding intent
Reflecting
IT IS NOT — Just about hearing
Just about remembering facts
Just about taking notes

CRITICAL THINKING
IT IS — Analyzing and synthesizing multiple resources and perspectives
Applying knowledge and creativity to problem-solve
Having perseverance
IT IS NOT — A quick response
Just about filling in the answer
Just about agreeing

EFFECTIVE COMMUNICATION
IT IS — Sharing in a clear and concise manner
Speaking confidently in front of others
Writing competently with purpose
IT IS NOT — Just speaking to be heard
Writing words to fulfill an assignment
Oversharing

Source: Courtesy of the Grosse Pointe Academy.

creating intellectually curious graduates who are empathetic and active listeners capable of thinking critically.

Maybe most important, though, is that the school didn't just lay out platitudes for what it wants its graduates to be able to do in the future. For each area, it also clarified what those phrases didn't mean so that there was greater clarity and less room for misinterpretation. For example, global citizenship is about "understanding the wider world and his/her place in it, respecting all cultures, and environmental and community stewardship." It's not just about traveling, fulfilling community service, or being bilingual.

Grosse Pointe Academy:
https://www.youtube.com/watch?v=-ALGjCrcYtc

My Take

At a high level, I contend that the purpose of K–12 schools is to help students become individuals prepared to:

- Maximize their human potential;
- Discover their purpose;[13]
- Build their passions and lead choice-filled lives;
- Participate civically in a vibrant democracy as thoughtful, informed citizens capable of acting through the proper levers of society;
- Contribute meaningfully to the world and the economy; and
- Understand that people can see things differently—and that those differences merit respect rather than persecution.

I hold this view based on my reading of what it takes for students to be prepared to lead successful lives—as they define success—in our complex world. But my take isn't what's important here. What's important is having that conversation in your community.

Once you have defined the end, the next step is to state how you would know if your school was successful so the school can learn and improve. What are the metrics that allow you to know if the school is fulfilling its purpose, and how will you measure them?

After you have done that, then you can start to think about the scope of activities it will take to get your graduates there. That's the topic of the next chapter.

KEY TAKEAWAYS

- The purpose of schooling isn't a straightforward topic.
- Schools suffer when they don't clarify the purpose as they seek to balance different priorities or struggle because of a lack of clarity.
- Beginning with the end—defining the destination—is imperative for each schooling community.
- Constructing a portrait of a graduate can be a powerful way to enter this conversation at a state, district, and school level.

NOTES

1. For a sample of the different views that parents prioritize as being the main purpose of schooling, see "National Tracking Poll #210362 Crosstabulation Results," Morning Consult and EdChoice, March 11–23, 2021, https://edchoice.morningconsultintelligence.com/assets/140102.pdf, pp. 16–43.
2. There are sometimes disagreements over that history.
3. Clayton M. Christensen, Michael B. Horn, and Curtis W. Johnson, *Disrupting Class: How Disruptive Innovation Will Change the Way the World Learns* (New York: McGraw-Hill, 2008), Chapter 2.

4. Some of these desires were fueled by racist, xenophobic, and anti-Catholic sentiments, for example.

5. "A Nation at Risk: The Imperative for Educational Reform," United States National Commission on Excellence in Education, 1983.

6. Stephen R. Covey, *The 7 Habits of Highly Effective People: Powerful Lessons in Personal Change* (Miami, FL: Mango, 2017), pp. 131–138.

7. Grant Wiggins and Jay McTighe, *Understanding by Design*, 2nd ed. (Alexandria, VA: Association for Supervision and Curriculum Development, 2005).

8. See, for example, "Portrait of a Graduate," Battelle for Kids, https://portraitofagraduate.org/.

9. "Utah Talent Mastery Autonomy Purpose," Utah State Board of Education, https://schools.utah.gov/file/bccb96eb-e6a6-47cf-9745-cf311675ad8b.

10. The Utah State Board of Education is working to implement competencies around the characteristics. Toward that end, Utah has broken down the competencies underlying the characteristics at different grade spans. "Utah Portrait of a Graduate Competencies," Utah State Board of Education, September 22, 2021, https://schools.utah.gov/file/4b9d1341-ddaa-47bc-8052-f029e794d513.

11. "Board Approves Statewide 'Portrait of a Graduate' Model," Utah State Board of Education, May 2, 2019, https://schools.utah.gov/file/91dfa870-3b06-4ef5-a60a-c1c02079595e.

12. "Portrait of a Graduate," Juab School District, https://www.juabsd.org/33-jsd/dgi/3404-board-approves-portrait-of-a-graduate.html.

13. The notion of purpose can feel like a grand exercise in self-importance and the stuff people talk only about in Ivory Towers, uppity cocktail parties, and professional sports. But it does not have to be abstract, grand, or erudite (yes, we just used that word). The point is to understand what you want to prioritize and make sure you will not live in violation of any deeply held values. This will also help you know what to prioritize when you need to make trade-offs between the things that you want more of in your life that you identified. Purpose can also be dynamic and a combination of one's goals and how one achieves those goals, which can evolve over time as circumstances change. Victor Frankl, a

neurologist, psychiatrist, Holocaust survivor, and the founder of logotherapy (a form of therapy based on the idea that people live in order to find meaning in life), wrote a famous book, *Man's Search for Meaning,* that addresses the topic of one's purpose as well. Frankl suggests that a person's purpose changes over time as a result of one's circumstances, and that we can discover our purpose at a given point in time in three different ways: "(1) by creating a work or doing a deed; (2) by experiencing something or encountering someone; and (3) by the attitude we take toward unavoidable suffering." For high schools, there is an entire course built around helping students create and clarify their current purpose that IDEO built. Called the Purpose Project (https://thepurposeproject.org), the course helps students clarify their purpose by focusing on a few questions. These questions derive from the earlier exercises we suggest in this section. What are you doing today? What do you like doing? What can you do so that you can get more clarity around what drives you, what you like, and what you don't? Action, in other words, and not talk, clarifies one's purpose. This overlaps with the first way that Frankl says people can discover their purpose.

Chapter 3

The Scope of Schools: How Do We Accomplish a School's Purpose?

As Julia's parents continued clamoring about all the things Spruce Peak should be doing, Dr. Ball's thoughts turned to another question.

If she were able to arrive at a common understanding of the purpose of the school with Julia's parents, what would Spruce Peak need to do to make sure it fulfilled that purpose—no, that promise— *for each student?*

Her mind started churning.

For Jeremy to maximize his potential, he'd not only need oppor-tunities to gain academic knowledge and skills, but the school would also have to provide him with food to help him learn.

It was doing that today, but as she thought about it more, she recognized that the school might also need to put more effort into making sure his hearing and vision were ready for academic work. The school would need to connect him to a variety of mentors and potential career paths to help him see what was possible. Jeremy would need to have rich real-world experiences to learn how he could contribute and to help him imagine a greater set of opportunities for his future. Ball realized the school would also have to figure out how to have tutors on hand.

Would the Owens family support all that?

For their own daughter, having the ability to stretch and learn things that she couldn't get access to at home would be important.

And every student Ball had seen would need help building their executive function skills and self-regulation.

Were Mr. and Mrs. Owens ready for that conversation? Ball realized that she wasn't, at least not yet. But she had the sense that it would be an important conversation to have soon.

* * *

Once a schooling community has defined its purpose, it should think about how to fulfill that purpose. There are at least six domains to consider:

1. Content knowledge

2. Skills

3. Habits of success

4. Real-world experiences and social capital

5. Health and wellness

6. Basic needs

Many of these domains creep into the portraits of a graduate that schools, districts, and states construct. For clarity, I think of these domains not as ends in and of themselves, but as means to realize the ends I laid out in Chapter 2: to help every student maximize their human potential, discover their purpose, build their passions and lead choice-filled lives, participate civically in a vibrant democracy, contribute meaningfully to the world, and understand and value that people can see things differently.

A way to think about these six domains is as the sets of experiences a school must provide so that it can ensure that it fulfills its purpose for all its students.

No matter what you conclude, when some people look at this list of domains, they grow uneasy. They aren't sure that schools should be involved in many of these areas. Educators often haven't been trained in many of these realms.

Some wish that schools would just stick to their knitting. Focus on the basics—like academic knowledge and skills. Reading, writing, and math.

But even for those individuals who might see schools as having a more limited purpose than I do, if we're going to redesign schools so that all students have the supports they need to fulfill a school's purpose, then schools will need to consider all these domains. Schooling communities will also have to acknowledge that different students in different situations will have different needs. One-size-fits-all solutions won't work.

SCHOOLS' SCOPE

Conversations around the proper scope of schools aren't new. All too often, however, they operate under bad theories or create false dichotomies.

A widely used theory to guide what an organization should or shouldn't do is to consider its "core competency." The idea is that if something lies inside your core competence, then you should do it yourself. But if it isn't core and someone else can do it better, then you should outsource it.

The problem with this line of thinking is that what an organization's core competency is today might become less important in the future, and what is a noncore activity today may become a critical competence in the future.[1]

Similarly, under the category of false dichotomies lies one of the more frustrating battles in education reform: the battle waged between school reformers and poverty relief advocates over what it takes to close the achievement gap.

Some scholars, like Abigail and Stephen Thernstrom, argue that school-based interventions are the most promising solution. Others, like Richard Rothstein, argue that schools are not the most efficient platform for fighting the effects of poverty. They say that society could better help low-income students succeed in school by spending scarce dollars on programs that target children's health and well-being. When Julia Freeland Fisher and I dug into this question for a research paper titled "The Educator's Dilemma: When and how schools should embrace poverty relief,"[2] we found both sides are simultaneously right and wrong.

A BETTER WAY FORWARD: THE THEORY OF INTERDEPENDENCE AND MODULARITY

A better theory from our research on innovation can help schools see through this paradox. This theory, called the theory of interdependence and modularity, can help schools understand where they can rely on outside partners and where they need to figure out how to do the work themselves.

When Organizations Are Underserving Their Users

The theory states that when there is a performance gap—the functionality or reliability of an offering isn't good enough for certain people—then organizations should improve by working to offer the best possible services. That's straightforward.

Here's the nuance. If the organization doesn't understand well how different parts of their offering should interact, organizations can't just tack on new features or functions to make the necessary improvements. That's because cobbling together "off-the-shelf" offerings takes too many degrees of freedom away from the designers of the system, so they cannot optimize performance.

That means the organization must control every critical component in the offering to make the system as a whole function adequately. A proprietary architecture is vital. That's because the parts in the offering are unpredictably interdependent, meaning two things: first, that the way one part is designed and functions is dependent on the way another part is designed and functions and vice versa and, second, how those parts interact isn't foreseeable. The rule of thumb is that when driving toward greater performance with parts that are unpredictably interdependent, to do anything, the organization must do nearly everything.

An extreme example helps clarify

In the early days of the mainframe computer industry, IBM faced this sort of problem. At the time, IBM could not have existed as an independent manufacturer of mainframe computers. That's because manufacturing was unpredictably interdependent with the design process for the machines, as well as the operating systems, core memory, and logic circuitry. IBM therefore had to integrate backward through all the parts of the value chain of its production that were not yet well understood to succeed in selling and making mainframe computers. It had to do nearly everything to do anything.

When Organizations Are Overserving Their Users

Conversely, when organizations overshoot what a set of users need in terms of functionality and reliability, those users redefine what isn't good enough. No longer do organizations need to optimize for raw performance. Customization, speed, and convenience instead become paramount.

In this world, there are few if any unpredictable interdependencies in the design of the service's parts. As a result, organizations can use a modular architecture. Modular parts fit and work together in well-understood, crisply codified ways. They can be developed in independent work groups or by different organizations working at arm's length. This is what enables fast customization, as organizations can plug and play and mix and match different best-of-breed components.

To illustrate, consider the "architecture" of an electric light. A light bulb and a lamp have an interface between the light bulb stem and the light bulb socket. This is a modular interface. Engineers have lots of freedom to improve the design inside the light bulb, so long as they build the stem such that it can fit the established light bulb socket specifications. Notice how easily compact fluorescent bulbs fit into our old lamps, for example. The same organization does not need to design and make the light bulb, the lamp, the wall sockets, and the electricity generation and distribution systems. Because standard interfaces exist, different organizations can provide products for each piece of the system—and we benefit with an array of customized options.

A Continuum

The reality is that the worlds of interdependence and modularity exist on a spectrum. An architecture is rarely fully one or the other.

There also exists a situation where something that an organization is offering isn't good enough for a set of users, but what it needs to do to improve the raw performance is well understood. There are no unpredictable interdependencies. That means the organization can improve by simply adding new features or functions.

There are two ways to do this. First, the organization can partner with an outside provider to offer the feature. Alternatively, it can vertically integrate, meaning that it takes ownership of adjacent steps in a system or offering. Vertical integration is prudent if no standalone service provider exists to supply the feature, or if it would be more costly and less reliable to partner with an outside provider.

APPLYING THE THEORY TO SCHOOLS

What does this mean for schools?

To deliver on a school's purpose for all students, schools need to take a systemic approach that considers the whole child across content knowledge, skills, habits of success, real-world experiences and social capital, health and wellness, and basic needs. Even for those who narrowly view the purpose of school as solely to improve academic results, if we don't take the full view that understands the different circumstances in which students enter school, we'll leave countless students behind. There's no one-size-fits-all solution.

When Schools Are Underserving Students

Society is asking the U.S. education system to deliver break-through results for the highest-need students. There's long been a performance gap. Our actions to date to close the gap have occurred in a world where we don't understand the precise solutions that can drive the desired outcomes, yet we have constrained our ability to succeed by structuring the school system in a modular, rather than an interdependent, manner. If schools' goal is to help high-need students who are underserved by existing schooling options succeed academically, they must integrate in an interdependent way into the nonacademic realms of these children's lives.

Over the past couple of decades, several educational institutions serving low-income students have begun to attack the effects of poverty. They've done so by integrating beyond schools' traditional academic domain. That means they are embracing the sorts of supports—mental health services, pediatric care, and mentoring, to name a few—for which poverty-relief advocates have long called. When we analyzed some of these efforts in our paper "The Educator's Dilemma," we made two key observations.

First, merely integrating backward to offer wraparound services with outside providers in a modular fashion is often not enough to help high-need students succeed academically. High-need students share a need for extra support, but what each student needs is different. The architecture must be interdependent so that the school can fine-tune the balance, mix, and type of services offered to each student. Personalization matters.

Second, the success of these models appears to depend on the end goal around which they are integrating. If helping students build academic knowledge, skills, and habits of success aren't the driving force that causes a school to integrate backward, then we're unlikely to see dramatic changes in academic results for high-need students.

This helps explain why many community schools' efforts or schools that integrate wraparound supports have seen only modest or mixed results. First, many community school models may not be sufficiently backward integrated to address fully the challenges of closing the achievement gap. Given their focus on coordinating outside service providers, rather than fully controlling the delivery, mix, and structure of the wraparound services offered, community schools may be unable to craft a coherent model that works well to serve its students' varying and often unpredictable needs. Second, it's possible that some community schools are properly integrated in terms of the mix of services they offer but aren't doing enough on the academic side to close the achievement gap. As Michael J. Petrilli, president of the Thomas B. Fordham Institute, said, "Yes, absolutely, let's make sure that we provide strong social supports for disadvantaged children, but let's not use that as an excuse to ignore what's happening or what's not happening inside of the school."[3] Coordinated service provision, in other words, may be a necessary but not sufficient driver of academic success.

When Schools Are Overserving Students

Strange as it may sound, there are some families that are over-served by today's schools. They don't need the full "bundle" that many traditional schools offer: the full sets of meals, the extended hours, the broad range of classes, and the many athletic, arts, and other special offerings. Their children are doing fine academically. Maybe the families are able to provide the at-home supports to help build their children's habits of success, ensure they have access to real-world projects and connections, and help them live healthy, fulfilled lives. Their concerns instead revolve around customization for their children's specific needs or interests.

These families are often happy for their children to enroll in a full-time virtual school so that they can continue to invest in their development as an athlete. Or they are thrilled by a hybrid homeschooling arrangement, in which they educate their child at home, but the child goes to the local school for a couple offerings each week. In these cases, modular offerings work well.

We were seeing more unbundled schooling offerings emerge before the pandemic, but COVID accelerated the interest in these arrangements. More families realized that they had specific preferences for their children's schooling and have sought customized offerings. Witness the myriad families finding tutors online, signing up for Outschool classes, and helping their children land online internships through various networking platforms.

Outschool:
https://www.youtube.com/watch?v=_lxiZFSwCvl

A Continuum

Most students sit somewhere in the middle of a continuum between needing a fully interdependent educational offering and a completely modular and unbundled offering. That means that many schools will be able to integrate offerings from other providers—food from places like Revolution Foods; health services from nearby clinics; or telemedicine, online speech therapy, social-emotional learning support, and other such therapies offered through entities like Presence Learning, EmpowerU, or Limbix. A wraparound approach could work in certain cases, in other words. The better question could be more whether schools have thought enough about the full breadth of wraparound services for certain students and on what they are trying to optimize, which falls back to the purpose conversation from Chapter 2.

New places where schools can modularize are also emerging. Chapter 7 discusses this phenomenon more, but the rapid rise of digital learning in schools means that delivering academic content is increasingly a commodity, not a differentiator. Disruptive innovations, like online coaching, mentoring, tutoring programs, and social networks, are changing how people connect. That's opening the door to allowing students to build relationships and radically expand their social capital. This can change students' views of what is possible and their ability to realize new dreams.

As these early innovations improve, savvy schools will use them to free up time and resources to focus on things like offering rich discussions, community projects, and enrichment; guaranteeing clean and pleasing physical environments; eliminating bullying; providing nutritious meals; supporting health and wellness; delivering a range of athletic, musical, and artistic programs; assessing children's widespread and varying needs; and developing students into master creators and innovators.

SIX DOMAINS TO CONSIDER IN YOUR SCHOOL'S SCOPE

As schools consider their scope to successfully serve students and fulfill their schooling purpose, there are at least six domains they should consider: content knowledge, skills, habits of success, real-world experiences and social capital, health and wellness, and basic needs. In practice, these domains aren't mutually exclusive, as they intersect and support each other in interdependent ways.

Content Knowledge

There is a mountain of research on the importance of academic achievement and content knowledge across a range of disciplines. Building academic achievement to at least a baseline is important for future life success[4]—after which other factors rise in importance. Without knowledge, preparing students for life success is a nonstarter.

Despite some claiming that content knowledge no longer matters in a world where everything is googleable,[5] possessing deep background knowledge remains imperative. Without it, students will struggle to be successful learners and read across a wide range of subjects and genres. Content knowledge is foundational. Without a working familiarity of a topic, Google will take you only so far when you must generate the right question to ask. As Maria Montessori reportedly said, "the mind constructs with what it finds."[6] Without knowledge, in other words, the mind can only do so much work and ask so many questions. Or as cognitive scientist Daniel Willingham wrote, "Every passage that you read omits information. . . All of this omitted information must be brought to the text by the reader."[7]

As students learn to read, they must build a strong and wide foundation of knowledge. They should engage with coherent bodies of content across subject disciplines. A learner's background knowledge is key to learning well and absorbing information from what they are reading and consuming. If students don't have a working familiarity with a body of knowledge, a new passage on a novel topic for that reader—no matter how elementary it may seem and no matter how strong the reader's fundamental decoding skills—will frustrate the reader.

A famous experiment about baseball illustrates the concept. Given a common passage about baseball, so-called "low-ability" readers who knew a lot about baseball significantly outperformed so-called "high-ability" readers who knew little. The reason is that the high-ability readers did not have the context to make sense of what they were reading.[8] Imagine, for example, the bewilderment of someone who knew nothing about baseball trying to understand why the crowd cheered when a runner stole a base—an act that would sound criminal without the proper context.

Yes, tapping into and developing children's interests and instilling in them a sense of ownership of their education is important. But this must be done with clear learning goals and boundaries in place. It's important that children don't miss out on building a broad foundation of knowledge. Nor should they be overwhelmed by having too many choices relative to their expertise.

One challenge for schools is that each student possesses different background knowledge. Students from affluent families, for example, tend to enjoy exposure to a range of experiences outside school that build their knowledge without them even realizing it. They can arguably get away with schools that are less intentional about building knowledge. Low-income students often have a far more limited set of experiences outside of school that leaves them further behind.

Within these broad groupings, the differences are even more disparate. Building learners' background knowledge in scalable ways that are personalized to their specific needs is challenging. As Chapter 8 discusses, this is one place technology can make a difference by helping educators personalize learning. But schools should consider these points as they determine their own role and scope for the students they serve.

As to what knowledge all students should learn, that's a topic for other authors.[9] Schools and the broader school system should, however, have a conversation about which topics are critical for all learners.

Education reformers often bemoan that schools never shed programs that are no longer needed or effective. New school initiatives are consequently layered on top of past practices. Schools therefore become overburdened. Educators struggle to implement new ideas. This practice of adding but not subtracting is costly. Reformers unfortunately often seem less likely to ask whether it's time to discard part of a school's curriculum, however, despite world conditions changing.

Algebra offers one example. It's seen as a gateway subject to college success, with a bevy of research to support the contention.[10] Reformers have often accordingly doubled down on efforts to help students pass algebra—and the Algebra 2 course more specifically. But what if the problem is whether an Algebra 2 class should be required in the first place for all learners? Are there better mathematical experiences to build students' fluency for today's world?

University of Chicago economist Steven Leavitt devoted an entire *Freakonomics* podcast to the question.[11] He concluded that the algebra requirement should be rethought. Leavitt noted that the primary reason high schools offer algebra is because Harvard began requiring knowledge of the subject in 1820 to gain admittance. As a result, secondary schools began teaching algebra. Fifty years later Harvard added geometry to its requirements—and secondary schools again followed suit.

Levitt concludes that every high school student should graduate with data fluency, which he describes as "an understanding of the difference between correlation and causality; the ability to evaluate claims that others make with data; maybe even to take a pile of data and make sense of it." Yet he points out that "only 10 percent of high school students take a statistics class—and even most statistics courses are primarily theoretical rather than requiring students to get their hands dirty with data."[12]

For most students, data fluency would be more relevant than a full course of Algebra 2. As Anthony Carnevale the director of the Center on Education and the Workforce at Georgetown University, told *Education Week*, just 11 percent of U.S. jobs involve work that requires understanding Algebra 2 concepts, and only 6 percent regularly use advanced algebraic operations.[13] Topics like data fluency and financial literacy, on the other hand, appear to be far more in demand—not just in the workplace, but also in everyday life.[14]

Some high schools are accordingly rethinking their algebra requirements. They still offer algebra so that students are exposed to it and can choose to pursue algebra and calculus if they enjoy them. But they are decreasing the mandated time on them to ensure that students are also exposed to data science and statistics. Escondido Unified School District in California, for example, has rethought its sequence of math courses; the state of Oregon is doing so as well.[15] Texas dropped its Algebra 2 requirement in 2014, although its districts didn't necessarily follow suit.[16]

To be clear, dropping algebra does not mean that students shouldn't learn algebraic concepts. Algebraic reasoning can be taught much earlier to students than in high school.[17] The bigger shift is from focusing primarily on how to calculate problems to helping students master computational thinking, a method of thinking that formulates problems and expresses solutions in an algorithmic manner.[18]

That starts to address critics' other complaint about reducing the time on algebra, namely that we will put a dent in developing individuals' problem solving and critical thinking skills. This worry leads us to the second domain that schools must pay attention to.

Skills

The purpose of knowledge isn't for its own sake, but so that an individual can apply it in useful ways.[19] Critical thinking, problem solving, collaboration, communication, and creativity are skills[20] that employers report consistently as being more and more important for their employees.[21] Mastering these skills helps prepare students for life success.

The ability to use these skills is dependent on having some domain knowledge. To illustrate this dependence: although I can think critically and communicate well about the future of education (some would agree with that statement, anyway!), if you drop me into a coding job at Google, because I can't code, I would be unable to think critically and communicate well in the job.

Some people go a step further and suggest that the expression of these skills is entirely discipline specific. They argue that these skills are only a function of content mastery and can't be taught in a way that transfers.

That's a bridge too far, however.

First, it's important to precisely codify what each of these skills are, something many schooling communities neglect or gloss over. Minerva University, a new, highly innovative liberal arts college, has done this work in rich detail, for example.

With that codification in place, educators can then provide structured learning opportunities that intentionally and repeatedly build these skills.

By doing so, over time, students can transfer and apply these skills across domains. That means that as individuals master these skills through deliberate practice in a variety of areas, they can more rapidly apply them in new areas as they master the knowledge and lexicon.[22]

As Jonathan Haber explains in his book *Critical Thinking*, several research studies support this approach. They show that the greatest learning occurs when skills like critical thinking are taught explicitly and in an integrated way with the other lessons in a class. That means that students must have consistent opportunities to deliberately practice and apply the skills.

Teaching these skills in a way that is divorced from the other material in a class doesn't work well. These findings echo the theory of interdependence and modularity. The best way to learn skills is interdependently with content knowledge.

The least effective method for helping build critical-thinking skills is when teachers just assume that students will learn them as a by-product of the content in a class. This is what often occurs in algebra or other math classes today.[23]

As Haber writes:

> One of the first opportunities students have to experience logical arguments occurs when they are taught geometric proofs. Yet how many math teachers take this occasion to show students how premises that provide reasons to believe conclusions can be applied to any form of argument, including arguments that, unlike math, are not based on deductive reasoning? Similarly, how many science teachers stress how the methods they teach can be applied in situations that do not involve the controlled experimentation so bound up in science, such as choosing which college you should attend, or which candidate deserves your vote?[24]

In addition to critical thinking, communication, creative thinking, collaboration, and problem solving, the foundations of reading—especially learning how to read—should also be included in the skills one must learn. Teaching how to read is perhaps the closest thing education has to an agreed-upon set of methods that are rules based and relatively reliable. The focus should be on teaching students to decode written words into spoken language. As Tavenner said, "Schools across the country are truly failing students right now in the early years by not ensuring that they learn to read. This is a solvable problem, and . . . should be what elementary schools are completely focused on nailing."[25]

Habits of Success

For students to be prepared for today's world, mastering habits of success is vital. This group of practices goes by a variety of names, ranging from character skills[26] to life skills, and from social-emotional learning[27] to dispositions and, my least favorite, non-cognitive skills.[28] According to Summit Public Schools, what I call habits of success through the remainder of the book revolve around 16 core practices[29]:

Healthy Development

- Attachment: Forming enduring bonds with caring individuals

- Stress management: Figuring out how to become calm and balanced when situations become stressful

- Self-regulation: Directing and maintaining attention and emotions

Academic and Life Readiness

- Self-awareness (reflection): Being aware of what one thinks, feels, does, along with one's strengths, weaknesses (metacognition), as well as one's impact on others

- Social awareness/relationship skills: Understanding how others feel and having the skills to maintain strong relationships

- Executive functions: Concentrating, staying organized, juggling multiple tasks, planning for the future

Positive Mindsets

- Growth mindset: Believing that intelligence can be grown and that one isn't born with a fixed amount

- Self-efficacy: Believing in one's capacity to do something successfully

- Sense of belonging: Feeling like one belongs in their community

- Relevance of school: Learning that education is valuable and seeing things learned as interesting

Perseverance

- Resilience: Bouncing back and dealing with challenging situations

- Agency: Making one's own decisions and acting on them

- Academic tenacity: Overcoming distractions and working toward longer-term goals

Independence

- Self-direction: Driving the actions needed to achieve goals, with or without help

- Curiosity: Being interested in lots of things and wanting to understand more

- Purpose: Charting a course for a life that is meaningful and will have an impact on the world

For each of these habits, there is evidence that they are measurable and teachable, align to the development of a learner, and impact academic achievement.[30]

Still, when educators look at this list, they have a Rorschach test moment. They either become excited because the list encompasses habits they believe should have been part of a whole-child learning experience all along, or they become wary as they worry about schooling overreach. Some worry because, as educator and founder of the Match Charter Public School Mike Goldstein put it, schools aren't all that good at teaching these habits—and those habits they do teach don't transfer from the academic context.

Part of the reason schools have struggled to teach these habits is that, similar to skills, schools have too often viewed these habits as something to teach students in a standalone lesson as opposed to interdependently with academic knowledge and skills.[31] Educators often treat them as one more thing on the long list of things schools should teach students. Indeed, less than a quarter of teachers say their schools implement these skills on a programmatic, schoolwide basis.[32] As the Introduction illustrates and Chapter 5 reinforces, the traditional zero-sum model of schooling also undermines these habits because schools don't reward students for developing them. In essence, schools come across as saying, "Do as I say, not as I do."

As a result, schools generally teach these habits poorly.

But that doesn't mean that helping students build these habits is a bad idea. After all, many schools have struggled to teach core academic knowledge or skills. That doesn't mean it can't be done well or shouldn't be done at all. Some schools, like Montessori schools or Summit Public Schools, are showing that it's possible to do this work well when the habits are taught in an interdependent way with core academics so that they are not an afterthought or something that is replacing academics. They should instead make the academic knowledge and skill acquisition more effective.[33]

Can some people survive without these habits being taught explicitly? Yes.

Are there different ways to teach these habits? Certainly.

But schools have expected students to acquire these habits without explicitly teaching them. They have implicitly assessed the habits for at least a century. That combination sets up many children to fail.

Real-World Experiences and Social Capital

Connecting school to the outside world is important so that students learn the different ways in which they can contribute to the world, what resonates with them, why what they are learning matters,[34] and why certain goals are worth attaining. Schools can connect students to the outside world through projects, extracurricular activities, externships, internships, and more. Chapter 5 shows some specific ways that high schools could better incorporate real-world opportunities—not contrived ones—into each student's day. For now, the point is that as students get older and move from novice toward expert learners in different areas, having more connections to the outside world becomes more important so they can develop a sense of purpose and be prepared for adulthood.

This is also something that students have long desired. According to "The Silent Epidemic: Perspectives of High School Dropouts," a report from 2006 that the Gates Foundation commissioned, the leading reason students dropped out was because of lack of relevance to their life, not academic challenges. The top suggestion for educators was to connect learning with real-world experiences.[35]

Although there are caveats as to how far to go in this endeavor,[36] many schools have thoughtfully heeded the call.[37] Summit Public Schools, for example, offers eight weeks each year during which students work off-campus with outside organizations. Students in Cajon Valley Union School District outside San Diego explore over 50 different careers from kindergarten through eighth grade through immersive, experiential opportunities. These help each child gain self-awareness about their unique strengths, interests, and values; a window into different academic and career opportunities; and the ability to ground and tell their own story.

Linking to the real world also creates more opportunities for students to connect with adults from different walks of life. If school isn't just about teaching academics but also about helping students have access to good life opportunities and careers, then those outside relationships are critical. As Julia Freeland Fisher argues in her book *Who You Know*, in today's world, schools need to engage in this activity. After building a baseline of academic knowledge and skills, who you know is often more important than what you know. Relationships help individuals gain access to opportunities and jobs; they help entrepreneurs raise capital; they help people learn about new pathways.

Researchers have long known that whom you know matters. An individual's social capital has significant impact on their success in life, as well as their health. Likewise, the robustness of a society's social capital impacts the wellness of that society.

Unfortunately, as *Who You Know* illustrates, schools have historically been built to keep the outside. . . outside of school.

This must change, particularly as the pandemic has showcased just how much relationships matter.[38] Leaving social connections to chance is a poor strategy, considering how unequally distributed relationships are. Given that society is already moving to hold schools accountable for the life outcomes students achieve, narrowing the opportunity gap means growing students' reservoir of social capital.

Relationships also impact what people know. Students who lack caring relationships are more likely to drop out of school, for example. They are more likely to suffer health challenges that impact their academic achievement. We also bemoan the fact that there are shortages of qualified teachers in certain academic subjects. Were schools to tap into the broader world of experts around the world, however, they could solve many of those staffing challenges.

This points to a bigger observation. As with the teaching of skills and habits of success, incorporating real-world experiences and social capital isn't an add-on to what schools are trying to accomplish. Indeed, the leadership team at Cajon Valley Union School District told me that students' reading has improved as students gained knowledge about different fields and careers.[39] As a recent Hoover Institute report said, "Coupling academic learning and exposure to people working on real-world problems can deepen student thinking and open possibilities for further learning. Even when teachers themselves do not have the tools or time to build rich materials on their own, organizations like Nepris offer curated collections of speakers, videos, and lesson plans for classroom use. Others, like Composer, specialize in providing globally connected civics education learning and action experiences."[40]

Health and Wellness

As schools have reopened since the pandemic, students have returned with a variety of social, emotional, and physical challenges. Some of these challenges have resulted in physical violence.

Many believe schools shouldn't be involved in health and wellness. After I suggested in an article that schools must focus on health and wellness, for example, one educator wrote me that there is a "robust market of alternative ways to produce health and wellness in kids"—and that public schools don't do well in this arena.

The challenge with that line of thinking is that if schools aren't working with students who are healthy and well, it will be harder for those students to learn successfully.

But there's some good news. As with building knowledge, skills, habits, real-world experiences, and social capital, schools don't have to see supporting students' wellbeing as an entirely separate exercise. Phyllis Lockett, CEO of LEAP Innovations, which works with schools to transform their learning environments to personalize for each student, wrote:

> Academic recovery is not the only crisis our educators and parents are facing. Students are reporting

significantly increased anxiety, stress, and suicidal thoughts, leading many to label the mental health fallout of Covid-19 the "second pandemic." Not surprisingly, the confluence of these dual crises is straining school system capacity during what has been a particularly difficult "back to school" season this fall as educators struggle to address the wider range of their students' academic and social-emotional needs. These challenges may seem unrelated, in part because we've created a false dichotomy between academic and social-emotional learning. But developmental and learning science tells us that they are, in fact, inextricably linked, and that one factor in particular—strong positive relationships between students and teachers—may drive academic and so-called nonacademic outcomes. Indeed, it may be more accurate to view our current "unfinished learning" challenge as a by-product of "disrupted relationships" and not just lost instructional time.[41]

U.S. schools also have experience in this arena with so-called newcomer programs, which support immigrant students who are new to the country and have both interrupted formal education and stress and trauma. As Audrey Cohan, a senior dean for research and scholarship at Molloy College in New York who studies these programs told *Education Week*, "A lot of the techniques and the strategies, the pedagogies that are used with newcomer schools, we can be using with every kid now that they're coming back to school." That includes providing social-emotional and mental health supports and helping build routines and connections to the community for students.[42]

Schools have also always played some role in health and wellness. Witness the long history of physical and health education in schools or the provision of meals and counseling. As Chapter 5 discusses, fitness, for example, helps prime students for learning. Therefore, even physical education should not be treated as something independent from learning knowledge and skills. Helping students and families build schedules that prioritize sleep is critical. And doing a better job to make sure that all students have consistent access to balanced meals with less sugar and fewer processed foods will directly help students improve several of their habits and ability to learn. Without some focus on wellness, it will be hard for every student to fulfill their potential.[43]

Basic Needs

The conversation around health and wellness bleeds into another domain that schools may have to consider: Are the basic needs of students around things like food, shelter, and clothing met? If they aren't, schools will have a difficult time achieving their purpose for students.

Most schools don't have the resources to tackle many of the questions this topic raises. But it's a question that we as a society should address. The SEED schools, for example, turn on its head the notion that boarding schools are for the most privileged members of society, as their students live and learn on campus tuition-free. Without asking these big questions, we won't be able to design equitable schooling solutions.

PERSONALIZING THIS APPROACH IN MY COMMUNITY

If schools accept these baseline ideas, they can take these domains and build SMART (specific, measurable, attainable, realistic, and time-bound) goals for each. The nuance of how each will land in any given schooling community will differ. Even trickier, the approach to implementing them should likely be personalized based on each student's distinct needs and background. A mistake for any school is to assume that all students sit in the same circumstances and need the same sets of supports. As the pandemic showed, that's not the case. Jennifer Orr, an elementary school teacher, wrote:

> It is clear that some students have food that is plentiful, healthy, and consistently available. Some students do not. Some students have access to reliable internet connections and multiple devices. Some students do not. Some students have tutors and families who are home and able to support with schoolwork at any time. Some students do not. Some students have families who are able to advocate fiercely on their behalf. Some students do not.[44]

During the pandemic, Spring Grove Public Schools in Minnesota became attuned to the fact that different students and families have different needs and preferences. According to the district's assistant superintendent, Gina Meinertz, as the district worked with students and parents to understand what they needed to feel safe, they realized there were "hidden voices" that had needs different from the majority.[45]

As Meinertz told me, "We might need to respond to a hidden voice because they have a valid reason that might not be everyone else's valid reason, and so we created this document that became very, very long of common themes and hidden voices. And from that we would create prototypes of this coming year, what do we keep, what do we not keep."

Spring Grove's leaders observed, for example, that having the ability for students to show up to school at different times could be beneficial. Staggered starts helped teachers create a calmer, less chaotic environment in which they could have a personal conversation with each child as they showed up to school. They learned that there was a divergence of views around where people ate lunch, so they offered different options.[46] Spring Grove's thinking is part of the logic behind schools starting their own microschools or schools within schools, which we discussed in Chapter 1, so that educators don't force all students and families to fit into certain arrangements that don't work best for them.

REMAINING CONCERNS

People reading this chapter will likely still have concerns about the scope of schools.

Some of these concerns may revolve around the financial costs of integrating into nonacademic realms. The theory of interdependence and modularity offers three answers.

First, if we stop seeing these different domains as independent tasks to tack on to an existing school and instead see them as something to be interdependently designed as core from the get-go, the costs will be lower than imagined.

Second, the theory shows that the costs of not integrating are higher to society. They are just hidden from the financial statements of any one organization.

Third, the theory also suggests that costs can come down over time. It predicts that as integrated schools start to succeed in serving low-income students, we will gain a clearer sense of the causal mechanisms that lead to this success. At that point, the education system will be able to modularize, which would create greater efficiencies.

A second set of concerns revolves around who will do the work. Many continue to have concerns about schools stretching into areas where their teachers haven't been trained and where they don't have experts today.[47] Modularity could work in schools' favor here by allowing them to bring in more people with deep expertise in other areas so that we are not forcing teachers who were trained for one set of roles to do things for which they are not trained. To the extent a school has had challenges filling educator roles during the pandemic, that may create a window for schools to contract, rather than employ, educators and staff to fill holes. If schools can sustainably staff their schools and retain the flexibility of these arrangements,[48] then they could more easily transition their staffing models over time to match what their community needs for their students to succeed.

The temporary infusion of federal dollars can also help. As discussed in Chapter 1, school finance experts have worried that many schools will make unsustainable investments in staff and programs. But knowing that these funds will go away, schools could contract for certain services to create a more flexible model that can adapt continually to what they need to offer students.

Even more intriguing from the perspective of crafting a properly integrated model is how community-based organizations in places like Cleveland and Boston ran microschools during the pandemic, which Chapter 1 detailed.[49] These organizations could create models that embed sound social supports in the places where students are learning while the content experts are remote.

THE FUTURE OF SCHOOLING

As more modular educational solutions emerge, the possibility of a more personalized, customizable version of schooling feels more within reach. When we look into the future of what school could be, we can imagine something like a community center with a range of academic, health, and support services available to students. In this new system, services and academics alike could be doled out in a flexible manner, with different resources, schedules, and supports for different students. This could facilitate more racial and socioeconomic integration than we see in schools today. To remain efficient and expand opportunities and choice, such a schooling system could welcome a range of providers that could plug into various interfaces at that schooling hub. Some students would still rely more on the services a school provides than others would, but the school would be positioned to serve many more types of students based on their needs.

This all sounds well and good. The problem remains that the current system has not integrated far enough. Schools—particularly those serving high-need students—cannot skip the early stages of integration.

Even where they can, schools must detail the sorts of things that their students will need to be prepared for their future. That means being clear about their purpose and then prioritizing what they must do versus what they must outsource versus what they don't need to worry about at all for each student along the domains of knowledge, skills, habits of success, real-world experiences and social capital, health and wellness, and basic needs.

Without that detailed consideration, helping all students maximize their human potential, discover their purpose, build their passions and lead choice-filled lives, participate civically in a vibrant democracy, contribute meaningfully to the world and the economy, and valuing that people can see things differently will remain a far-off dream.

KEY TAKEAWAYS

- Once a school has defined its purpose, it can then consider the activities it must undertake to deliver on that purpose by considering the whole set of experiences a student will need to succeed.

- The theory of interdependence and modularity offers a better way for schools to think about their scope than traditional ideas of "core competency."

- Students who are underserved need more supports offered in an interdependent way.

- Students who are overserved want more customized offerings enabled by a more modular architecture.

- To think about the sets of services a school offers and how it should offer them, schools should think through at least six domains: content knowledge, skills, habits of success, real-world experiences and social capital, health and wellness, and basic needs.

- There are no one-size-fits-all answers. Customization is critical.

NOTES

1. Clayton M. Christensen and Michael Porter, *The Innovator's Solution* (Boston, MA: Harvard Business Review Press, 2003), p. 125.
2. Michael B. Horn and Julia Freeland Fisher, "When and How Schools Should Embrace Poverty Relief," Clayton Christensen Institute, June 9, 2015, https://www.christenseninstitute.org/wp-content/uploads/2015/06/The-Educators-Dilemma.pdf.
3. Caroline Porter, "More Schools Open Their Doors to the Whole Community," *Wall Street Journal*, July 28, 2014, http://www.wsj.com/articles/more-schools-open-their-doors-to-the-whole-community-1406586751 (accessed April 27, 2015).
4. Jesse Singal, "The False Promise of Quick-Fix Psychology," *Wall Street Journal*, April 9, 2021, https://www.wsj.com/articles/the-false-promise-of-quick-fix-psychology-11617981093.
5. Anya Kamenetz, "Q&A: Exit Interview with a Nationally Known School Leader," NPR, February 15, 2021, https://www.npr.org/sections/ed/2015/02/15/385774711/q-a-exit-interview-with-a-nationally-known-school-leader.
6. "Constructing Specific Knowledge: The Importance of Non-Fiction Children's Books," Resurrection Episcopal Day School, New York.See also "Montessori Meets Core Knowledge in Memphis," CoreKnowledge, August 9, 2018, https://www.coreknowledge.org/blog/montessori-meets-core-knowledge/.
7. Daniel Willingham, "School Time, Knowledge, and Reading Comprehension," *Daniel Willingham–Science & Education* (blog),

March 7, 2012, http://www.danielwillingham.com/daniel-willingham-science-and-education-blog/school-time-knowledge-and-reading-comprehension.

8. Donna R. Recht and Lauren Leslie, "Effect of Prior Knowledge on Good and Poor Readers' Memory of Text," *Journal of Educational Psychology* 80, no. 1 (1988): 16–20.

9. In our *Class Disrupted* podcast, Tavenner offered a helpful framework that replaces a "required" curriculum, or canon, for all learners with a common framework. That framework is inherently personalized but also communal. In it, each student would learn through concentric circles—starting with themselves, then expanding to their community and the society in which they live, and from there they could follow where their curiosity leads them.

"What Schools Should Teach," *Class Disrupted*, Season 3, Episode 2, September 21, 2021, https://www.the74million.org/article/listen-class-disrupted-s3-e2-what-schools-should-teach/.

As Tom Vander Ark, CEO of Getting Smart, wrote, "High school should be an opportunity to figure out who you are, what you're good at, and where you want to make a contribution. That should start with problem finding—spotting big tough problems of interest."

Tom Vander Ark, "The Math Youth Need to Make a Difference," *Forbes*, November 14, 2019, https://www.forbes.com/sites/tomvanderark/2019/11/14/the-math-youth-need-to-make-a-difference/#1a38e3e34bd6.

Tavenner's framework mirrors some of the thinking from Montessori education. That philosophy holds that children must first understand the concrete world they inhabit. Over time they can then learn about things that are increasingly abstract or distant from their reality.

Schools that intentionally create coherent experiences will provide a leg up for their learners. That means that schools should take a less atomized and more integrated view of the subject disciplines of science, social studies, math, language, music, art, and so on. They should instead view all of them as opportunities to reinforce each other with content that is connected and coherent. That's something that many schools don't do particularly well today. Nor have many done it well as students progress through grade levels in schools. As Stephen Sawchuk wrote in *Education Week*, "the evidence suggests that core reading, math, and science instruction, even within the same school, lacked cohesion from grade to grade *before* the pandemic."

Stephen Sawchuk, "What Is the Purpose of School?," *Education Week*, September 14, 2021, https://www.edweek.org/policy-politics/what-is-the-purpose-of-school/2021/09?utm_source=nl&utm_medium=eml&utm_campaign=eu&M=63798075&U=67948&UUID=2a97314eb8614a7f8123bed720cdf420.

10. Linda M. Gojak, "Not 'If' but 'When,'" National Council of Teachers of Mathematics, https://www.nctm.org/News-and-Calendar/Messages-from-the-President/Archive/Linda-M_-Gojak/Algebra_-Not-_If_-but-_When_/.

11. Steven D. Leavitt, "America's Math Curriculum Doesn't Add Up," *Freakonomics*, October 2, 2019, http://freakonomics.com/podcast/math-curriculum/.

   See also Jo Boaler and Steven D. Levitt, "Opinion: Modern High School Math Should Be about Data Science—not Algebra 2," *Los Angeles Times*, October 23, 2019, https://www.latimes.com/opinion/story/2019-10-23/math-high-school-algebra-data-statistics.

12. The figure, according to the National Center of Education Statistics, was 10.8 percent in 2009. See "Table 179. Percentage of public and private high school graduates taking selected mathematics and science courses in high school, by sex and race/ethnicity: Selected years, 1982 through 2009," National Center for Education Statistics, 2012 Tables and Figures, https://nces.ed.gov/programs/digest/d12/tables/dt12_179.asp.

   A more recent analysis suggests that 23 percent of high school students take a probability or statistics course. Low-income students are less likely to take such classes. Liana Loewus, "Just 1 in 4 High School Seniors Have Taken Statistics," *Education Week*, September 7, 2016, https://www.edweek.org/leadership/just-1-in-4-high-school-seniors-have-taken-statistics/2016/09.

13. "Questions Arise About Need for Algebra 2 for All," *Education Week*, June 11, 2013, https://www.edweek.org/ew/articles/2013/06/12/35algebra_ep.h32.html.

14. "Investing in America's Data Science and Analytics Talent," The Business-Higher Education Forum, 2017, https://www.bhef.com/publications/investing-americas-data-science-and-analytics-talent.

15. Catherine Gewertz, "Should High Schools Rethink How They Sequence Math Courses?," *Education Week*, November 13, 2019, https://www.edweek.org/teaching-learning/should-high-schools-rethink-how-they-sequence-math-courses/2019/11.

16. Stephen Sawchuk, "Texas Dropped Algebra 2 as a Requirement. Its Schools Didn't," *Education Week*, February 8, 2018, https://www.edweek.org/teaching-learning/texas-dropped-algebra-2-as-a-requirement-its-schools-didnt/2018/02.

17. If schools shift to mastery-based learning, as I argue in Chapter 5, we also would move away from thinking about discrete courses for fixed durations and instead focus on the competencies that a student has mastered.

18. "Conrad Wolfram on Computational Thinking," *Getting Smart*, August 5, 2020, https://www.gettingsmart.com/podcast/conrad-wolfram-on-computational-thinking/.

19. Many may observe that committing multiplication tables to memory—although not by rote learning per se—is also antiquated. But the reason it is important is that it has value in developing automaticity that allows us to do higher order math and application of complex concepts. But that's not as true of Algebra 2, in which concepts are used rarely in the real world. The deeper point is that understanding algebra is not the only way to learn critical thinking skills—and it certainly isn't the most direct. Algebra need not be the gateway to critical thinking skills, let alone the gateway to college success.

20. "These Skills Prepare Kids for Any Future," *Prepared Parents*, https://preparedparents.org/editorial/universal-skills-for-kids-to-succeed/ (accessed November 14, 2021).

21. "Key Attributes Employers Want to See on Students' Resumes," National Association of Colleges and Employers, January 13, 2020, https://www.naceweb.org/talent-acquisition/candidate-selection/ key-attributes-employers-want-to-see-on-students-resumes/.

22. Ben Nelson and Stephen Kosslyn, eds., *Building the Intentional University: Minerva and the Future of Higher Education* (Cambridge, MA: MIT Press, 2017).

    See also Robert Pondiscio, "How to Help Students Think Critically," July 10, 2019, https://www.robertpondiscio.com/blog/ how-to-help-students-think-critically.

23. What might that look like for different skills?

For critical thinking, according to Haber, it would include structured thinking or logic—being clear about what one's thinking, the reasons behind that belief, and the ability to evaluate if the reasons are justified. It would include language skills, including the ability to translate arguments into systems of logic, as well as persuasive communication, rhetoric, and argumentation, which requires background knowledge and the ability to locate, evaluate, organize, synthesize, and communicate information.

For the skill of communication, it's important to help students master these across multiple modalities. As Minerva University shows, it's important to be able to analyze others' works and to be able to communicate by writing, speech, visual and musical arts, and different technological mediums, as technology changes the way communication occurs and across different subject matters. Minerva University includes learning about word choice, grammar, style, logic, facts, organization, evidence, emotion, rhetorical tools, persuasion, and more. See Nelson and Kosslyn, *Building the Intentional University*, Chapter 5.

Creative thinking at Minerva is paired with empirical analyses. The University emphasizes the iterative and creative aspects of empirical research and problem solving. It explicitly builds in concepts like recognizing and overcoming biases, characterizing or defining a problem, deriving novel and creative solutions to problems, evaluating those solutions, employing both inductive and deductive reasoning in the scientific method, synthesizing, and more (*Building the Intentional University*, Chapters 6 and 7).

24. Jonathan Haber, *Critical Thinking* (Cambridge, MA: MIT Press, 2020), Chapter 3.

25. Emily Hanford, "Hard Words: Why Aren't Kids Being Taught to Read?," *APM Reports*, September 10, 2018.

    Emily Hanford, "At a Loss for Words: How a Flawed Idea Is Teaching Millions of Kids to Be Poor Readers," *APM Reports*, August 22, 2019.

    Sarah Schwartz, "Popular Literacy Materials Get 'Science of Reading' Overhaul. But Will Teaching Change?" *Education Week*, October 13, 2021, https://www.edweek.org/teaching-learning/popular-literacy-materials-get-science-of-reading-overhaul-but-will-teaching-change/2021/10?utm_source=nl&utm_medium=eml&utm_campaign=eu&M=64176508&U=67948&UUID=2a97314eb8614a7f8123bed720cdf420.

26. "Character," Character Lab, https://characterlab.org/character/ (accessed January 21, 2022).

27. "Fundamentals of SEL," CASEL, https://casel.org/fundamentals-of-sel/ (accessed January 21, 2022).

28. For a good overview of several of the different habits of success frameworks that exist, see Eliot Levine, "Habits of Success: Helping Students Develop Essential Skills for Learning, Work, and Life," Aurora Institute, October 2021, https://aurora-institute.org/wp-content/uploads/Aurora-Institute-Habits-of-Success-Helping-Students-Develop-Essential-Skills-for-Learning-Work-and-Life-2.pdf. In the piece, Levine not only gives an overview of several of the frameworks that exist, but he also helps underscore their importance, how they can be taught, and the issues that exist with assessing these skills.

29. This is based on the Building Blocks for Learning Framework developed by Dr. Brooke Stafford-Brizard for Turnaround for Children. "Practice the 16 Habits of Success," *Prepared Parents*, https://preparedparents.org/wp-content/uploads/2020/03/Habits-of-Success_Prepared-Parents-1.png.

"Focus on Habits Instead of Test Scores," *Prepared Parents*, https://preparedparents.org/editorial/focus-on-16-habits-of-success-not-test-scores/ (accessed January 21, 2022).

For a deeper dive on the evidence base behind this framework, as well as around the importance of content knowledge, cognitive skills, and sense of purpose, see "The Science of Summit," Summit Public Schools, August 7, 2017, https://summitps.org/wp-content/uploads/2018/09/The-Science-of-Summit-by-Summit-Public-chools_08072017-1.pdf.

K. Brooke Stafford-Brizard, "Building Blocks for Learning," Turnaround for Children, 2016, https://turnaround.ams3.digital-oceanspaces.com/wp-content/uploads/2016/03/14034511/Turnaround-for-Children-Building-Blocks-for-Learningx-2.pdf.

30. According to Tavenner, the one exception is curiosity, which is difficult to teach. There are practices to teach curiosity, but there is also evidence that today's schools strip away curiosity. Therefore, reshaping schools to not strip out the curiosity that individuals possess naturally is important. And as Tavenner told me, we can also enable people to remain curious as they enter adulthood by helping build their growth mindset, sense of belonging, resilience, and tenacity.

    See also "Encourage Your Kid to Be Curious," *Prepared Parents*, https://preparedparents.org/tip/encouraging-my-kids-interests/ (accessed January 21, 2022) for an overview of curiosity and its importance toward being successful in school and life.

31. Others emphasize that educators haven't been trained to help students build these habits.

32. John M. Bridgeland and Francie Richards, "Where Does Social-Emotional Learning Go Next?," *Education Week*, May 11, 2021, https://www.edweek.org/leadership/opinion-where-does-social-emotional-learning-go-next/2021/05?utm_source=nl&utm_medium=eml&utm_campaign=eu&M=59971982&U=67948&UID=2a97314eb8614a7f8123bed720cdf420.

33. Indeed, curiosity and persistence are "most closely linked to better academic performance for both 10- and 15-year-olds, according to the first international survey of social-emotional skills." Sarah D.

Sparks, "The SEL Skills That May Matter Most for Academic Success: Curiosity and Persistence," *Education Week*, October 29, 2021, https://www.edweek.org/leadership/the-sel-skills-that-may-matter-most-for-academic-success-curiosity-and-persistence/2021/10?utm_source=nl&utm_medium=eml&utm_campaign=eu&M=64194894&U=67948&UUID=2a97314eb8614a7f8123bed720cdf420.

34. This is one example where these domains overlap with each other. Understanding why what one is learning matters overlaps with the habit of success in which students develop an understanding of the importance of education.

35. John M. Bridgeland, John J. Dilulio, Jr., and Karen Burke Morison, "The Silent Epidemic: Perspectives of High School Dropouts," Civic enterprises in association with Peter D. Hart Research Associates for the Bill & Melinda Gates Foundation, March 2006, https://docs.gatesfoundation.org/documents/thesilentepidemic3-06final.pdf.

36. With this said, this isn't to say that schools should blindly follow what students desire and like from a surface-level perspective. There are clearly limits to that approach. As Jason L. Riley wrote in his intellectual biography of the economist Thomas Sowell, "At the end of the first semester, [Sowell] approached the department chairman to ask for permission to drop the course because he didn't think he was learning anything. Permission was granted, and it would be decades later before Sowell realized his mistake. In an emotional column written after Becker died in 2014, Sowell said that his former professor had been 'introducing his own analytical framework that was destined to change the way many issues would be seen by the economics profession in the years ahead.' Becker was teaching 'something important, but I just wasn't on the same wavelength.' Sowell described his youthful arrogance as 'a continuing source of embarrassment to me over the years, after I belatedly grasped what he was trying to get across.' His takeaway from these episodes and others was that students often don't know—because they can't know at the time—what is 'relevant' to their education." Jason L. Riley, *Maverick: A Biography of Thomas Sowell* (New York: Basic Books, 2021), p. 82.

More to the point, we often forget how much of the mysterious world is of genuine interest to students. Trying to connect concepts to something that they express interest in today—because of a students' own (perhaps limited to this point) background experiences—that may distract from the intent of the learning may be unnecessary. Posing interesting questions up front that spark curiosity to unpack more may be enough in many cases to leverage a child's "interests." As Daniel Willingham wrote in *Why Students Don't Like School*, problems that students believe they can solve, questions, and stories all can provoke interest from students. Margaret (Macke) Raymond, "COVID-19, High School, and the 'Both And' World," Hoover Institution, May 1, 2021, https://www.hoover.org/research/covid-19-high-school-and-both-and-world.

37. Indeed, a slew of states and foundations have made embedded innovative career and technical education programs in schools to try and lure disengaged students back. Beth Hawkins, "Fueled by Grants, States Bet Innovative Career Programs Will Lure Disengaged Youth Back to School After COVID—Starting in Middle School," The 74, November 9, 2021, https://www.the74million.org/article/fueled-by-grants-states-bet-innovative-career-training-programs-will-lure-disengaged-youth-back-to-school-after-covid-starting-in-middle-school/.

38. According to Next Generation Learning Challenges, those schools that prioritized relationships were well prepared for the pandemic. "What Made Them So Prepared?," NGLC, https://www.nextgen-learning.org/prepared-project (accessed November 14, 2021).

    Yet again, this is also an area that connects to the habit of success of attachment.

39. "Behind the Innovation in Student Purpose at Cajon Valley Union School District," YouTube, July 7, 2021, https://www.youtube.com/watch?v=7pL4OGfFaYI.

40. Raymond, "COVID-19, High School, and the 'Both And' World."

41. Phyllis Lockett, "Why We Must Look to the Science of Learning to Strengthen Student-Teacher Relationships," *Forbes*, September 22, 2021, https://www.forbes.com/sites/phyllislockett/2021/09/22/why-we-must-look-to-the-science-of-learning-to-strengthen-student-teacher-relationships/?sh=7572bc925f59.

42. Sarah D. Sparks, "Helping Students Bounce Back from a Disrupted Year: Strategies for Schools," *Education Week*, May 24, 2021, https://www.edweek.org/leadership/helping-students-bounce-back-from-a-disrupted-year-strategies-for-schools/2021/05?utm_source=nl&utm_medium=eml&utm_campaign=eu&M=60321929&U=67948&UUID=2a97314eb8614a7f8123bed720cdf420.

43. More broadly, there is significant research that backs up these observations about the importance of knowledge, skills, habits of

Essential Guiding Principles for Equitable Whole-Child Design

Derived from SoLD Practice Principles: Darling-Hammond, L., Flook, L., Cook-Harvey, C., Barron, B., and Osher, D. (2019). Implications for educational practice of the science of learning and development. Applied Developmental Science. 2.

success, real-world experiences and social capital, and health and wellness. The Science of Learning and Development Alliance, a partnership of leaders and organizations focused on the science of learning and development to support education systems and help each young person achieve their full potential, published a framework with guiding principles to ensure equitable whole-child design, for example. Although their categories are different from the ones I present here, they arrive at a similar list, with the exception that by including wellness as well as basic needs in my health bucket, my list is broader than theirs. They focus on five categories—positive development relationships, environments filled with safety and belonging, rich learning experiences and knowledge development (which includes real-world experiences), development of skills, habits, and mindsets, and integrated support systems. Their diagram is shown below to illustrate how these elements come together in an integrated whole.

Pamela Cantor, Linda Darling-Hammond, Merita Irby, and Karen Pittman, "How Can We Design Learning Settings So That All Students Thrive?," SoLD Alliance, April 8, 2021, https://www .soldalliance.org/post/how-can-we-design-learning-settings-so-that-all-students-thrive.

44. Larry Ferlazzo, "The Pandemic's Glaring Lessons for District Leaders," *Education Week*, September 28, 2021, https://www .edweek.org/leadership/opinion-the-pandemics-glaring-lessons-not-yet-learned/2021/09?utm_source=nl&utm_medium= eml&utm_campaign=eu&M=63853099&U=67948&UUID=2a97 314eb8614a7f8123bed720cdf420.

45. That led to the district creating robust outdoor learning spaces. Spring Grove didn't simply re-create the classroom outside. The district took advantage of the natural environment. It also built learning pods.

46. "Behind the Innovations at Spring Grove Public Schools," YouTube, August 17, 2021, https://www.youtube.com/watch?v=0sJ6cVlw2SY.

47. As Robert Pondiscio wrote in a brief for the American Enterprise Institute, schools should be wary about extending into "social and emotional learning," as it "alters fundamentally the role and nature of

schooling." In particular, Pondiscio argued, "The tendency to borrow ideas and tactics from therapy carries with it the risk of pathologizing childhood and encouraging educators to view children—particularly children from disadvantaged subgroups—not as capable and resilient individuals but as fragile and traumatized." The explicit emphasis on teaching habits of success around agency, resilience, academic tenacity, self-direction, purpose, sense of belonging, and growth mindset are at direct odds with some of the roots of Pondiscio's concerns. But many of his concerns rotate on whether we ask untrained teachers to take on some of these additional roles. Robert Pondiscio, "The Unexamined Rise of Therapeutic Education: How Social-Emotional Learning Extends K–12 Education's Reach into Students' Lives and Expands Teachers' Roles," American Enterprise Institute, October 2021, https://www.aei.org/wp-content/uploads/2021/10/The-Unexamined-Rise-of-Therapeutic-Education.pdf?x91208.

48. "Leaders We Need Now," National Association of Elementary School Principals, 2021, https://www.naesp.org/leaders-we-need-now/.

49. In Boston, a group of organizations—the YMCA of Greater Boston, Inquilinos Boricuas en Accion, The BASE, and Latinos for Education—have banded together to create a Community Learning Collaborative to run 12 pods serving 125 students to create smaller settings for students to have individualized attention to their learning needs connected to the community. James Morton, "Morton: Combining Summer School & Summer Camp—How a Group of Boston Nonprofits Is Reimagining Public Education," The 74, May 15, 2021, https://www.the74million.org/article/morton-combining-summer-school-summer-camp-how-a-group-of-boston-nonprofits-is-reimagining-public-education/.

Chapter 4

Student Experience: Lose Learning Loss

While her parents sat in Dr. Ball's office, Julia kept her head down in her fifth-grade classroom. Her class was in the middle of a history lesson, and she was bored.

They were reviewing the practice of indentured servitude—again. She already understood it, and she was itching to move on.

She caught Jeremy's eye from across the room. Maybe he could help her with her kicking again during kickball today at recess, she thought. That might keep her away from some of the fights that had been happening.

Jeremy smiled at her, looked at their teacher, Mrs. Alvera, and then rolled his eyes.

Julia giggled.

"Ms. Owens," Mrs. Alvera said sternly.

Julia's head swiveled to the front of the room. "Yes, Mrs. Alvera," she said. Shoot, she had been caught.

"I don't think indentured servitude is a laughing matter. Would you like to share just how long you'd be stuck in this classroom if you were my indentured servant?"

"Seven years," Julia gulped. Her eyes looked down again as Mrs. Alvera continued.

Jeremy cast his eyes downward, too. He felt badly that he had made Julia laugh. He was also bored, but that was because he was totally lost. He couldn't square how indentured servitude made up the largest segment of the early Virginia population and yet stayed stuck in this arrangement. And how did it connect with slavery again? He couldn't remember.

* * *

If it wasn't apparent to people beforehand, the pandemic made it more obvious. School for its own sake isn't a priority in most students' lives.[1]

Were it otherwise, more students would have dug into remote and hybrid forms of schooling and remained engaged no matter the quality of the experience. But, for the most part, that didn't happen.

Yet there was a seeming paradox. Many families and educators witnessed their children clamoring to go back to in-person school. Why?

It wasn't that they were demanding school per se.

For many, it was that they were desperate to be in a place where they could have fun and socialize with friends.[2] As one parent relayed, his children wouldn't let him go on vacation during the pandemic when they were in hybrid schooling because they didn't want to be away from their friends—no matter how few days were in person. They had seen what they stood to lose in the spring of 2020. They didn't want that to happen again. Not even for a trip to Disney.

Schooling, in other words, wasn't a priority. It was a conduit to something else.

This phenomenon isn't unusual. Nor is it confined to the world of education.

Individuals rarely consume an offering for its own sake. They are generally trying to make progress in a struggling circumstance (what we refer to as a "Job to Be Done"). They use a particular service or product to help.

The famous Harvard marketing professor Theodore Levitt summarized it as such: "People don't want a quarter-inch drill. They want a quarter-inch hole!"

WHAT DO STUDENTS WANT?

I have studied this question over the past 15 years in K–12 schools and was curious whether the findings would hold up during the pandemic. They have.

At a macro level, children have two Jobs to Be Done. First, they want to do things that help them feel successful—that they are making progress and accomplishing something, rather than experiencing nothing but repeated failure or running up against walls. Second, they want to do things that help them have fun with friends. They want positive, rewarding social experiences with others, including peers, teachers, coaches, and advisors.[3]

What about those students for whom remote schooling worked well—a minority perhaps, but still a significant number?

Some of those students found a place where they could be successful and make progress. Some percentage of them had struggled to do that in traditional in-person schools. Alternatively, some were now in a setting where they were able to have more positive interactions with others around them—something that they may have struggled to do when they were in person. Those struggles could have been caused by their dispositions and personal circumstances or factors such as bullying.

With this knowledge, as educators seek to build better schools, how should they engage students? What's the experience that will help students meet with success and have fun with friends?

TRADITIONAL SCHOOLS FALL SHORT

For most, it's not the traditional experience.

The opportunities to experience success in the traditional classroom occur infrequently. For example, in many classes, the only real opportunity to feel successful is on end-of-unit tests, which occur only every few weeks. Students often don't receive timely feedback on these assessments—or even their day-to-day assignments—so the opportunity to feel successful is separated from the work.

Progress is also decoupled from the learning because students advance on the pacing guide's schedule, not based on their own learning. That's because in today's school system, time is held as fixed and each child's learning is variable. Teachers are required to move students through a set of standards each year based on their grade level or the course in which they are enrolled. In most schools, the class marches accordingly through the curriculum.

At the end of each unit, which occurs at fixed times when students typically take an assessment, some have inevitably failed to master the material. They therefore don't experience success. The privilege of feeling successful is reserved for only a few. By design, the rest experience something short of that.

The challenges the Jeremys and Julias of our country face because of sorting stem directly from this phenomenon. As they receive grades on the work they submit—grades that generally can't be changed—labels emerge. Being labeled often means individuals will see themselves as someone who is fixed as opposed to someone who can grow. Being sorted into different groupings and tracks because of those labels can damage a child's self-efficacy. Any kind of label that implies a fixed and immutable set of characteristics or realities works against a growth mindset, as

Carol Dweck argued in her bestselling book *Mindset: The New Psychology of Success*. Negative labels carry extra baggage that discourage most from even trying.

Despite the reams of advice telling us to learn from our failures, rare is the individual who wants to *feel* like a failure in anything and seeks out activities that reinforce that feeling. As Northwestern University professor Lauren Eskreis-Winkler argues, there is evidence that failure thwarts learning.[4]

By moving to mastery-based learning, however, we can help individuals reframe failure as part of the learning process on the road to success. Doing so follows the advice of bestselling author Jessica Lahey to see failure as a gift, rather than a permanent label.

Worse still, school activities in which students can experience success are often explicitly separated from the core educational experience. Pursuits such as athletic teams and musical and dramatic arts performance groups, which are mechanisms for feeling successful, are called *extracurricular* activities rather than curricular ones. That speaks volumes.

During the pandemic, for example, former Vermont governor Peter Shumlin authored a piece in which he made the case for the benefits of such extracurricular activities: the advancement of "prosocial" behaviors, improved mental and physical health, and a more creative mind. If, as he wrote, "participation in extracurricular activities is positively associated with consistent school attendance, higher grades, and greater aspirations for continuing education beyond high school,"[5] one of the reasons is because the students who participate are able to experience success in these activities and have fun with friends.

But why not embed the chance to experience success and have fun with friends into the core experience as well?

Lest we use the fact that many children wanted to return to school as evidence that the traditional core experience is a good social experience, that's hardly the case. It's just better than the alternative, which for many was being stuck at home and maybe interacting online with friends. Being together in masks was preferable to that.

The traditional experience isn't great at helping children have fun with friends. At the extreme end, roughly 20 percent of students ages 12–18 report being bullied in school.[6] Among parents with children in grades K–12, more than a third believe that bullying is a problem at their child's school, according to a Harris poll.[7]

Although not all students experience negative relationships like this, the question arises: Are traditional classrooms optimized to help students form positive relationships?

Teachers are responsible for instructing large batches of diverse students and have limited time to connect with each student one-on-one. Whole-class instruction offers little opportunity for students to form relationships with each other or with the teacher.

Schools are stretched to provide a full suite of academic, extracurricular, and social services. The elimination of bullying and the assurance of a safe, positive environment can fall through the cracks.

Even more to the point, as Diane Tavenner said, "We all believe that school should be a social experience, that it should be joyful, that our kids should like it, and that they should actually be learning... But what parents are thinking of as social learning actually isn't."[8]

If you take a step back and remember some of your own schooling experience, you can likely see her point. If a student seeks to be social during class, that student typically gets in trouble in a traditional school. Just remember the fate of the class clown. Or, in my case, why many of my middle school teachers perhaps thought I had written an autobiography when *Disrupting Class* was first published. Or how students who ask a friend for help in understanding something get in trouble for doing so in the middle of class.

It is true that in addition to the extracurricular activities discussed earlier, schools do afford some other opportunities for social interaction—during recess or in the hallway before, between, and after class. But the fact that these are all outside of the classroom as opposed to woven into the fabric of schooling itself shows that schools have a ways to go.

As a result of these dynamics, schools are essentially in competition with a number of nonacademic options that allow students to experience success and have fun with friends, including playing video games, participating in the arts, competing in sports, dropping out of a school to take a job or hang out with friends, and joining a gang. Too often, schools are sorry competitors for these alternatives.

This means that students who focus their attention on things besides education are not unmotivated. They are plenty motivated—to feel success and have fun with friends. The problem is that many students just don't or can't feel successful each day and find rewarding relationships at a traditionally structured school. Instead, school makes them feel like failures—academically, socially, or both.

LOSE LEARNING LOSS

Once we understand what individuals are trying to accomplish in their lives—the progress they are seeking, and the social, emotional, and functional dimensions of that progress—we can start thinking about what experiences are important to help an individual make that progress. Then we can figure out how to knit together the right assets—people, facilities, technologies, curriculum, the use of time, training and professional development, and the like—to help create the progress students crave.

How should schools build their student experience?

An important place to start is reversing the practice of sorting that breeds a sense of failure. It's instead important to refocus schooling on cultivating success for each child every day.

That means ditching the notion of learning loss that has been such a national obsession during the pandemic. Yes, the initial focus on learning loss as a threat was critical to marshal resources, as Chapter 1 discussed. Keeping this framing, however, won't help students now.

The interruptions that occurred to many students' learning remain heartbreaking. But leaning into that loss and testing ad nauseum just to show how much students missed is unlikely to help.

Students don't want to hear about how they're failing. It's the opposite of motivating. And if we're to help accelerate students' learning, then they need to buy in because they will need to do a lot of the work. There's a reason why legendary football coach Vince Lombardi's speeches dwell on winning and success, not losing and failure.

To be clear, taking this direction isn't because educators should hide from what knowledge and skills students need—and have yet—to learn. Instead it is to harness students' natural motivation to make progress in their lives. The idea is to align that progress with the goals of educators and schools.

What would that look like? That, along with how to embed the ability to have fun with friends into the school day, is the topic of the next chapter.

KEY TAKEAWAYS

- Schooling isn't the top priority in most children's lives.
- Their top priorities are to experience success—that they are making progress and accomplishing something—and to have fun with friends on a daily basis.
- Traditional schools fall short on these dimensions.

- Focusing on learning loss helps make students feel like failures and doesn't contribute to allowing them to experience success.

NOTES

1. Multiple surveys showed that on average students became less engaged during remote learning as the pandemic interrupted schooling. See, for example, Matt Barnum and Claire Bryan, "America's Great Remote-Learning Experiment: What Surveys of Teachers and Parents Tell Us about How It Went," *Chalkbeat*, June 26, 2020, https://www.chalkbeat.org/2020/6/26/21304405/surveys-remote-learning-coronavirus-success-failure-teachers-parents. The article reads, "Two-thirds to three-quarters of teachers said their students were less engaged during remote instruction than before the pandemic, and that engagement declined even further over the course of the semester."

2. See, for example, this survey from Bellevue School District in Washington: "BSD Second Grade Back-to-School Feedback Survey," Bellevue School District, January 21, 2021, https://bsd405.org/wp-content/uploads/2021/01/grade-two-first-day-back-family-survey-results.pdf.

3. As Arthur Brooks wrote in *The Atlantic*, "For many children, school is not just hard work, but also intensely isolating. Research shows that 80 percent of children face loneliness at times in school; that emotion is linked to boredom, inactivity, a tendency to withdraw into fantasy, and a passive attitude toward social interactions." Conversely, friendship at school is by far the biggest predictor of enjoyment and positive behaviors. Gallup has found that having a best friend at school is the best predictor of student engagement in both fifth grade and 11th. Similarly, a study from the Hebrew University of Jerusalem, the University of Warwick, and the National Bureau of Economic Research shows that students with "reciprocal friendships" (wherein both sides see the relationship

the same way) are more likely to enjoy school and are more successful in the classroom.

Arthur C. Brooks, "The Real Reason Kids Don't Like School," *The Atlantic*, August 26, 2021, https://www.theatlantic.com/family/archive/2021/08/how-help-kids-like-school-better-loneliness/619881/?utm_source=feed.

4. Lauren Eskreis-Winkler and Ayelet Fishbach, "Not Learning from Failure—the Greatest Failure of All," *Psychological Science*, November 8, 2019.

5. Peter Shumlin, "Kids Are Missing More Than Classroom Learning Due to COVID-19. Why States Must Also Use Relief Funds to Restore Student Engagement via In-Person Extracurriculars," The 74, April 26, 2021, https://www.the74million.org/article/gov-shumlin-kids-are-missing-more-than-classroom-learning-due-to-covid-19-why-states-must-also-use-relief-funds-to-restore-student-engagement-via-in-person-extracurriculars/.

6. "How Many Students Are Bullied at School?" National Center for Education Statistics, https://nces.ed.gov/fastfacts/display.asp?id=719 (accessed November 14, 2021).

7. "6 in 10 Americans Say They or Someone They Know Have Been Bullied," The Harris Poll, February 19, 2014, https://theharrispoll.com/wp-content/uploads/2017/12/Harris_Poll_17_-_School_Bullying_2.19.2014.pdf.

8. "LISTEN—Class Disrupted Podcast Episode 2: Why Is My Child Doing So Many Worksheets Right Now?" *Class Disrupted*, May 25, 2020, https://www.the74million.org/article/listen-class-disrupted-podcast-why-is-my-child-doing-so-many-worksheets-right-now/.

Chapter 5

Student Experience: Guarantee Mastery

Jeremy started daydreaming. He remembered the early days of the pandemic when there was no school. Well, there was, but he hadn't gone to remote school those first couple of months. By May he was back.

He recalled fondly how his second-grade teacher had mailed home a simple sheet with the big ideas he was supposed to learn. Each idea had its own square on a colorful path that looked like the road in Candy Land,[1] *his favorite board game back then.*

Whenever he learned something, he showed his teacher he could do it on Zoom. If she agreed he had mastered it, then he got to color in the corresponding square—and she did as well on her screen.

It made each lesson so clear—and it meant he was always working on his own map at his own pace. He liked that.

The next year, his third-grade teacher kept the practice up so she knew exactly where he was when he returned in the fall. She didn't need to give him any tests to see where he was in his learning. They just did some little refreshes and then he was off.

"Jeremy," Mrs. Alvera said, as she interrupted his reverie.

Oh no. Now he had been caught.

"Well, what's the answer?" she asked.

"I dunno," he muttered. He sighed as he longed for those days when he knew what he was supposed to learn and his teacher knew where he was in his learning.

By the end of the third grade, after most of his classmates had returned to in-person learning, his teacher had stopped using the Candy Land-type boards as she marched the class through a bunch of lessons before the state tests in April.

Well, at least he could play with his friends at recess later and show off his big leg during kickball.

* * *

As we seek to reinvent schools to best serve each individual student, a reframe is in order. Rather than focus on learning loss, we should focus on what students have mastered. Instead of a deficit mindset, let's understand the positives. What have students accomplished? And how might we make schools a place where students can have fun with their friends as they experience success in their learning?

A LEARNING CYCLE BUILT ON SUCCESS

Start with success instead of loss.

The learning cycle that students at Summit Public Schools move through achieves that reframe by creating a pathway to success for each student (see Figure 5.1).

The cycle starts with goal setting. Educators work with students to articulate what they are trying to accomplish. Students then make a plan to reach those goals. From there, students learn and then show evidence of their learning. That evidence could be

Figure 5.1 Summit learning cycle

through a conventional assessment, a project, a written paper, a presentation, and so forth. Finally, students receive feedback and reflect on what they learned in the process, which informs the next goal they set. Implementing this cycle builds in the habits of success of self-awareness, agency, and executive functions as students set their own goals, plan on how they will get there, and reflect on how well they executed.

The cycle moves away from a focus on learning gaps, unfinished learning, or learning loss to focusing on mastery. That means throwing off the yoke of today's time-bound system to focus on mastery-based—also called competency-based—learning.

Summit Public Schools:
https://www.youtube.com/watch?v=6IG7KnQ8zek

HOW TOYOTA ILLUSTRATES THE POWER OF GUARANTEED MASTERY

To show the power of a mastery-based approach, an analogy helps. The analogy is from a story MIT lecturer Steve Spear tells in his book *Chasing the Rabbit*.[2] It's one that I've written about in several books, including *Disrupting Class*, to help frame what mastery-based learning can look like.

While a doctoral student, Steve took temporary jobs, working first on an assembly line at one of the Detroit Big Three plants and then at Toyota at the passenger-side front seat installation point.

In Detroit, the worker doing the training essentially told Steve, "The cars come down this line every 58 seconds, so that's how long you have to install this seat. Now I'm going to show you how to do it. First, you do this. Then do that, then click this in here just like this, then tighten this, then do that," and so on, until the seat was completely installed. "Do you get how to do it, Steve?"

Steve thought he could do each of those things in the allotted time. When the next car arrived, he picked up the seat and did each of the preparatory steps. But when he tried to install it in the car, it wouldn't fit. For the entire 58 seconds he tried to complete the installation but couldn't. His trainer stopped the assembly line to fix the problem. He again showed Steve how to do it. When the next car arrived, Steve tried again but didn't get it right. In an entire hour, he installed only four seats correctly.

Historically, one reason it was so important to test every product when it came off the end of a production line like the Detroit Big Three's was that there were typically hundreds of steps involved in making a product, and the company could not be sure that each step had been done correctly. In business, we call that end-of-the-line activity "inspection." In education, we call it "summative assessment."

When Steve went to work at the same station in Toyota's plant, he had a completely different experience. First, he went to a training station where he was told, "These are the seven steps required to install this seat successfully. You don't have the privilege of learning step 2 until you've demonstrated mastery of step 1. If you master step 1 in a minute, you can begin learning step 2 a minute from now. If step 1 takes you an hour, then you can learn step 2 in an hour. And if it takes you a day, then you can learn step 2 tomorrow. It makes no sense for us to teach you subsequent steps if you can't do the prior ones correctly."

Testing and assessment were still vital, but they were an integral part of the process of instruction. As a result, when he took his spot in Toyota's production line, Steve was able to do his part right the first time and every time. Toyota had built into its process a mechanism to verify immediately that each step had been done correctly so that no time or money would be wasted fixing a defective product. As a result, it did not have to test its products when they came to the end of the production process.

That's quite a contrast between the two methods for training Steve Spear. At the Detroit Big Three plant, the time was fixed, but the result of training was variable and unpredictable. The "exam"—installing the seat—came at the end of Steve's training.

At Toyota, the training time was variable. But assessment was interdependently woven into content delivery, and the result was fixed. Every person who went through the training could predictably do what he had been taught to do. It was guaranteed.

Not only that, but success was also built into the Toyota process. Although someone might struggle and experience small failures en route to learning how to install the right front seat, failure wasn't the end point. Because learning was fixed, so, too, was success in the equation. In other words, learning in this way builds in success and meaningful progress. That's motivating, not discouraging.

TIME-BOUND VERSUS GUARANTEED LEARNING

The traditional learning system, which is akin to the process in the Detroit factory, looks like what is shown in Figure 5.2.

Figure 5.2   Time-fixed, learning variable

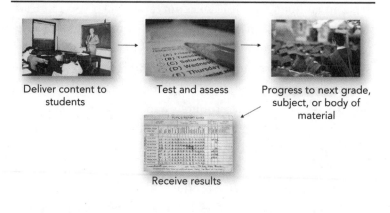

Deliver content to students

Test and assess

Progress to next grade, subject, or body of material

Receive results

We offer learning experiences, test and assess, and then students move on to the next unit or grade; only afterward do they receive feedback.

Although we hear a lot about the importance of data-driven decision making and feedback in learning, it turns out that data and feedback are not always good for learning. When a student receives feedback but cannot do anything useful with that data— meaning they can't use it to improve their performance or learning, as in the time-fixed, learning variable system—then it has a negative influence on student learning. Conversely, when the student can do something with the data, then it has a positive impact on learning.[3]

This is where mastery-based learning can start to help. Figure 5.3 shows what it roughly looks like.

With clear learning goals established, we still offer learning experiences and then test and assess. But students then receive feedback that they use to inform what they do next. Only after they demonstrate mastery do they fully leave a concept.

Success is built into the process. The use of data and feedback is to allow students to successfully master concepts. The feedback can be delivered frequently and in bite-sized pieces, as necessary, to help each student feel successful.

Figure 5.3 Learning fixed, time variable

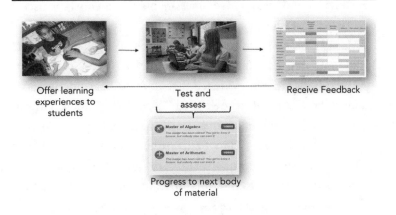

Offer learning experiences to students

Test and assess

Receive Feedback

Progress to next body of material

In traditional instruction, in contrast, exams are offered every few weeks. Then, because this system is designed to categorize students as excellent, average, and below average, it causes most students to not feel successful as they learn.

Some psychometricians, experts in the science of measuring mental capacities, say that assessments can either drive instruction or be used for accountability, but not both. The Toyota experience suggests otherwise if the assessments are implemented in a mastery-based learning system in which time is variable and learning is guaranteed.

This gives a window into how the public education system can move past end-of-year summative assessments for accountability that essentially tell us what percent of students have failed. We can instead use a combination of short assessments to verify mastery of objective concepts along with rich projects that measure several competencies—what a student can do with the knowledge and skills they've acquired. As Chapter 6 discusses, the projects should be reviewed by people other than the student's teacher—be that other teachers in the school, district, state, or outside experts. This is how the Mastery Transcript Consortium, a nonprofit seeking to reinvent the transcript for college, works.

This vision for the use of assessments is different from formative, benchmark, and summative assessments. It's a constant use of evaluation that is both *of* learning and *for* learning.

Mastery-based learning has another benefit, which connects to students' desire to make progress and experience success.

There is significant evidence that students' learning is maximized when content is delivered "just above" their current capabilities—not too much of a stretch, and not too easy. As cognitive scientist Daniel Willingham wrote, "Working on problems that are of the right level of difficult is rewarding, but working on problems that are too easy or too difficult is unpleasant." A key to helping students experience success is borrowing a concept from the world of gaming and allowing students to learn at the point that will maximize their chances of success while still being sufficiently challenging or interesting that they will experience that triumph as a real moment of progress—with all the endorphins that produces—so that they will want to keep learning.[4] Customization to the "just above" level for each student is natural in a mastery-based model, whereas it's anathema to the time-based traditional model of most schools.

DON'T JUST CHANGE GRADING WHEN IMPLEMENTING MASTERY-BASED LEARNING

When educators implement mastery-based learning, they often start by changing how they grade. The temptation is to move away from today's letter-based grades and instead move to standards-based grading. In standards-based grading, educators assign a rating for each competency, such as "mastered (4 on a 4-point scale)," "proficient (3)," "needs more work (2)," and "not yet started (1)."

Problems with the Traditional Grading System

The traditional grading system has many problems that need to be fixed.[5]

The system doesn't accurately represent what someone knows and can do. If someone earns a C in Algebra, for example, which 30 percent of the learning standards do they not understand? A single grade for a given class or subject does not provide enough specificity or granularity.

It's also possible a student received that grade for reasons apart from their understanding of the learning goals. For example, if someone has mastered a subject by the end of a class but did poorly on early assignments, their averaged grade may be a C. But that grade doesn't accurately showcase what they now know and can do. Students sometimes alternatively earn an A because of the extra-credit work they did—which may or may not have anything to do with their mastery of the subject. The traditional grading system also often takes into account other factors beside the academic standards in play, like behavior or tardiness, that would be better represented through feedback about students' habits of success. As Diane Tavenner wrote in her book *Prepared: What Kids Need for a Fulfilled Life*, "Grades offer little in the way of objectivity, as two-thirds of teachers acknowledge their grading reflects progress, effort, and participation in class."[6] At one talk I gave to a prominent teachers' organization, one member confided that this trend is increasing. Teachers worry about failing students for doing little work, the member said. They instead want to make sure students receive some credit for the nonacademic elements that schools should help cultivate in students. This points to the reality that traditional grades are often inequitable and idiosyncratic, as most teachers have different grading standards for the same subject.

The traditional grading system also casts fixed labels on people. Students will grow to view themselves as a "C student in math" or an "A student." If one is in the latter bucket, that can be detrimental because they might feel like they shouldn't have to ask for help if they struggle later.

Begin with the End

Yet fixing grading alone is akin to a doctor treating a sick patient's symptoms rather than the root cause of the underlying problem. Moving to a mastery-based learning system is a systemic change, not a simple initiative. It's hard work that involves changing the underlying priorities and processes of our education system.

When implementing mastery-based learning, educators should begin with the end by clarifying the learning goals. What is the end destination? What will students master? These goals should span knowledge, skills, dispositions, and habits.

Educators should then spend time clarifying how they would know that someone had demonstrated mastery for each learning goal. What is the evidence they would need to see? What is the rubric by which educators would judge mastery? Do students need to consistently demonstrate their understanding over a certain time period to show true mastery? How will educators ensure consistency and rigor across a school and district so that students don't attain mastery because of the whim of a teacher, because a teacher liked or disliked a particular student, or because teachers were using different assessments, rubrics, or scales?

From there educators need to figure out how to facilitate the new system of learning in which each individual will learn based on their individual needs, will use assessment to receive timely and actionable feedback that informs what they do next, and will progress based on evidence of mastery, not time.[7] This leads into architecting the day-to-day student experience and the specific curricula and learning opportunities.

Once a school community has worked through this process to redesign the system, then it can delve into grading through the prism of measuring and reporting what students know and can do at any particular point in time. Attending to the grading system, in other words, is a change that occurs naturally at the end of the process. It's not the end itself.

Focus on Success and Learning, Not Grades

Although tackling the problems with traditional grading can be a gateway to deeper changes, starting with grading can also be fraught with challenges and traps unless educators are "prepared to lift up the conversation," as competency-based learning expert Chris Sturgis argues.[8] Why? Besides that it starts with the end-point of a broader change process, the A–F grading system is synonymous with schooling in the minds of many communities. It's what they experienced and how they think school "should be." Unless you've helped a community reconceptualize the purpose of schooling and how to motivate students, starting one's journey into mastery-based learning by upending the traditional grading system risks stalling progress before you start by focusing on a what—grades—instead of the why.

A conversation with my own mom from several years ago showed me how powerful the A–F grading system is in the minds of many.

Before the pandemic, when I traveled frequently, my mom and I would often chat on the phone while I was waiting in the airport. Several years ago, as I stood in an airport in Tennessee, my mom called. She started the conversation by yelling for 10 minutes. The source of her irritation? It was a story she had read in the *Washington Post* about a school that had abandoned A–F grading.

She kept asking, "Can you believe how they're dumbing down schools now?" She was incensed.

After listening to her and not saying anything, at the end of the conversation I replied meekly. "Mom, this sounds kind of like what I work on and what I try to get schools to do!" I then tried to explain how mastery-based learning is in fact more rigorous because it means that all students will eventually master each competency rather than just languish and skip fully learning fundamental blocks of knowledge and skills.

Her point has stayed with me, however.

The cost of challenging the letter-grade system in which parents grew up and replacing it at the outset with an unfamiliar nomenclature can be high. A new grading system can feel less rigorous. It's also often confusing. And it can worry parents that their children will be at a disadvantage when they apply to college. Many are concerned that colleges won't understand alternative ways of representing achievement.

It turns out that parents needn't worry. Many colleges already successfully navigate this dynamic today. A growing number of colleges are showing interest in other ways of understanding who students are and what they can do by working with groups like the Mastery Transcript Consortium. Still, it is a worry that parents have and educators will need to address.

More interesting perhaps is that none of the challenges with letter grades are inherently built into the nomenclature of A–F itself. Schools can move to mastery and standards-based grading with letter grades partially intact.

A story about the struggles of a suburban middle school principal in Massachusetts illustrates why.

The middle school principal implemented standards-based grading well before the pandemic. His primary motivation was to create a more equitable grading system. But a subset of parents cared only about how it would impact their children's college prospects.

A struggle ensued that drained resources. Chapter 7 directly addresses this parental dynamic more, but to handle the conflict, the district ultimately reached for a compromise. It suggested that the middle school could keep standards-based grading for sixth grade, but should then move to a traditional grading system for seventh and eighth grades to prepare students for what they would confront in high school.

As a group of us counseled him on what to do, one conclusion was that sticking to a novel grading system might not be the best way forward. Perhaps he could move the three-point grading scale his school was using to an "A, B, or Incomplete" grading system for each competency. In a mastery-based learning model, keeping the familiar letters but changing other aspects of the grading system could work relatively seamlessly.

Finally, one other reason starting with grading is often counterproductive is that it causes people to focus on what they are losing. This includes the ability to sort the Jeremys and Julias of the world into neat categories. Some parents may also feel like they are giving up a sense of whether their child is ahead of their peers. By focusing on what they're losing, they're unlikely to embrace the gains of better opportunities for all students.

It's important not to innovate behind parents' backs or push changes onto their children. Instead, create the conditions under which parents and the broader schooling community will pull in changes so that you're innovating *with* your community.

Chapter 11 on the Tools of Cooperation further addresses this dynamic and gives leaders ways to navigate these challenges. But for now, know that this may mean that creating a small school within the broader school is your best bet so that you're not imposing a set of changes on anyone. If you take this path, let parents self-select into the mastery-based model that has been framed as an opportunity, much as Kettle Moraine did, as we discussed in Chapter 1.

Either way, the big message to parents should be that you're making sure all students will succeed and master each of the required competencies. That's the bottom line.

What Should Gradebook Reports Look Like?

Many districts are actively working to change grading policies. Some of these efforts, like that of the Mastery Transcript Consortium, were underway before the pandemic. The pandemic has accelerated the shift in many other districts and schools.

Instead of thinking of a report card as the final say on a student's grades for a particular subject, reframe it as a snapshot check-in. Teachers, students, and parents should all be able to access this snapshot on demand because the purpose is to communicate what students know and can do—and help understand what else they need to learn to be successful.

Part of the challenge for many mastery-based grading efforts is that showing all the competencies and where students are in their learning can be confusing and overwhelming. But a snapshot check-in could instead convey simple metrics, such as whether the student is on track, ahead of where they need to be, or behind for any given area. Beyond that, it could convey what percent of different grade-level standards a student had mastered. It could also show what students had started but not yet mastered.

From there, the snapshot check-in could allow students or parents to double click (or turn the page) on places of interest for more detail. Here they could review a more detailed list of competencies that the student has mastered, is still working on, or hasn't yet started, as well as a portfolio of evidence—projects, assessments, and the like—that showcase the students' work for any given standard.

If comparison is important for some reason, the check-in could theoretically also give a comparison to the class to show where a student chose to go deeper. That could indicate a deeper interest or passion. It could also theoretically provide a snapshot of where a student ranked relative to others in terms of the competencies mastered. But this wouldn't ultimately have much meaning, as what's more important is whether students are mastering the required competencies at a fast enough rate to graduate on time.

The big shift should be toward understanding how fast, far, or deep a student went in their mastery versus what percentage they got right or wrong.

ANSWERS TO FOUR CRITICISMS OF MASTERY LEARNING

You will likely encounter some pointed questions from skeptics of mastery-based learning. Here are four common ones, along with some answers.

1. This Isn't How the "Real World" Works

Some may wonder why we're not letting students sink or float on their own merits to prepare them for the "real world." Isn't it unfair to let students keep redoing work until they get it right, they might ask?

The purpose of school shouldn't be to *model* the real world. It should be to prepare students to *succeed* in the real world.

Yes, the world isn't always fair. But putting students into a system that judges them at arbitrary points in time and then sorts them with little opportunity to change their grouping makes little sense. Compare that to a system in which all children have learning experiences to help them master the skills to successfully do jobs once they graduate. A better system would provide students with clear feedback to let them know when they have mastered those skills. That's what true preparation for the real world would look like.

Think of Michael Jordan, for example. Widely considered one of the best basketball players ever, there's a famous story about how Jordan was cut from his high school's varsity basketball team as a sophomore. Were this our education system, he would have received a grade—perhaps a C. That grade would have stuck on his transcript and impacted his future college opportunities.

Basketball thankfully doesn't operate like our education system.

Jordan improved and was able to become a star player on his varsity team. He was evaluated for the skills he mastered and displayed in games, not what he had done at one arbitrary point in his life. As a result, the University of North Carolina and its legendary coach Dean Smith recruited him to play basketball. The rest, as they say, is history.

The point is that allowing students to improve their performance and "redo" work is a feature in this system, not cheating. As long as the assessment is robust—and not mindless multiple-choice questions that can be gamed—working to improve performance and obtain mastery is the goal. In many ways, that's how the real world actually works.

If we also agree that embedding the habits of success like perseverance and growth mindset are important, our current time-based system of education works systematically against instilling these skills in students. But mastery-based learning, in which redoing and improving upon one's work is the expectation, naturally embeds these habits of success.

Why is that? As discussed in the Introduction, today's system signals unambiguously to students that it doesn't matter if you stick with something because you'll move on to the next unit or body of material regardless of your results, effort, and understanding. This approach undermines the value of perseverance along with the fostering of agency and curiosity. That's because it does not reward students for working more on a topic.

It also demotivates students in the context of school. Many become bored when they don't have to work at concepts that come easily to them. Or they fall behind when they don't understand a building-block concept, but the class continues to progress.

Contrast this with a mastery-based learning model in which time becomes the variable and learning becomes the constant. Students only move on once they demonstrate mastery of the knowledge and skills at hand. If they fail, that's fine. They stay at a task, learn from the failures, work until they demonstrate mastery, and then move on.

Without talking about perseverance, mastery-based learning embeds the building of that habit into its design.

Mastery-based learning has one other benefit for enhancing our understanding of the habits of success. In a mastery-based system, we can measure these sorts of skills by observing the daily work students do, not what they say on a questionnaire.

When students struggle, do they pick themselves up and attack the work again and exhibit resilience? Do they need time and space—and can they create that time and space intentionally—before diving back in? Or do they just struggle to re-engage? And how are these reactions the same and different across different subjects? Similarly, how do students tackle novel topics about which they know little? How do they manage themselves? By watching students in a mastery-based system, we can learn a considerable amount about their habits of success—something Montessori teachers have long known as they observe students to evaluate and support them.

There's ironically a flip side to the "real world" argument. Some argue that mastery-based learning is too focused on students mastering knowledge and skills fit for the economy and the workforce. This is an argument one hears more in higher education than in K–12, but nonetheless, it's worth considering its validity.

What's ironic is that those who express this concern fail to note that the existing assembly-line education system is also aligned to the economy and work—but to an industrial economy that is no longer with us. As we've discussed, today's education system prioritizes sorting, not learning. It deals a grave injustice to learners in today's world. A mastery-based learning system, however, prioritizes each individual's learning so that we can guarantee that all have the foundation to navigate today's knowledge economy.

2. Does Mastery-Based Learning Preclude Spiraling and Other Useful Techniques?

The answer is no.

The notion of spiraling stems from psychologist Jerome Bruner's work. It's one in which students revisit topics over time, but also build on and deepen their understanding of the topic by delving into more complex ideas at each turn.

Scott Ellis is the founder of MasteryTrack, which offers free dashboards for mastery learning to make it simple for teachers, schools, and districts to move to mastery-based learning. He argues that mastery-based learning isn't at odds with these ideas. To see why, we need more precision when talking about mastery-based learning.

When a student masters a particular idea and then moves on to a deeper concept, that means that they are now tackling a different learning objective, Ellis argues. That means that each learning objective is effectively binary in the sense that a student has either achieved mastery or hasn't yet done so. If a student hasn't yet mastered a learning objective, educators can give ratings like "near mastered," "started," and "not started" to provide more nuance, transparency, and a deeper sense of progression. Lexington Montessori School, for example, employs this practice and uses the ratings of "Consistently" to denote a student that consistently shows mastery of a learning objective, "Practicing," "Beginning," and "Not Applicable." That's preferable to a standards-based grading approach that suggests there are different kinds of mastery and depth possible for a given concept—a 4 for "mastered" instead of a 3 for "proficient."

When people resist this idea, Ellis argues, it's because the learning objective hasn't been defined in a way that is specific enough, clear enough, and demonstrably shows a clear threshold for consistent mastery.[9] This is yet another reason why it's so important to define learning goals and what would constitute evidence of mastery up-front. Ellis's ideas aren't just applicable to areas like math, where there are clear right and wrong answers, or foundational classes. MasteryTrack has been implemented in subjects ranging from college psychology to a graduate course in physical therapy and from high school social studies teachers teaching the College, Career, and Civics (C3) Framework for Social Studies to a district measuring the skill area of collaboration.[10] And Lexington Montessori School uses the consistently, practicing, beginning, and not applicable terms for areas like social-emotional learning.

There's a related question. What if a student is struggling to master a particular learning objective and moving on would be a wise step rather than banging their head against a wall and growing frustrated?

It turns out that the phrase most used to describe mastery-based learning—move on upon mastery—can be misleading.[11]

Although students might not master a particular concept on which they're working, they can move on to other concepts or subjects if they aren't dependent on the one on which they're stuck. They can then return to the challenging competency when it makes sense to do so and visit the concept multiple times.

The point is that students don't get to leave entirely a foundational concept that they haven't yet mastered. In essence, they will continue to have a designation showing that they are still working on something until they exhibit mastery. But the demonstration of mastery can occur at their own pace. For certain concepts that are optional, students might decide something isn't for them and make the decision to skip it. That would be okay. Their record would show they started something but never mastered it.

Educators can also specify that students can only master a learning objective after demonstrating their mastery in ways spaced out over time. This shows a more durable, consistent mastery—in stark contrast to the kind that comes from cramming at the last minute for a test. It is also more consistent with our understanding of learning and memory. Practicing a concept over time—where the spaced intervals between working on that concept increase—leads to more durable mastery.[12]

3. In the Absence of Valid, Reliable, and Objective Assessments, Mastery-Based Learning Can Become Less Rigorous and Cause Schools to Overlook Important Habits

The rigor criticism is related but separate from the "real world" criticism. The critique has two elements.

First, by focusing on mastery of academic knowledge and skills and separating that from behaviors—like whether a student turns in her work on time—schools risk not preparing students for the importance of those behaviors. This is a possibility, but it's simple to counteract. It's not enough to just focus on academic knowledge and skills. Schools must also constantly assess students' behaviors and habits of success and indicate—within each domain—whether students are exhibiting mastery of them or still need work. Students shouldn't be able to skate by on these dimensions. They should still have deadlines for their work based on where they are in their learning. Moving to mastery-based learning ought to create more transparency and a greater focus on these habits, not less than the present system.

Second, critics worry that teachers might say that students have mastered key competencies when they haven't in fact done so. This is a problem in the current system as well. But it's a critique worth taking seriously because the incentives are different in a public mastery-based system where policy and funding focus on outcomes and accountability. The incentives are to support each learner in obtaining mastery. As a result, there are arguably more pressures in place for teachers to pass students through any number of mechanisms—cheating, a lack of rigor in grading, or a lack of knowledge in how to assess key competencies.

The next chapter addresses this topic in more depth, but the basic principle is this: in these environments, teachers shouldn't be the final arbiter of mastery for their own students. A third-party teacher or assessor that, ideally, the students don't know should be the judge of whether the students have mastered the learning goals.

4. There's No Way to Assess Mastery of Complex Activities

Some, like Peter Greene, a retired teacher, argue that focusing on mastery risks reducing learning to atomistic parts that don't add up to anything holistic. Greene's argument is essentially that although you can demonstrate mastery of being able to shoot a free throw—and we might agree that mastery means you're making 70 percent of your attempts—the notion of mastering basketball is absurd.

It's true that we could reduce a complex skill to its component parts at the risk of the whole. Many would argue that we do that today in traditional education through the use of learning standards. Of course, today's system isn't mastery based, which suggests Greene's worry might be broader.

Still, to stick with the basketball analogy, we could overly obsess with someone's mastery of shooting, passing, and dribbling. We might even combine some of these into more complex skills. Maybe we'd focus on mastery of a sequence of moves— someone's mastery of taking a jab step from a triple threat position and seamlessly shooting a jumper, for example.

But if someone can't do these things in a game, what does it matter?

This is one reason those who practice mastery-based learning tend to focus on how students perform while doing real tasks—called performance-based learning. In this way, educators aren't simply assessing whether someone has mastered foundational knowledge and skills, but whether people can put the building blocks together in something more complex. WG Coaching, which works with some of the top coaches, athletes, teams, and sporting organizations around the world, exemplifies this with a framework that defines different levels of mastery that range from being able to perform a specific skill to being able to perform the skill very well, at speed, under fatigue, and under pressure consistently in competition conditions.[13]

More broadly, there's an extensive body of work to assess mastery in a given field. Frameworks from the Lumina Foundation, the United Kingdom, and Europe, for example, exist to measure mastery in a specific field. They contain criteria to denote what level of mastery someone has demonstrated in a certain profession on a 1 to 8 scale, where an 8 would be akin to the Lebron James of basketball.[14] This also shows that reporting on someone's mastery can take into account that one's mastery over knowledge and skills is dynamic and can change over time—not just toward mastery of more challenging objectives, but also in the reverse direction.

As we guard against any learning becoming overly reductionist, projects that contain a performance by the student are important. Projects are also a great way to have fun with friends as a student learns—the other Job for which students would like to hire school.

HAVING FUN WITH FRIENDS

Moving to mastery-based learning also changes the nature of the relationship between the student and the teacher. We'll talk more about this in the next chapter. But rather than seeing the teacher as someone who is there to judge and label them, in a mastery-based environment students can see their teachers as advocates for them. That's because the teacher's job is to ensure that everyone achieves mastery. As a result, that enables students to have more fun with their teachers in the course of their learning.

But students also want to have fun with their peers. What are ways that they can do so?

One path is intentionally building time in the day to allow for mentorship and peer-to-peer learning.

Another is the addition of small-group learning. Mark Van Ryzin, a professor at the University of Oregon, has researched the many benefits of effective small-group instruction, which he defines as four or fewer students in a K–12 school. Among the academic benefits he cites are boosts in learning achievement, deeper processing, and greater retention. But his research focuses more on the positive social experiences that can accrue in small-group settings. For these to occur, educators must establish the proper structures and scaffolding so students can create "positive interdependence"—a condition when people realize that working together is better both for them as individuals and the collective whole.[15]

Making Projects More Central

Still one more path to allowing students to have fun with friends is through making projects a more central part of the learning experience.

Although many definitions exist around project-based learning and other similar concepts in education, when I'm speaking about the use of projects in K–12 education, I'm using a definition similar to that of Adam Carter. Carter is the executive director of Marshall Street, a coalition of educators working to improve opportunities for students.

In Carter's words, a project involves authentic problem solving and a performance. It should consist of the merger of high-quality, rigorous content with a set of skills. Students can master knowledge, skills, and habits of success in the course of doing a project. The performance can be anything from a written product to a presentation or dramatic reenactment in front of an audience. It's critical because the performance is where students receive feedback so that they can improve and master the knowledge and skills at the heart of the project.

It's also important to make sure that a project doesn't overwhelm a learner's working memory by asking them to do too much. This is one reason that when you give a novice learner a project, it should be simple and short enough with proper scaffolding, which should include direct instruction that ideally involves active learning.[16]

A good project also follows the Summit learning cycle, in which there are multiple opportunities for planning, feedback, and reflection. In other words, iteration is embedded. This is important so that students don't create flashy products without much substance, which is a common problem with school projects.

A project should also start with a question or problem that captures students. That question may perplex them. It could be on a topic about which they care or one about which they don't know much but are intrigued by. The point is that students should be motivated to address the challenge.

As Jonathan Haber wrote in *Critical Thinking*, "ill-defined problems engage student curiosity by instilling doubt in their minds, doubt that, according to [John] Dewey's Pragmatist philosophy, we are all highly motivated to eliminate."[17]

Or as cognitive scientist Daniel Willingham wrote in *Why Don't Students Like School?*, "Curiosity is provoked when we perceive a problem that we believe we can solve . . . it's the question that piques people's interest. Being *told* an answer doesn't do anything for you."[18]

An important component, yet again, is that students must believe that they can solve the problem or answer the question. It can't be too far out of their reach and expertise, nor should it be too easy.

A sound project also incorporates feedback not just from the teacher, but also from students' peers. Learning to provide feedback can help the student who receives it. But it also helps the student who is giving the feedback by allowing them to clarify what mastery means. That also means that even if a project is a solo experience, it naturally allows students to start working— and having fun—with each other.

Projects can also be collaborative or team-based, although for novice learners in a particular domain, too much collaboration could detract from their learning.[19] If students work together on a project, it's important that educators provide explicit coaching and scaffolding to help students learn how to work together. This helps to avoid another challenge with group projects: the free-rider problem where one student does most of the work and the others hang on for the ride.

FROM ZERO SUM TO POSITIVE SUM

Moving to a mastery-based system where students can offer feedback to improve each other's performance offers yet one more way that students can have fun together as they learn.

In a traditional education system, teachers often subconsciously compare their students. They do this explicitly when they use a curve to grade the class.[20] In the traditional system, supporting your peers and having fun with each other in the learning process has a clear downside. It undermines your own chance for success and opportunity. Because students are attending school in a system that is sorting and comparing them to each other and doling out scarce opportunity in the form of admission to selective colleges, there are few incentives to cooperate rather than compete. All of this works against helping students have fun with each other as they learn.

Competition isn't bad. But competition for extrinsic reasons—out of a desire to be the best for its own sake, not for the intrinsic value of the experience—has clear downsides. Experts ranging from the *New York Times*'s Frank Bruni to Harvard's Michael Sandel have offered observations on the current system and raised questions about how healthy this is—for the individuals themselves as well as for society writ large.[21]

"Our credentialing function is beginning to crowd out our educational function," Sandel said in an interview with the *Chronicle for Higher Education*.

> Students win admission to [exclusive institutions] by converting their teenage years—or their parents converting their teenage years—into a stress-strewn gauntlet of meritocratic striving. That inculcates intense pressure for achievement. So even the winners in the meritocratic competition are wounded by it, because they become so accustomed to accumulating achievements and credentials, so accustomed to jumping through hoops and pleasing their parents and teachers and coaches and admissions committees, that the habit of hoop-jumping becomes difficult to break. By the time they arrive in college, many find it difficult to step back and reflect on what's worth caring about, on what they truly would love to study and learn.[22]

As Todd Rose shared, this competition to be the best for its own sake is insane.

"Literally you gotta be the same as everyone else only better," he said. "Take the same test score, [but just get] higher. Right? Take the same classes. Get better grades. [And the assumption is that] is going to give way to something that I think is really cool."[23]

As we discussed in the Introduction, the problem, according to Rose, is that our current system of education—and selective higher education in particular—is zero sum. For every winner, there's a loser.

The good news is that moving to a mastery-based system and measuring students against a standard instead of each other can lift students and teachers out of this spiral into a positive-sum system. That's because success isn't at the expense of other students. Incorporating projects and small-group learning where students are actively giving each other feedback and supporting each other also helps lift students and educators into a positive-sum system.

As students seek to carve out their own pathway in life and be the unique individuals they are, comparisons can shift from trying to label someone's ability on a narrow set of measures to instead understanding who they are becoming. Where comparison is still important, we can look at students' depth of learning to understand where their passions are, their progress against their goals, or even their rate of learning to see which areas are truly their strengths and aptitudes. This offers a better way for educators to help all students build their passions, fulfill their potential, and understand how they can best contribute to society.

SUCCESS AND FUN WITH FRIENDS IN ACTION

What might a learning environment that helps students experience success and have fun with friends look like on the ground? Here are a few examples.

Summit Public Schools

Summit doesn't use a traditional schedule. It remixes time, teachers, content, technology, and place to allow it to build an environment in which students constantly experience success and have fun with friends. Here's an example daily schedule:

7:30	Begin to arrive; work on personalized learning plan
8:25	School starts with project time (math and science)
10:20	Break
10:35	Personalized learning time
11:35	PE or sustained reading time
12:35	Lunch and recess outside
1:20	Project time (English and history)
3:15	School ends; can stay and work on personalized learning plan
Note	On Fridays, the student spends most of the day on her personalized learning plan and has a one-on-one check-in with her mentor.

When students arrive, they begin working on their personalized learning plan. That starts with their personal goals, which they set, master, and track through the Summit Learning Platform. This technology platform provides access to everything from content to the projects and learning goals students choose to tackle.

At around 8:30, school begins officially and students dive into a two-hour block of math and science project time that is interdisciplinary. Having interdisciplinary projects is another way to combat Greene's concerns about an overly reductionist view of mastery.

After a brief break, students move back into personalized learning time for an hour. The challenge of the project builds a need to learn content. That drives the use of direct instruction in the platform.

Afterward, the students have an opportunity to move physically or read—also critical for building background knowledge to help them be capable of tackling bigger projects. Lunch and recess outside are next. Students then enter another two-hour block for an interdisciplinary project in English and history. When school ends, students are free to stay to work on their personalized learning plan.

The schedule on Fridays looks different. The entire day is open to personalized learning time, which means that there is built-in time for each student to meet with their mentor at the school—meetings that students learn to lead. Each teacher mentors roughly 15 students per year.

Summit also provides its students with eight weeks a year of "expeditions," in which students learn largely off-campus in the real world. Students explore their passions and learn about career options through everything from elective courses to real internships. Expeditions give students the chance to build strong relationships with their expedition teachers and people in outside community organizations.

All of this contributes to an environment in which students can make meaningful progress and have fun with friends. As students partake in the personalized learning time and work to develop content mastery, for example, when they feel they are ready, they can take assessments. These are available on demand to show evidence that they have mastered the concepts or skills. That means that if students believe they already understand a concept, they can take an assessment at the outset and skip ahead. If they fail, then they work through their individual playlist until they can demonstrate mastery. Success is built into the design.

After taking assessments, students receive pass/fail feedback, as well as a detailed explanation of their performance. This short-cycle feedback loop allows students to make progress—and feel ownership of their progress—in steady, frequent increments. It also gives them access to actionable data. With that data in hand, each Friday students sit down with their mentors to reflect on their weekly progress, how they feel about their learning experience, what worked well, and what to improve. The data and the meetings are all designed to help students bolster and deepen their success.

Because students can progress as fast as they master material, Summit has developed a full coherent scope, suggested sequence, and associated playlists of resources for the entire set of competencies a student should master through high school. That means teachers don't have to plan lessons the night before. The other benefit of this is that Summit posts this scope and sequence in its software so that students can see what's ahead—and helps them know what it will take to graduate. That clarity around what success looks like further helps students with understanding how they can continually make progress and feel successful each day. Summit even has a graphical line in its student-facing data system that moves with the calendar to help students see where they should be in their learning if they want to complete high school on time, and that allows them to adjust accordingly.

Making time for reading and fitness is also part of how Summit helps its students experience success. Although having opportunities for students to engage in productive group work is vital so that students can master teamwork skills and have fun with friends, Summit's philosophy is that all too often schools overlook the importance of providing students with quiet time when they can immerse themselves in a book. Students often do not have an environment at home conducive to this type of experience. Without it, they may struggle to build the background knowledge and in-depth reading capacity they need to be successful in so many other parts of their schooling.

Through constructive coaching that helps students build their ability to work in teams, Summit's extensive time dedicated to projects and expeditions creates lots of opportunities for students to have fun with friends that is productive. Given that Summit fosters a positive-sum environment, not a zero-sum one that is competitive and cutthroat, it's not unusual to see students pop over to coach other students as they learn. The mentorship time also creates a relaxed environment for students to have fun with their teachers. Summit supplements its schedule with 45 minutes per week of community time, in which students meet in small groups to engage in discussions about issues important to them.

Fitness is also a critical part of priming students to learn successfully. John Ratey, a neuropsychiatric expert at Harvard Medical School, has written extensively about the importance of physical fitness—and how many students get far too little of it, which inhibits their ability to be successful. Even 30 minutes of exercise before a chunk of learning can help prime the brain to focus. If structured well, time for fitness and recess can also be a great opportunity to have fun with friends.

Transforming PE

Although fitness can bolster students' academic success, the place where fitness should occur in most schools—PE class—is all too often focused on teaching organized sports and games rather than ensuring that each student is moving daily and improving their fitness.[24] Far too often, PE class makes some individuals feel like failures.

Peter Driscoll, a PE teacher at Hartford High School in the Hartford School District of Vermont, has spent much of his teaching career changing that dynamic. An avid CrossFitter, Driscoll brings an ethos of CrossFit into his classes with a focus of helping build a foundation of fitness in each individual. Other teachers in the building have told Driscoll that they notice the students are in a much better space for learning after his class.

But Driscoll hasn't just helped students be successful in other parts of school. He's changed the methodology of his class so that all students can experience success in PE itself.

The first change he implemented was when he was teaching elementary school. At the start of each class, he had the children do a "Tabata Workout," in which an individual works out for 20 seconds followed by 10 seconds of rest for four minutes total. In many cases, that working out was just running back and forth across the gym. Because it was time based, no child finished before any other child. The students loved it.

This practice changed what Driscoll had observed previously. "The kids who really loved PE were the kids who were innately good at fleeing, chasing, and dodging, and they had the coordination and agility skills, and they were just supersized," he told me. "And the other kids didn't. They didn't have that self-confidence from our class that I wanted them to. So when I switched to kind of a fitness-based approach and got away from team games and the competitive side of team sports, the program has blossomed, and the kids would go home and rave about what they did in class. And I got a ton of support from the parents."[25]

Driscoll has since expanded his work.

His high school students now set personal fitness goals with clear numbers attached to them. This is to ensure that each student is competing only against themselves, not anyone else in the class or school.

Students plan how they will tackle the workout of the day. What's their strategy and how will they pace themselves? Where do they need to scale a given movement, for example, so that they can safely and successfully complete the workout?

Finally, after the workout, they receive immediate feedback on how they did. They use the information to reflect with Driscoll on what they can do better to realize their personal goals.

The result is one where each student is essentially enjoying a personalized PE class.[26] They also experience a learning cycle that isn't too different from Summit's, as it includes goal setting, planning, executing the plan, and using their performance to reflect. This allows students to experience the feelings of daily success and the endorphins and dopamine produced from both the sweat and authentic accomplishments.

Hartford High School:
https://www.youtube.com/watch?v=sN94F2BODjc

Teacher, School, and District Implementations of Mastery-Based Learning and Projects

Increasing numbers of schools moved to mastery-based learning during the pandemic. According to the Christensen Institute, 10 percent of school systems reported facilitating mastery-based learning during the pandemic, up from 7 percent beforehand.[27]

Rogers High School in the state of Washington, for example, adjusted its policies in November of 2020 to take some steps toward mastery-based learning by changing its grading to reflect mastery of learning, as opposed to how many assignments were turned in, according to the *Wall Street Journal*.[28] The goal, its principal Roger Smith said, was to help overwhelmed students see that there was a manageable way out of their current challenges.

In many other cases, individual teachers have adopted tools like MasteryTrack to operationalize mastery-based learning. Many school districts, including large ones like Cleveland and Columbus, Ohio, are moving to mastery-based learning not only as a solution to COVID learning loss, but also as a superior way to learn. Both Cleveland and Columbus have joined the Mastery Transcript Consortium to help move beyond traditional grading policies and better reflect and report students' achievements in mastery-based systems.[29]

Like Ohio, many districts in Utah have also experimented with mastery-based learning. The Iron County School District, for example, created a new high school in 2020 called the Launch High School[30] to combine mastery learning with hands-on projects that focus on entrepreneurship. The school creates opportunities for students to share their projects with community members throughout the year—part of the culminating "performance" of the projects. It also allows students to do their extracurricular activities at their local traditional high school. The district is planning the launch of magnet programs within existing schools for students who are looking for a similar experience in elementary and middle school.

Northern Cass District 97 in North Dakota and Parker-Varney Elementary School in Manchester, New Hampshire have likewise moved to mastery-based learning.[31] The Canopy Project, started by the Christensen Institute and stewarded by Transcend Education and the Center on Reinventing Public Education, also has information on a variety of other schools that use mastery learning.[32]

Mastery Transcript Consortium:
https://www.youtube.com/watch?v=PQlgbf3Z6-4

Iron County School District's Launch High School:
https://www.youtube.com/watch?v=YnCqMthWLnk

RESULTS

Many schools that commit to mastery-based learning over longer periods of time, like the Kettle Moraine school district we learned about in Chapter 1, are, perhaps unsurprisingly, seeing positive results. To achieve these results, the district can't just be paying lip service to mastery-based learning; it must also make a real commitment to ensure that students move along only as they master competencies. Doing so embeds results in the process and engages students in a cycle of success. In the two examples that follow, both started from different points from each other and Kettle Moraine as they embraced mastery-based learning.

Lindsay Unified

One of the most noteworthy examples of mastery-based learning across the country is Lindsay Unified School District, a small district with a little over 4,100 students in rural California. In 2007, over 90 percent of its students qualified for free and reduced price lunch—a measure of students who hail from families with lower incomes. Eleven percent were homeless; over 40 percent classified as English-language learners, and roughly 95 percent were Hispanic. Lindsay's schools were also struggling. Its test scores and graduation rates ranked among the lowest in California. Its annual teacher turnover was above 50 percent.

With broad consensus among all stakeholders that the district was failing its students, its superintendent, Tom Rooney, was able to bring together a broad group of individuals across the community to launch over a decade of work to redesign the district's processes. The focus was on mastery-based and personalizing learning for each student's learning needs.

Students no longer move in lockstep through their learning. As in Summit's model, students take ownership for their goals and progress. Each school has significant autonomy to tweak its model to meet its distinct needs so long as it aligns with the district's overall vision.

The work is paying off. In 2014–2015, for example, just 26 percent of its students were proficient on the Smarter Balanced Assessment Consortium (SBAC) tests used by the State of California. Five years later 47 percent were. The district soared from the 33rd percentile rank in the SBAC's English Language Arts (ELA) achievement compared to other similar school districts in the state to the 87th percentile. The graduation rate rose to above 94 percent. Double the number of its graduates enrolled in four-year universities.

Student engagement has also improved. Attendance rose to over 96 percent. Suspension rates fell by 41 percent. Gang membership fell from 18 percent to 3 percent, which suggests the district is competing more successfully for the time and attention of its students. The school's Student Climate Index, a measure derived from a statewide instrument called "The California Healthy Kids Survey," shows Lindsay's ranking rising from the 52nd percentile in 2011 to the 97th percentile in the state in 2018, with its absolute score rising nearly 40 percent.[33]

NYOS

In Austin, Texas, the NYOS Charter School—NYOS stands for Not Your Ordinary School—is similarly turning heads. The school, which was launched in 1998, was known for serving both struggling students and those who were excelling. With a mix of students from different backgrounds—one-third of its 1,000 students are from low-income neighborhoods, but many others are from well-off areas, and the school is 40 percent White, 36 percent Hispanic, and 14 percent Black—there's a long waitlist of 3,000 students hoping to enroll.

Five years ago, the school decided to move to mastery-based learning out of a realization that serving students in small groups was superior to working with large numbers of students with varying levels of academic achievement.

As Beth Hawkins wrote in The 74, researchers working with four universities—Texas A&M, Johns Hopkins, Duke, and the University of Wisconsin–Whitewater, used data from the 2016 NWEA MAP assessments to show that the average fifth-grade classroom contained roughly a third of students who were performing at or below a third-grade level in math; roughly a third at fourth grade; only 25 percent at fifth grade, and the rest above grade level. Said differently, the average classroom likely contained students achieving at seven different grade levels.

COVID exacerbated the spread. Using preliminary data from NWEA that many have suggested may have overstated the amount of learning that occurred during the pandemic, the researchers said that the span of levels in any given fifth-grade classroom has likely widened to a whopping nine grade levels.

Seeing this spread on the ground convinced the NYOS Charter School to change its learning model. In the move to reconfigure time and space so that students could move on as they mastered content—meaning at their own pace—the school has seen strong results. In the 2018–2019 school year, Hawkins reported, students in every grade met or exceeded state and district averages in both reading and math. The school earned an A on Texas's 2018–2019 state report card, compared to a B for the Austin Independent School District. It also earned 96 out of 100 points for student achievement and 100 out of 100 for closing achievement gaps.[34]

IMPLEMENTATION OF PODS AND MICROSCHOOLS

One thing that's notable about both the Iron County, Utah and Kettle Moraine examples are that both have used microschools to help implement their strategy.

Likewise, Cleveland isn't just moving forward with mastery-based learning. The district is continuing to explore using pods and microschools to help create the right greenfield structures that alter the use of time, personnel, and location in learning. As Chapter 1 discussed, Cleveland put pods in place during the pandemic in partnership with a variety of community organizations. It is now looking to use pods in the future to address a range of student needs. Eric Gordon, Cleveland Metropolitan School District's CEO, has mused that these needs could range from having supervised outlets for inquiry for students who are bored in class because they have already mastered the material to helping students removed for disruptive behavior stay on track rather than be suspended. The district has even explored having student-run pods in which students would act as tutors to help their peers catch up on lost learning.

Microschools create more opportunities for students to have both the personalized supports necessary to be successful and the close communities in which they can have fun with friends. It also does one other thing: acknowledge that there isn't one best arrangement for everyone to learn and allow districts to create a variety of options and choices that allow students and families to find the best fit for them. Among these is custodial care. One of the purported benefits of schools is the custodial care they provide, but for many working parents, the coverage is lousy. Childcare that lasts from 8 a.m. to 3 p.m. isn't in sync with the conventional 9 a.m. to 5 p.m. workday or the longer and less consistent work schedules that have spread. Chapter 7 delves deeper into these dynamics, but suffice to say, more schools are playing with these structures to create the right opportunities for students to make progress. They don't assume there's a one-size-fits-all way to do so.

Flipping the School Day

Along these lines, many have started to question how high schools might reimagine the school day to better set up their students for success. One structure for which Bob Harris, the former head of human resources for the Pittsburgh Public Schools, as well as Lexington Public Schools in Massachusetts, advocates is flipping the school day.[35]

Harris advocated for this before the pandemic. But the wisdom behind the concept appears even clearer now for a number of high schoolers and their parents who experienced liberation from what is often an excruciatingly early school start time for adolescents. The opportunities for enriched learning that stem from not being tethered to a physical campus are another enticing benefit.

In a flipped school day, students would start their day later—say 9 a.m.—by reporting to a workplace in their community, which they could rotate every semester or year.

After working half a day, the students would then break for lunch and head to school to do their extracurricular activities and work on projects with their fellow students.

Finally, in the evenings, students would take their classes online from home when their parents are more likely to be around. They wouldn't have homework per se, as work would simply be woven into their online-learning experiences, their projects with their fellow students, and, ideally, the projects they are tackling while on-site at a workplace in the morning.

Having students *take only one to two online courses at a time* so that they can focus deeply on what they are learning without distraction, not have work that stretches on too late such that it cuts into their sleep, and so they can attain mastery before they move on to other courses would also have many benefits and further throw off the limits of the traditional seven-period high school structure. In this vision, each course would last roughly a month—the time would ideally vary based on each student's mastery—such that over the course of a year students could take a full course load but not be overburdened. Plus, with less chance for conflicts between classes, students could delve more deeply into bigger projects. These projects could integrate with their afternoon on-campus work or the work they are doing in a workplace. Alisa Berger, co-director of deeper learning for all at Harvard, said that this idea has a big upside. A high school she worked with in British Columbia moved during the pandemic to have students take just one course at a time and saw pass rates rise.

Alternatively, if students took two courses at a time, the classes could be done in an interdisciplinary way. Students could thereby dig into meaty projects that allow them to learn the content in the context of something more meaningful.

The benefits of this approach would be significant for certain students. The schedules would align with adolescent circadian rhythms. It would be both more in line with the research around when teenagers should wake up and start their days and also more in line with research that suggests students tend to perform better in courses that meet later in the day.[36] This would likely have both academic and health benefits.

There would also be more opportunities for deep engagement in course work. As Michael Petrilli has observed, "students only learn when they are focused, engaged, and putting in effort. Yet surveys have long shown that teenagers spend most of their day bored, zoned out, and only pretending to listen. For many students—especially the most motivated ones—they'd be better off, not to mention happier, if they spent much more of their time reading, writing, and completing projects than going through the motions in our industrial-style schools."[37]

Students would also have more chances to learn about potential careers, build their social capital, forge connections with mentors outside of school, and develop their passions. This is all critical given that, according to our research in *Choosing College*, many students leave high school without a strong sense of purpose or passion, which contributes to them making subpar college choices that often results in them dropping out with debt.

Big Picture Learning schools, a network of schools that focus on cultivating curiosity and sparking passion, helps illustrate the opportunities that arise with more engaged students working outside of schools as part of their formal learning. As one student at a Big Picture Learning school in Nashville, Dayvon, said, "I have friends who want to be veterinarians, OB-GYNs, orthodontists, and the fact that they actually get to work in an orthodontist office or actually go to a vet clinic is very engaging. Then they actually say, 'Hey, I'm doing this exhibition, and I'm going to focus on what I want to learn.' You get to support them and say 'I'm here for you' and 'I support everything you're doing.' And when you get that same love back it drives you. Like hey, I can actually do this."

Another Big Picture Learning student in San Diego, Izzy Fitzgerald, told me that, unlike Dayvon and some of his friends, she didn't yet know what she wanted to do with her future. But her school allows her to build an understanding of herself and the different pathways that exist. "There's so many different opportunities that the school provides for me to investigate every single one. And that's really what drives me because I am a little indecisive so it really just shows me, hey, you don't really want to do that, or that's a little too scary, or oh don't go into being a doctor, you don't like blood. Different things like that. I think that's a lot of students as well, we just don't know yet. So that we get to experience every single thing, [which] is really amazing."[38]

If schools creatively stagger schedules to meet different student scheduling needs, they can also realize health and cost benefits through less densely filled school buildings that can be better utilized over the course of a day and year.

And finally, it will also better prepare high school students for college and the world of work, as it will create a scaffolded and intentional approach to releasing them into the "real world" and helping them build their habits of success like agency, executive functions, and relevance of school.

Big Picture Learning:
https://www.youtube.com/watch?v=Idimr1Of37o

---

* * *

The point isn't that flipping the school day will be right for every student or even every school system, but that it's time for schools to think through the opportunities to use time, space, and personnel very differently to create dramatically better opportunities for students to experience success and have fun with friends as they learn. If we do so with an eye toward what *each* student needs, we have big opportunities to bolster *every* student's ability to maximize their human potential.

KEY TAKEAWAYS

- Instead of focusing on what students have lost, schools should focus on what students have accomplished.

- By guaranteeing mastery, educators can embed success into the design of schools.

- Mastery-based learning isn't just about changing the flawed grading system, but also about changing the system of learning to ensure students succeed.

- In so doing, mastery-based learning also embeds several habits of success into its design—unlike the traditional time-bound system that undermines many of those habits.

- Making projects more central in schools alongside mastery-based learning also creates opportunities for students to have fun with their friends as they learn.

- There are several great examples of schools and districts making the shift to a positive-sum education system that prioritizes each student's success and the ability to have fun with friends.

NOTES

1. This *Candy Land* concept and analogy is adapted from a real school featured in a *Washington Post* article. The school is Parker-Varney Elementary School in Manchester, New Hampshire. See Nancy Walser, "Emerging from the Pandemic, Districts Look to Expand Personalized Competency-Based Education," *Washington Post*, August 13, 2021, https://www.washingtonpost.com/local/

education/schools-competency-based-education/2021/08/13/a8faac98-fac0-11eb-9c0e-97e29906a970_story.html.

2. Steven J. Spear, *Chasing the Rabbit: How Market Leaders Outdistance the Competition and How Great Companies Can Catch Up and Win* (New York: McGraw-Hill, 2008).

3. Richard A. DeLorenzo and Wendy J. Battino, *Delivering on the Promise: The Education Revolution* (Bloomington, IN: Solution Tree Press, 2009), Kindle Edition Locations 1624–1630.

4. Daniel Willingham, *Why Don't Students Like School? A Cognitive Scientist Answers Questions about How the Mind Works and What It Means for Your Classroom* (San Francisco, CA: Jossey-Bass, 2009), Chapter 1.

5. For a wonderful history of today's A–F grading system, see Jack Schneider and Ethan Hutt, "Making the Grade: A History of the *A–F Marking Scheme*," *Curriculum Studies* 42, no. 2 (March 2014), https://www.researchgate.net/publication/263259031_Making_the_grade_a_history_of_the_A-F_marking_scheme.

6. Diane Tavenner, *Prepared: What Kids Need for a Fulfilled Life* (New York: Currency, 2019), p. 83.

7. In essence, educators should establish a system that mirrors the Aurora Institute's definition of competency-based learning and its seven points. See Eliot Levine and Susan Patrick, "What Is Competency-Based Education? An Updated Definition," Aurora Institute, 2019, https://aurora-institute.org/wp-content/uploads/what-is-competency-based-education-an-updated-definition-web.pdf, p. 3.

8. Chris Sturgis, "Progress and Proficiency: Redesigning Grading for Competency Education," *CompetencyWorks*, January 2014, https://aurora-institute.org/wp-content/uploads/progress-and-proficiency.pdf, p. 27.

   More to the point, Sturgis convincingly argues that starting with changing the grading system often has the effect of drawing public attention on grading as opposed to learning and "it fails to help people understand 'why' schools need to change."

   See Chris Sturgis, "Missteps in Implementing Competency Education: Introducing Grading Too Early," *CompetencyWorks*, September 24, 2018, https://aurora-institute.org/cw_post/missteps-in-implementing-competency-education-introducing-grading-too-early/.

9. To be clear, Ellis's argument does not mean that in order to demonstrate mastery, a student must get something right 100 percent of the time. The key is to have a clear threshold of mastery defined. This seems particularly important in more complex topics and in the humanities, according to Ellis, and speaks to the wisdom of communicating that someone has achieved mastery by using the word "consistently."

Also, the importance of creating learning goals that are clear speaks to another principle of the theory of interdependence and modularity, which is that in order to move to a modular architecture, the standard must be specifiable and verifiable. Many learning standards are not constructed cleanly with this principle in mind.

10. See more at https://masterytrack.org/blog/.

11. The Aurora Institute offers a deeper, seven-part definition of what competency-based learning is. See "Introduction to Competency-Based Education," Aurora Institute, https://aurora-institute.org/our-work/competencyworks/competency-based-education/ (accessed November 15, 2021).

12. As Stephen Kosslyn wrote, "Students learn more effectively if they are asked to use previously taught information repeatedly during a course. Spaced practice is effective in part because it allows students to associate different contexts to the same material, which later provides more possible cues to help them recall that material." Stephen M. Kosslyn, *Active Learning Online: Five Principles that Make Online Courses Come Alive* (Boston: Alinea Learning, October 2020).

13. "Sports Skills: The 7 Sports Skills Steps You Must Master in Every Sport," WG Coaching, https://wgcoaching.com/sports-skills/ (accessed March 3, 2022).

14. See the Degree Qualifications Profile in "Connecting Credentials: Building a System for Communicating About and Connecting Diverse Credentials," Lumina Foundation, May 2015, https://connectingcredentials.org/wp-content/uploads/2015/05/ConnectingCredentials-4-29-30.pdf, p. 4.

See also "European Qualifications Framework," Wikipedia, https://en.wikipedia.org/wiki/European_Qualifications_Framework (accessed January 24, 2022).

To be clear, this framework is not at odds with Ellis's notion of mastery being essentially binary, as each of these levels represents its own discrete learning goal where one either has crossed the threshold of mastery or hasn't yet.

15. The Small-Group Learning Advantage, YouTube, October 22, 2021, https://www.youtube.com/watch?v=EEvxOs7_mQI&t=4s.

16. Indeed, as Daniel Buck summarized in a piece for the Thomas B. Fordham Institute, the research on project-based learning remains weak. Part of this is because incorporating projects well is challenging. Properly scaffolding a project for a particular learner is critical. And just because you're doing a project or learning something in the context of a larger question or problem doesn't mean that starting with direct instruction first—from a computer or teacher—isn't important. For a novice learner, it generally is. See Daniel Buck, "Sorry Edutopia, the Research Base on Project-Based Learning Remains Weak," Thomas B. Fordham Institute, October 14, 2021, https://fordhaminstitute.org/national/commentary/sorry-edutopia-research-base-project-based-learning-remains-weak.

   Doug Lemov has also written specifically about how project-based learning can work well for experts but be a poor fit for novice learners. See Doug Lemov, "Op-Ed: Pandemic Learning Loss Is Real. Schools Must Follow the Science to Make Up for It," *Los Angeles Times*, October 6, 2021, https://www.latimes.com/opinion/story/2021-10-06/schools-must-follow-the-science-to-make-up-for-pandemic-learning-loss.

17. Jonathan Haber, *Critical Thinking* (Cambridge, MA: MIT Press, 2020), Ch. 3.

18. Daniel Willingham, *Why Don't Students Like School?* (San Francisco, CA: Jossey-Bass, 2009), Kindle Edition Location 428.

19. According to a study by Christian J. Grandzol and John R. Grandzol (both of Bloomsburg University of Pennsylvania) titled "Interaction in Online Courses: More Is NOT Always Better," "Cognitive theory suggests more interaction in learning environments leads to improved learning outcomes and increased student satisfaction. . . . Using a sample of 359 lower-level online, undergraduate business courses, we investigated course enrollments, student and

faculty time spent in interaction, and course completion rates. ... Our key findings indicate that increased levels of interaction, as measured by time spent, actually decrease course completion rates. This result is counter to prevailing curriculum design theory and suggests increased interaction may actually diminish desired program reputation and growth." Cognitive scientists suggest this makes sense. As a novice in a field, one has limited information stored in background memory on a topic, which means their working memory capacity is filled with details they are learning. That means there is little space to do hard, unfamiliar work. Working with others, especially one's friends and peers, likely further takes up space in working memory, which would squeeze out one's ability to focus on the foundational knowledge and skills one is trying to master. See Michael B. Horn, "More Interaction in Online Courses Isn't Always Better," Christensen Institute, December 17, 2010, https://www.christenseninstitute.org/blog/more-interaction-in-online-courses-isnt-always-better/.

20. This is one reason why criterion-referenced assessments that evaluate students relative to a clear learning goal rather than norm-referenced ones that evaluate students relative to their peers are preferable.

21. Frank Bruni, *Where You Go Is Not Who You'll Be: An Antidote to the College Admissions Mania* (New York: Grand Central Publishing, 2016).

    Len Gutkin, "The Insufferable Hubris of the Well-Credentialed," *Chronicle for Higher Education*, September 30, 2020, https://www.chronicle.com/article/the-insufferable-hubris-of-the-well-credentialed?cid=gen_sign_in&cid2=gen_login_refresh.

22. Gutkin, "The Insufferable Hubris of the Well-Credentialed."

23. "Help! My Child and I Are Overwhelmed," *Class Disrupted*, Season 1, Episode 6, June 22, 2020, https://www.the74million.org/article/listen-class-disrupted-podcast-episode-6-help-my-child-and-i-are-overwhelmed/.

24. Daniel Fulham O'Neill, *Survival of the Fit: How Physical Education Ensures Academic Achievement and a Healthy Life* (New York: Teachers College Press, 2021).

25. Michael B. Horn, "How This School's Fitness Is a Good Model for All Learning," Substack, July 14, 2021, https://michaelbhorn.substack.com/p/how-this-schools-fitness-is-a-good.

26. Although online PE class may sound odd to those who haven't seen one, a high-quality online learning PE class accomplishes the same thing and focuses on ensuring students build daily healthy habits.

27. Thomas Arnett, "Carpe Diem: Convert Pandemic Struggles into Student-Centered Learning," Clayton Christensen Institute, August 2021, p. 15, https://www.christenseninstitute.org/wp-content/uploads/2021/08/Carpe-Diem.pdf.

28. Yoree Koh, "Lessons from Remote School, Captured by Twin Sisters Who Pulled Through," *Wall Street Journal*, May 14, 2021, https://www.wsj.com/articles/twin-sisters-lean-on-each-other-to-survive-a-year-of-remote-learning-11621001883.

29. Patrick O'Donnell, "Helping Students Learn at Their Own Pace: Why Some Ohio Schools Are Adopting a 'Mastery' Approach in Hopes of Closing COVID Learning Gaps," The 74, July 19, 2021, https://www.the74million.org/article/helping-students-learn-at-their-own-pace-why-some-ohio-schools-are-adopting-a-mastery-approach-in-hopes-of-closing-covid-learning-gaps/.

30. Launch High School, https://launch.ironk12.org/ (accessed February 4, 2022).

31. Yoree Koh, "How Schools Are Rewriting the Rules on Class Time for Students—and Even Ditching Grade Levels," *Wall Street Journal*, August 9, 2021, https://www.wsj.com/articles/how-schools-are-rewriting-the-rules-on-class-time-for-studentsand-even-ditching-grade-levels-11628517648?mod=article_inline.

   Nancy Walser, "Emerging from the Pandemic, Districts Look to Expand Personalized Competency-Based Education," *Washington Post*, August 13, 2021, https://www.washingtonpost.com/local/education/schools-competency-based-education/2021/08/13/a8faac98-fac0-11eb-9c0e-97e29906a970_story.html.

32. Canopy Project Research, https://canopyschools.transcendeducation.org/research (accessed February 4, 2022).

33. Elliot Levine, "Strong Evidence of Competency-Based Education's Effectiveness from Lindsay Unified School District," Aurora

Institute, March 2, 2020, https://aurora-institute.org/cw_post/strong-evidence-of-competency-based-educations-effectiveness-from-lindsay-unified-school-district/.

Barry Sommer and Abinwi Nchise, "Building Solid Evidence—It's Working at Lindsay Unified," Lindsay Unified School District, https://drive.google.com/file/d/0B6QRjuxlEcioUmUtSVNIQn RaelZ6al8yN1V1eld6R0R5cUc4/view?resourcekey=0-K-LWv BybeTgtnDVLIx5_Vw.

Amanda Avallone, "A Decade On: Lindsay Unified's Personalized Learning Journey," *Education Week*, September 21, 2018, https://www.edweek.org/leadership/opinion-a-decade-on-lindsay-unifieds-personalized-learning-journey/2018/09.

34. Beth Hawkins, "With Up to 9 Grade Levels per Class, Can Schools Handle the Fallout from COVID's K-Shaped Recession?" The 74, August 5, 2021, https://www.the74million.org/article/with-up-to-9-grade-levels-per-class-can-schools-handle-the-fallout-from-covids-k-shaped-recession/.

Beth Hawkins, "New Research Predicts Steep COVID Learning Losses Will Widen Already Dramatic Achievement Gaps Within Classrooms," The 74, June 9, 2020, https://www.the74million.org/article/new-research-predicts-steep-covid-learning-losses-will-widen-already-dramatic-achievement-gaps-within-classrooms/.

35. Michael B. Horn, "Don't Just Flip the Classroom, Flip the School Day," *Forbes*, October 10, 2019, https://www.forbes.com/sites/michaelhorn/2019/10/10/dont-just-flip-the-classroom-flip-the-school-day/?sh=2e35702f6dfb.

36. Perri Klass, "The Science of Adolescent Sleep," *New York Times*, May 22, 2017, https://www.nytimes.com/2017/05/22/well/family/the-science-of-adolescent-sleep.html.

37. Michael J. Petrilli, "Half-Time High School May Be Just What Students Need," Fordham Institute, May 27, 2020, https://fordhaminstitute.org/national/commentary/half-time-high-school-may-be-just-what-students-need.

38. Michael B. Horn, "Maintaining Engagement During Remote Learning," Substack, January 20, 2020, https://michaelbhorn.substack.com/p/maintaining-engagement-during-remote?utm_sq=gmz33hib55.

Chapter 6

T in Teachers Is for Team

Mrs. Alvera didn't love that she had just called Julia and Jeremy out in front of the class. It didn't make her feel good. And she was sure it didn't make them feel good or more motivated to learn.

But what was she supposed to do?

She scanned her students' faces from the front of the classroom. Twenty-five pairs of eyes stared back. Mostly, anyway.

Here we go again, she thought.

For most of the 2020–2021 school year, she hadn't been in-person with her students. And then the 2021–2022 year brought many interruptions, as different students had to quarantine and learn remotely at different times. Kicking off this school year with a full classroom was similar to how she had felt as a first-year teacher, where it seemed like she had been thrown into the deep end of the pool and left to sink or swim on her own.

It felt lonely then, and it felt lonely now.

Which was somewhat surprising. Despite the physical isolation of the pandemic, in some ways she had never felt more connected to her fellow teachers. They had worked together and split certain duties—teaching lessons, answering student and parent questions at different hours of the day and night, planning, moving lessons to digital formats, picking good digital curriculum, and more. Plus, with the school's temporary move to mastery-based learning during the pandemic and ditching A–F letter grades, for the first time she had felt like she wasn't judging her students against each other, but instead was invested in seeing all of them master the knowledge and skills at the heart of the fifth-grade curriculum.

Even now as she stared out at the children sitting in the rows of desks, her mind was speculating subconsciously on who her A students were—and which would be the B, C, and D students. Jeremy was falling fast on that scale, and she wasn't sure what to make of Julia, either.

Remote learning wasn't all roses, of course. Far from it. But as she ground through another year, she wondered why she couldn't hold on to a few of the tricks she had picked up during the pandemic. At the very least, as the 50 eyes stared at her and she prepared to transition them from history to science, she wouldn't have minded having another teacher alongside her.

* * *

Schooling during the pandemic unquestionably took a toll not just on many students, but also on many teachers. On the heels of the 2020–2021 school year, roughly 25 percent of teachers reported that they were considering quitting, according to the RAND Corporation.

But even before the pandemic, nearly 17 percent of teachers reported that they would likely leave the profession each year.[1] Thirty percent of college graduates who become teachers typically leave the profession within six years. That ranks as the fifth-highest turnover by occupation, behind secretaries, childcare workers, paralegals, and correctional officers—and higher than policing and nursing.[2]

Although in Chapter 3 we discussed how a more flexible staffing model could help schools, educators and communities shouldn't just be asking how to design a better schooling experience for students. They should also seek to create a more sustainable and gratifying teaching profession. There are many needed steps in this endeavor. Key among them are figuring out ways to reduce and simplify the many tasks on teachers' plates and reimagining teaching as a team sport—not something that one teacher is expected to do on their own, but something that each teacher gets to do on an everyday—even every minute—basis with their fellow teachers.

MOVING PAST NORMAL

In the months after the 2020–2021 school year, I spoke to dozens of educators. Their landscape had changed in many ways. Among them, the curtain between how they worked with students in the classroom and what parents saw and understood had been pulled back further than ever before.

That had many implications, one of which is that language that was formerly consigned to the jargon of education was now commonplace and mainstream, as discussed in Chapter 2. Educators expressed a desire to move past focusing on these phrases.

But the line that the educators with whom I spoke[3] were most tired of was the idea of "getting back to normal." They didn't want things to return to normal. They wanted to create a better teaching and learning experience that better serves every single student. They recognized that wasn't happening before. If that was normal, it was better to leave it behind.

What's more, their students didn't just want to get back to in-person schooling to have fun with their friends. Many of them were desperately seeking connection and support from their teachers.

To deliver on these desires, the traditional one-to-many teacher-to-student model must change. The teaching profession needs to be rethought to create a web of support for children, not just single isolated strands.

THE BEST USE OF FACE-TO-FACE TIME

Given the near-ubiquitous technology and digital curriculum that now exists in and for schools and that we discuss more in Chapter 8, delivering content is not the best use of a teacher's time. Although digital content could still benefit from plenty of improvements, dynamic delivery of content to help students build their background knowledge is no longer the scarce resource it once was.

With that in place, the teacher's role can shift to what many education researchers argue they should be doing anyway, which is—to adapt a line from the musical *Hamilton*—talking less and listening more.

Reducing teacher talk time to increase the amount of active learning that students do has long been a goal of educators and researchers. According to education professor John Hattie, studies on the topic of teacher talk show that, on average, teachers talk for 70 to 80 percent of class time. Hattie's own research suggested that that number was even higher—a whopping 89 percent. All that talking doesn't produce good learning. One study, for example, showed that middle and high school students' engagement fell the most when their teachers were talking.[4]

The question has always been, what should teachers be doing instead? Many promote asking penetrating questions that push students to deepen their thinking. But if students are in a mastery-based learning environment that is personalized for each student's level, what else might teachers do instead of talking and leading whole-class instruction? Teachers I've spoken to over the years have highlighted several ideas, including:

- Tutoring students one-on-one or in small-group instruction: This takes advantage of the insights from the research on the value of tutoring and creates more opportunities for students to engage in dialogue with teachers.

- Mentoring students: Many district leaders and teachers who have adopted Summit's learning model have told me that the most valuable part of it is the way they are now able to create dedicated time for teachers to mentor students each week. More students need teachers to serve as mentors—not just to help them build positive relationships and have fun with friends, but also to help them succeed in life. The pandemic laid bare the number of students who needed a strong mentor in their lives. Although schools can't step in for an engaged parent, reapportioning some educator time to mentoring can help.

- Facilitating conversations and rich projects: Discussions and dialogue have an important place in learning environments. With much of the content delivery off their plate, teachers can spend more time focusing on the questions they ask, the art of facilitating insightful conversations,[5] and the variety of groupings they might employ for those conversations. They can also make sure the student projects are meaty and content rich.

- Serving as a concierge: Being the conduit to help students explore different areas of interest in the world and help them build passions—either through content or connections to professionals outside of school—can unlock pathways students would never have otherwise imagined.

- Curating resources: Robert Pondiscio,[6] an education researcher and former teacher, makes an important argument that teachers should not be spending the bulk of their time assembling curriculum. They aren't trained as instructional designers and others are. But when students are struggling to grasp fundamental concepts, teachers do have an important role to play in finding other ways of explaining concepts or filling in gaps in students' background knowledge. Teachers don't have to create the curricular material themselves to explain these concepts or misunderstandings. There is an abundance of high-quality learning resources in the world that they can curate for students so that children have access to coherent curriculum.

- Evaluating and offering timely feedback on student work: One of the hardest things for teachers to find time to do is give robust and timely feedback to students so that they can improve their performance and deepen their understanding of concepts. Given that feedback is one of the most critical parts of learning, creating more time for it in a teacher's day offers huge value for students—and is necessary to facilitate mastery-based learning and good projects.

- Data mining: One of the most oft-repeated phrases in education is "data-driven instruction." Data can be used by teachers to make sure they are helping students with the support they need when they need it, as well as to create dynamic groupings of students. There are times when having a homogenous group of students learning at the same level is ideal. And there are other times when a heterogenous group of students is ideal so that students at different levels can teach and learn from each other or those with different background knowledge can engage in a conversation and complement each other's strengths.

- Counseling: As discussed in Chapter 3, a large number of students had important social and emotional challenges that needed attention before the pandemic; since the pandemic that need has increased significantly. Supporting students as part of the daily routine is critical to unlock their learning. Many teachers have already been thrust into this role, particularly during the pandemic and its aftermath. Given that today the average guidance counselor-to-student ratio is roughly 464-to-1, leveraging educators who have far more daily interaction with students is important to creating a much better web of support for students.

- Many will rightly observe that teachers haven't been trained for certain of these tasks. But the point is that if delivering content isn't a teacher's primary role, then schools can start to reimagine what educators should do and be trained for and who should fill these different roles.

NO TEACHER SHOULD DO ALL OF THESE ACTIVITIES

Reading this list is daunting because it isn't just a list of things that teachers could do with their freed-up time. It's also a list of things that many students need the adults around them to do if they are to be successful.

Yet for a single teacher to successfully do all this work at once, they must act as a superhero—which is what we are asking many of our teachers to be today. Many ably step into that role.

But creating a job in which teachers must serve as a superhero is fraught with stress and unsustainability, at best, and a path to failure for many. Asking teachers to do things for which they haven't been trained also creates downside risks for students.[7] It's the same problem with the education movie *Waiting for Superman*. If the only way for all students to realize their potential is for a high percentage of the 3.8 million teachers across the country to successfully be all or even many of these things, it's an impossible job to do at scale. As Pondiscio memorably wrote when describing one of the reasons teachers shouldn't build curriculum, "[Having teachers build and select curriculum is] like expecting the waiter at your favorite restaurant to serve your meal attentively while simultaneously cooking for 25 other people—and doing all the shopping and prepping the night before. You'd be exhausted, too."[8]

Although some servers have had to do just that during the pandemic, it isn't a recipe for success.

That was true for teachers before the pandemic. It's arguably even harder now, given the vast array of experiences that students have had since the pandemic. Technology that takes content delivery off teachers' plates may help, but it's not enough.

TEAM-BASED CO-TEACHING

One change that could significantly help teachers is to make teaching a team sport to distribute these different crucial roles across several individuals.

By team teaching, I don't mean assigning teachers to teams but still having them remain in their separate classrooms and only meeting during collective planning periods or off-hours. Schools have done that for decades.

I'm instead referring to co-teaching in which groups of teachers actively work together as they support large groups of students. There are a variety of ways to accomplish this.

Larger Learning Environments, More Teachers

Creating larger learning environments or combining classrooms to create more open learning spaces is one way to create team teaching. This has echoes of the open-classroom movement from the 1970s, which failed as educators spent the 1980s and 1990s erecting walls again.

There is a key difference now, however. In the 1970s, there was an assumption that any learning activity could occur anywhere. In other words, you wouldn't need to design specific spaces for specific modalities of learning. In trying to be all things to all modalities, however, the spaces were suboptimal for any activity. On top of that, in the absence of any technological advances, the dominant model of instruction was still a teacher talking to their class, which produces noise that could disturb a neighboring lesson or silent learning activity. The use of technology can change this dynamic because it can eliminate whole-class instruction. Still, it's important to remember that spaces in new buildings may need to be purpose-built and not universal in nature.

That said, once you have a larger learning environment with more teachers and students, you can allow teachers to disaggregate their roles in a variety of ways—and help eliminate the loneliness that certain teachers like Mrs. Alvera feel.

As one example, imagine that in a learning environment of three or four educators, one might love geeking out on data. In this environment, she can focus on data and assessment and what to do with that data, such as creating different groupings of children or giving rapid feedback. Another might want to steer clear of data as much as possible, but loves playing the role of mentor, counselor or caseworker, and facilitator. A third might want to lean in on tutoring and facilitating rigorous projects, as well as curating those projects from the surrounding community. At any given point, a different educator might step up to play the role of content expert to teach a lesson depending on what students are working on at the time. The educators may also fill a smattering of roles. But the opportunities to focus, develop one's expertise, and create a web of support for students can alleviate the burden on any individual teacher.

Allowing educators to specialize also allows them to master the areas of teaching where they have passion. They can also spend less time on those areas in which they are less excited or less talented. That might be based on a particular area of content expertise or a specific function related to teaching and learning.

Creating these environments could alternatively lead to less structured and specialized roles that allow teachers to ping-pong off each other to create a web of support for their learners and each other. This is the goal of professional learning communities today, but there is a benefit to giving teachers the support in real time.

There are several models for what this can look like.

In the Elizabeth Public Schools district in New Jersey, five schools have created open spaces of roughly 3,000 square feet—plus a teacher preparation area and storage. They have implemented Teach to One, an education model that the nonprofit New Classrooms developed to personalize math learning for middle schoolers.[9] In the model, each student receives an individualized learning playlist every day—the precise set of activities and concepts on which each student would work based on their needs. While students cycle through a variety of modalities to learn, ranging from independent online work to peer-to-peer learning and traditional teacher instruction,[10] the teachers do everything from traditional teaching to tutoring to monitoring how individual students are faring in their assigned modalities.

Summit Public Schools offers another example. Multiple teachers with a variety of roles work together in large learning studios with large groups of students. Summit's teachers take on the roles of everything from subject matter experts to mentors and coaches. They work with each other in an environment that mirrors the open-office environments of the companies in the surrounding areas of the San Francisco Bay Area in California.

Although the Summit and Teach to One learning models are relatively new and make extensive use of digital technology, the notion of having multiple teachers working with students isn't new. For decades, Montessori schools, developed originally in Italy by Maria Montessori, have generally had two teachers working with multi-age students in a prepared learning environment. According to Montessori, the ideal size for a learning environment is 28 to 35 students—or even more—with two educators.[11]

For most teachers and parents, the idea of a larger class being ideal is counterintuitive. But because students are engaging in self-driven work—be that independently or in small groups—teachers can spend their time observing and assessing students, gently directing them, and teaching with direct instruction in small groups. Having two teachers in the environment allows the teachers to play off each other and make sure to serve each student with what they need. Although Montessori classrooms aren't typically thought of as having "technology," they actually have lots of technology. It's just not necessarily of the digital variety. It's instead in the form of the curriculum—consisting of manipulatives and other materials—that students can use to drive their own learning.

According to a report from the Fordham Institute, during remote schooling, schools that embraced a team approach to teaching with a common curriculum did better than those that didn't. At charter school networks like Achievement First, DSST Public Schools, and Success Academy, for example, lead teachers planned lessons across the network of schools. Master teachers recorded the lessons. And other teachers spent time grading and offering feedback to students. Still others focused on the caseworker and tutoring aspects of teaching. They checked in with families and had one-on-one video calls with students. The division of labor, Fordham reported, "allowed networks to deploy teachers according to their skills, strengths, interests, and experience, while also allowing teachers closest to the students to follow up with them in groups and individually."

This could take different forms. At Success Academy, for example, one master grade-level teacher taught 125 students in synchronous sessions. The other teachers reviewed student work, provided individualized feedback, held office hours, and checked attendance. For DSST, while one teacher facilitated the online learning session, another managed the technology and chat. Key to all of this was having a common curriculum with clearly defined learning goals—just as Elizabeth Public Schools through its partnership with Teach to One, Summit Public Schools, and Montessori schools have. This takes curriculum development off teachers' plates and allows them to collaborate.[12]

Multi-Classroom Leaders

There is another approach to creating co-teaching environments that may be more practical in many schools. Knocking down walls and creating larger learning environments or having the money to pay for multiple educators in a learning environment isn't possible in some places. An alternative is to create multi-classroom leaders of teachers.

Public Impact, an education consultancy, has done lots of research on innovative staffing models through its Opportunity Culture work—an effort to restructure schools to "extend the reach of excellent teachers, principals, and their teams to more students, for more pay, within recurring school budgets."[13] A core tenet of the work is the creation of a new position called a multi-classroom leader (MCL).

The MCL leads a team of teachers. He or she provides guidance and frequent on-the-job coaching; co-teaches specific lessons to model what certain teaching should look like; plans, which can include offloading lesson planning for her teachers; analyzes data, which often frees up the teachers she oversees from doing so; and does limited teaching of small groups of students, which can help teachers provide personalized feedback for their students.

An additional benefit stems from the management of schools.[14] In a typical elementary school, a principal might have at least 20 direct reports, if one imagines that each teacher essentially reports up to the school principal as the instructional leader. By instituting an MCL structure, each MCL reports to the principal. The other teachers report to the MCLs. That simplifies the principal's job, as many studies suggest that the ideal number of direct reports for a manager is somewhere in the neighborhood of seven.[15] It also means that teachers are able to receive far more regular live feedback and coaching on their teaching from an expert, something that can be difficult to do in a conventional schooling structure.

Ranson IB Middle School in the Charlotte-Mecklenburg school district in North Carolina was among the first in the country to adopt the Opportunity Culture structure. A high-poverty and struggling school, after implementing the MCL model schoolwide, Ranson experienced the highest student achievement growth among Title I district schools in North Carolina. Teachers who take on the MCL role, like Okema Owens Simpson, a sixth-grade MCL for English Language Arts (ELA), typically oversee three other ELA teachers. Simpson is in turn responsible for the performance of those teachers' 275 students. Because of the structure, she's not only able to take some work off the plate of the teachers she oversees, she's also able to observe them regularly and provide coaching to improve their teaching—up to at least three times per week.[16] Independent research from the Brookings Institution has suggested that this MCL model yields statistically significant learning improvements for students in math, based on data from the three largest school districts implementing this model at the time: Charlotte-Mecklenburg, Cabarrus County Schools in North Carolina, and Syracuse in New York.[17]

More broadly, research from the Christensen Institute shows how important it is for students to have a strong network of supports around them. By taking stock of who students know, schools can intentionally build up a unique team of supports for each child. This team would include professional connections and mentors. It would also benefit from technology that connects students to different relationships.[18]

Ranson IB Middle School:
https://www.opportunityculture.org/2017/11/28/days-in-the-life-mcl-video/

UNBUNDLING TO TAKE THINGS OFF TEACHERS' PLATES

There is a common undercurrent in many of these ideas: taking tasks off individual teachers' plates to give them a higher likelihood of success and making sure students have a stronger web of support.[19]

For example, online learning should take significant amounts of content delivery off teachers' plates.

Employing mastery-based learning that allows students to move as fast as they can demonstrate mastery means that there must be a full curriculum in place. That means teachers don't have to create or curate the core curriculum themselves, just as Pondiscio recommends. Recall how Summit has developed a full coherent scope, suggested sequence, and associated playlists of resources for the entire set of competencies a student should master. That means there is no lesson planning the night before for teachers. The Teach to One and Montessori models operate in the same way. This doesn't diminish teachers' professionalization; it bolsters it. In other professions—from law to medicine—we consciously cultivate a variety of roles that have different responsibilities to ensure that trained professionals can practice at the top of their respective craft.

Similarly, having students do more of the work themselves—as occurs in the Summit and Montessori models—takes a significant burden and role off teachers' plates. What's interesting is that the schools that employed team-based teaching models weren't the only ones that fared better during the pandemic. Another set of schools that did well were those that had intentionally built their students' agency and made student ownership of their learning a priority prior to the pandemic. Why? When it was hard for some to receive directions from teachers on what to do as schools scrambled to move online, students who already knew what to do and how to make their own learning decisions—and already knew the curriculum ahead of them—didn't have to miss a beat. Schools that used the Summit Learning Platform, as well as those in districts like Menlo Park in California that were using the Altitude Learning platform to help manage its curriculum, benefited from the approach.

As Brian Greenberg, founder and CEO of the Silicon Schools Fund, said, the theory of school reform for many decades has essentially been that we have over 3 million teachers and some 50 million students on a giant rowboat, which represents our sprawling and decentralized school system. We've historically shouted at the teachers that they aren't rowing hard or fast enough. But what if, rather than shouting at the teachers to do more of the rowing on that metaphorical rowboat, we gave those 50 million-plus students each an oar for themselves and let them do more of the work by allowing them to direct more of their own learning?[20] If students have that ownership of learning—where they set their own goals, plan how they will learn, do the learning, show evidence of their learning, reflect, and then repeat the cycle that we discussed in Chapter 5—what might we then see? What else might we enable teachers to be and do for their students?

No More Grading Your Own Students

One other thing that should be taken off many teachers' plates is grading their own students.

That may sound odd, for it seems as American as apple pie. Teachers are solely responsible for a whole class of students and their grades.

But what if, like the sugar in apple pie, being graded by your teachers isn't actually good for students—or teachers and maybe even society? What if there are other ways to organize schools so that teachers get to work with other teachers and are solely pulling for their students, not judging them?

There is ample evidence to suggest we ought to ask the question.[21]

In her bestselling book *Mindset: The New Psychology of Success*, Stanford professor Carol Dweck wrote, "When teachers are judging [students], [students] will sabotage the teacher by not trying. But when students understand that school is for them—a way for them to grow their minds—they do not insist on sabotaging themselves."[22]

Why would students ever get the impression that their teachers are judging them? Because their teachers are responsible for grading them—which involves judging how well they have done in a subject.

In *The Gift of Failure*, Jessica Lahey talks about how students learn more when their "families are involved in their education." Yet, in many cases, parents and teachers have become adversaries—to the point that many teachers "cite the challenge of dealing with their students' parents as the main reason for abandoning the classroom." Why the tension? Grades.

As Lahey wrote, "Many of my students express tension and outright fear for weeks before report cards come out, and in the days before parent-teacher conferences, they look as if they are bound for the gallows. Even when they adore their parents and respect their teachers, loyalty to one gets in the way of the relationship with the other, sort of like negotiating divorcing parents. My students cannot possibly trust me completely when I am locked in battle with their parents."[23]

One reason this tension feels like a battle is that students are stuck in a high-stakes, zero-sum system that parents rightly perceive as being averse to failure. Moving to a mastery-based learning system, as we discussed in Chapters 4 and 5, allows for the embrace of failure as part of the learning process. It reframes the failure as a low-stakes event that is a step on the journey to success for each student.

Even in a mastery-based learning system, however, teachers doling out the final grades for their students still creates a conflict of interest that is unfair to both the students and teachers.

As Tavenner wrote in *Prepared*, "Teachers then have two jobs that are in opposition to each other. On the one hand, they are responsible for students' learning. . . Their second responsibility is ensuring students' grades show what the student has done, and that they grade their student in a fair and ethical way."[24]

This conflict connects to other reasons to be wary of teachers grading their own students, which we touched on in Chapter 5.

Teacher grades, for example, are subject to grade inflation. One explanation for why standardized tests have stubbornly remained a part of education is that they serve as a check on teachers going easy on their students.[25] Mastery-based learning doesn't inherently fix this dynamic. As Chapter 5 discussed, it might even exacerbate it because the incentives for inflating reports of student mastery could conceivably grow.

Chapter 5 laid out other reasons that teachers' grades of their own students can be inequitable and idiosyncratic.

So what to do about it?

In higher education, Western Governors University (WGU) has illuminated one pathway forward. WGU is the largest online, competency-based university in America, as it serves well over 100,000 learners. Founded in 1997, the university embraces the unbundling of the teacher role with a five-part faculty model. There are three student-facing faculty roles:

1. Program mentors, who are assigned to a student upon enrollment. They help that student all the way through graduation with a variety of non-academic supports;

2. Instructors, who are subject-matter experts that provide proactive and reactive academic support to students;

3. And evaluators, who review assessments to see if students have demonstrated mastery.

There are also two faculty roles that are behind the scenes: assessment faculty, who are experts in creating a variety of high-quality assessments that are valid and reliable, and curriculum faculty, who are experts in curriculum development and the science of learning.[26]

Having a separate staff of impartial evaluators allows WGU to accomplish a few specific things for students.[27]

First, students can never say they received a bad grade because their teacher didn't like them. That's because the faculty doing the grading doesn't know them.

Second, WGU can protect against grade inflation and, more generally, different grading practices among faculty members. It does so by having multiple faculty members grade a subset of work to establish interrater reliability. The University also invests in training its evaluators in the science of assessment—a skill that receives short shrift for most teachers. Because its evaluators specialize, they are able to spend more of their time on acquiring these skills and perfecting their craft. As a result, although WGU uses some assessments that are automated and computer scored, WGU's most significant assessments are robust performance tasks rather than narrow measures that look like those that would appear on a standardized test and be the subject of educators' scorn (or Greene's criticisms from Chapter 5).

These practices are in opposition to today's K–12 schools where, as Tavenner wrote, "Grades offer little consistency, as grading rigor varies from teacher to teacher and from school to school. And grades offer little in the way of specificity; most parents and some students don't know the reasoning behind a letter grade."[28]

Finally, students at WGU don't have an adversarial relationship with their program mentors and instructors, because they aren't judging the students. They are instead doing everything they can to support and advocate for the students to help them attain mastery of different concepts and skills.

On the face of it, implementing this in K–12 school districts would seem to be much more difficult. Some districts only have one teacher for a given subject or grade level, which means that districts would have to create or join systems and agreements with other districts around how to use other teachers to grade their students. That would in turn mean that districts would need some agreement on the competencies to master, which assessments to use, the rubric through which to grade students, and what level of work constitutes what corresponding grade—or, better yet, demonstrates mastery.

Yet there are hopeful signs ahead. The Khan Academy, through its tutoring platform Schoolhouse, offers assessments to certify mastery of certain concepts.[29] The Graide Network offers rapid feedback for students from expert readers. Perhaps this could turn into a more robust network of assessing mastery were schools to move to a mastery-based system where assessments were both for and of learning.[30] And, as mentioned earlier, the Mastery Transcript Consortium seeks to facilitate these evaluation practices across its member schools.

This is worth a serious investment in time, thought, and building educator capacity because students deserve schools where teachers are their advocates and supporters, not their final judge and jury. Teachers deserve the same.

TEACHER MOTIVATION

Creating co-teaching opportunities and chances for teachers to advance in their areas of expertise—and shed the tasks that bring them less joy and fulfillment—sounds like a set of ideas that would make the teaching profession more sustainable and offer students more supports. It also has backing in research about how to improve motivation for professionals at work.

In 1968, Frederick Herzberg published an influential body of research showing that it's possible to both love and hate your job at the same time.[31]

This is possible because two sets of factors affect how people feel about their work. The first set, called hygiene factors, affects whether employees are dissatisfied with their jobs. The second set, called motivators, determine the extent to which employees outright love their jobs. It's important to note that in Herzberg's categorization scheme, the opposite of job dissatisfaction is not job satisfaction, but merely the *absence* of dissatisfaction. Similarly, the opposite of loving your job is not hating it, but the *absence* of loving it.

To help eliminate one's dissatisfaction, Herzberg found that it was important to address "hygiene" factors, which are listed here in their order of impact on job dissatisfaction (from highest to lowest):

- Company policy and administration
- Supervision
- Relationship with supervisor
- Work conditions
- Salary
- Relationship with peers
- Personal life
- Relationship with subordinates
- Status
- Security

But to make someone satisfied in their job, you need to make the job more motivating—or use motivators, in Herzberg's parlance. The motivators are listed here in order of their impact on satisfaction (from highest to lowest):

- Achievement
- Recognition
- Work itself
- Responsibility
- Advancement
- Growth

What does this mean?

Allowing employees to find places to achieve, gain recognition, exercise responsibility, and have a career path has a greater tendency to motivate employees than do salary levels or vacation time. But conversely, these other factors can make people dissatisfied with their jobs. To put it another way, to make teachers perform better in their jobs, schools should work on improving the motivators. Financial incentives and the like will not do much. But to keep teachers from leaving because of dissatisfaction, schools need to ensure adequate hygiene factors.

What's interesting is that the traditional teacher job lacks many of the motivators.

Teachers often work in isolation from other adults, which means there is little or no opportunity for recognition for their efforts.

There is also no real career track for teachers in traditional schools and districts. Opportunities for increased responsibility and career advancement are slim. Aside from becoming the head of a department, the only other way for most teachers to move up in this line of work is, in fact, to stop teaching so they can be "promoted" into an administrative job.

Aside from occasional workshops or required training programs, teachers have limited opportunities for growth in the job after the first few years.

Yet from creating multi-classroom leaders to allowing people to specialize and take on more responsibilities to being recognized for their work by their peers on a more regular—even everyday—basis, there are a lot of opportunities to redesign the teaching role to include more motivators, as well as improve the hygiene factors that lead to dissatisfaction.

WILL TEACHERS EMBRACE THE SHIFT?

What I'm proposing here amounts to a large set of changes. These changes will be difficult to implement for a variety of reasons. Ideas like these often fall flat because teachers aren't buying what people like me are proposing—even if they would likely improve satisfaction for educators, students, and parents once fully in place. For any change in a school to be successful, the teachers in that school must buy in and execute it well. Trying to impose it in a top-down way in a public school is unlikely to work.

My colleagues Tom Arnett, Bob Moesta, and I conducted research to understand why teachers make significant changes to their teaching practice.[32] The work was akin to understanding the Jobs to Be Done students experience as they try to make progress.

What we learned is that there are four Jobs to Be Done that teachers have when they make big changes in their teaching— ranging from implementing project-based and blended learning to changing their work arrangements and use of time with other teachers in the building.

Some teachers change because they are forced to. They essentially say, "Help me to not fall behind on my new school's initiative." But they aren't excited about the change being implemented.

Teachers experiencing this Job are like Cindy, a pseudonym for one teacher we talked to. Before leaving the teaching profession to be a stay-at-home mom, Cindy had loved teaching, getting to know her students, and designing creative ways to engage them. But when she came back to teaching, she was told that she was going to have to use computers to do blended learning. As a technology neophyte, Cindy felt anxious.

Cindy stayed with the blended learning because the rest of the school was doing the initiative. She wanted to show her new colleagues that she was trying. She went through the motions and had her students use the computers a few times a week. But her enthusiasm wasn't in the effort, which showed in her lackluster execution.

Better was to implement something new in a circumstance like Rachel's, another teacher we talked to. Rachel's principal asked her to be part of a county-wide leadership team working on project-based learning, a topic about which Rachel knew nothing. But after five years of teaching fifth grade at her school, she was ready to take on a new challenge and develop a reputation with all her colleagues by contributing to the broader school, not just the students in her classroom.

Teachers in a circumstance like Rachel's—ready to embrace a change because of a desire and ability to contribute to the broader school—were in what we called the "Help me lead the way in improving my school" Job. People who experience this Job are not "early adopters" because they are enthusiastic about a particular initiative or technology, but because they want to contribute to something school wide.

The other two Jobs we uncovered were also more positive places in which to implement something new with a teacher. One was "Help me engage and challenge more of my students in a way that's manageable" and the other was what we call "Help me replace a broken instructional model so I can reach each student." Trying to get someone in the "replace a broken instructional model" Job to do something that felt incremental or tinkering was unlikely to gain traction, but asking someone in the "Help me engage and challenge more of my students" Job to do something transformational was likely a nonstarter because it would feel overwhelming. And neither cared about the impact on the whole school per se.

Why does this matter? Understanding these dynamics should help leaders better design and position initiatives to meet different teachers' goals. Trying to get a teacher to do something radically different, like take down the walls between her classroom and those of two other teachers when all she is trying to do is boost the engagement of her students, is unlikely to get traction. It might even force that teacher into the "Help me to not fall behind" Job that is marked by compliance and a lack of enthusiasm.

On the flip side, showing how some simple swapping of groups between classes could create more engagement by allowing a teacher to play off her strengths with those of another teacher down the hall might work. It could also then create momentum for more changes down the road that, because of the groundwork in place, will be more incremental and less radical. Spending time educating the teacher in this circumstance about the flawed traditional educational model and the opportunities that arise in mastery-based learning could also help move a teacher to the transformational Job of replacing a "broken instructional model."

On the other hand, a teacher who is looking to replace a broken instructional model to reach each student is probably ready to dive into the deep end with mastery-based learning and co-teaching right away. Any initiative that falls short of that radical promise might push that teacher to leave.

If we understand teachers' circumstances, their struggles, the progress they desire, and what will make them anxious or excited, we stand a much better chance of making progress together.

That's particularly true if the ideas will result in a more sustainable teaching job that creates a better web of support for students and teachers—and a better relationship between teachers and parents. That progress is of course likely to be halted, marked with fits and starts, and different in different places. But it would be progress, which is a lot better than what's happened with so many of the change efforts people have tried in the past. And remember, progress is what people are trying to make in *their* lives—which means as they define progress, not as you might. So help them to help you.

KEY TAKEAWAYS

- Delivering content to a whole class of students, particularly in today's age of near-ubiquitous technology and digital curriculum, is not the best use of a teacher's time.

- That should allow teams of educators to focus on other aspects of what students need to succeed, including tutoring, mentoring, facilitating conversations and rich projects, serving as a concierge, curating resources, evaluating and offering timely feedback, data mining, and counseling.

- No teacher should do all of these activities.

- Team-based co-teaching offers a promising path forward to distribute these roles across several individuals.

- One thing teachers should stop doing is grading their own students.

- Creating co-teaching opportunities and chances for teachers to advance in their areas of expertise supports the research on what motivates people at work.

- Important in implementing any of these changes is making sure they align with the progress that educators desire. When educators make big switches in their practice, they are looking to not fall behind on their school's initiative, lead the way in improving their school, engage and challenge more of their students in a way that's manageable, or replace a broken instructional model to reach each student.

NOTES

1. Abigail Hess, "'I Felt Like I Was Being Experimented On': 1 in 4 Teachers Are Considering Quitting After This Past Year," CNBC, June 24, 2021, updated June 25, 2021, https://www.cnbc .com/2021/06/24/1-in-4-teachers-are-considering-quitting-after-this-past-year.html.
2. Leslie Kan, "How Does Teacher Attrition Compare to Other Professions?," *Education Next*, July 14, 2014, https://www .educationnext.org/teacher-attrition-compare-professions/.
3. To clarify, these educators weren't necessarily representative of the sentiments of the teaching profession.
4. Catherine Gewertz, "How Much Should Teachers Talk in the Classroom? Much Less, Some Say," *Education Week*, December 10, 2019, corrected January 3, 2020, https://www.edweek.org/ leadership/how-much-should-teachers-talk-in-the-classroom-much-less-some-say/2019/12.

   See also John Hattie, *Visible Learning for Teachers* (New York: Routledge, December 2012).
5. The R.E.A.L. Discussion skills offers a helpful way to facilitate these discussions. See https://www.realdiscussion.org/ (accessed February 4, 2022).
6. Robert Pondiscio, "How We Make Teaching Too Hard for Mere Mortals," *Education Next*, May 16, 2016, https://www.educationnext .org/how-we-make-teaching-too-hard-for-mere-mortals/.
7. As Pondiscio wrote, "The tendency to borrow ideas and tactics from therapy carries with it the risk of pathologizing childhood and encouraging educators to view children—particularly children from disadvantaged subgroups—not as capable and resilient individuals but as fragile and traumatized." Pondiscio, "The Unexamined Rise of Therapeutic Education: How Social-Emotional

Learning Extends K–12 Education's Reach into Students' Lives and Expands Teachers' Roles," American Enterprise Institute, October 13, 2021.

8. Pondiscio, "How We Make Teaching Too Hard for Mere Mortals."

9. DMR Architects, https://www.dmrarchitects.com/projects/k12-education/elizabeth-public-schools-teach-to-one/ (accessed August 19, 2021).

10. Douglas D. Ready, Katharine Conn, Shani S. Bretas, and Iris Daruwala, "Final Impact Results From the i3 Implementation of *Teach To One: Math*," Consortium for Policy Research in Education, Teachers College, Columbia University, January 2019, https://newclassrooms.org/wp-content/uploads/Final-Impact-Results-i3-TtO.pdf.

11. "Essential Characteristics of Association Montessori Internationale (AMI) Environments Comprehensive Description," Association Montessori Internationale Canada, https://www.ami-canada.com/essentialcomprehensive.html (accessed January 25, 2022).

12. Gregg Vanourek, "Schooling COVID-19: Lessons from Leading Charter Networks from Their Transition to Remote Learning," Thomas B. Fordham Institute, August 2020.

13. "What Is the Opportunity Culture Initiative?," Public Impact, https://www.opportunityculture.org/what-is-an-opportunity-culture/#:~:text=The%20Opportunity%20Culture%20initiative%20helps,possible%20before%20teaching%20and%20leading (accessed January 25, 2022).

14. John Danner, an entrepreneur, former teacher, investor in education technology companies, and co-founder of Rocketship Public Schools, first suggested this idea to me.

15. Jim Schleckser, "How Many Direct Reports Should You Have? Most Leaders Miss This Critical Culture Element," *Inc.*, March 5, 2019, https://www.inc.com/jim-schleckser/how-many-direct-reports-should-you-have.html.

16. "The Opportunity Culture Principles," Public Impact, https://www.opportunityculture.org/what-is-an-opportunity-culture/#principles (accessed August 19, 2021).

"Days in the Life: The Work of a Successful Multi-Classroom Leader: A Profile of Okema Owens Simpson," Opportunity Culture: An Initiative of Public Impact, 2017–2018, https://www.opportunityculture.org/wp-content/uploads/2017/11/MCL_Vignette_Okema_Simpson-Public_Impact.pdf.

17. Benjamin Backes and Michael Hansen, "Reaching Further and Learning More? Evaluating Public Impact's Opportunity Culture Initiative," National Center for Analysis of Longitudinal Data in Education Research, American Institutes for Research, January 2018, https://caldercenter.org/publications/reaching-further-and-learning-more-evaluating-public-impacts-opportunity-culture.

18. Julia Freeland Fisher and Mahnaz Charnia, "5 Steps for Building & Strengthening Students' Networks," Clayton Christensen Institute, May 2021, https://whoyouknow.org/wp-content/uploads/2021/05/playbook.pdf.

19. For more on how technology and innovation can aid this work, see Thomas Arnett, "Teaching in the Machine Age: How Innovation Can Make Bad Teachers Good and Good Teachers Better," Christensen Institute, December 7, 2016, https://www.christenseninstitute.org/publications/teaching-machine-age/.

Also see Thomas Arnett, "A New Framework to Unlock Edtech's Potential for Teachers," December 11, 2018, https://www.christensen-institute.org/blog/a-new-framework-to-unlock-edtechs-potential-for-teachers/.

20. "Blended Learning: Personalizing Education for Students," Coursera, 2013, https://www.coursera.org/learn/blending-learning-personalization.

21. For more on this topic, see:

Michael B. Horn, "Why Teachers Shouldn't Grade Their Own Students," Forbes, December 5, 2019, https://www.forbes.com/sites/michaelhorn/2019/12/05/why-teachers-shouldnt-grade-their-own-students/?sh=264065e3236b.Thomas Arnett, "Teachers Grading Students Hinders Education," Christensen Institute, June 26, 2015, https://www.christenseninstitute.org/blog/teachers-grading-students-hinders-education/.Thomas Arnett, "Teachers Shouldn't Have to Be Their Students' Judges,"

Christensen Institute, September 25, 2019, https://www
.christenseninstitute.org/blog/teachers-shouldnt-have-to-be-their-
students-judges/.

22. Carol Dweck, *Mindset: The New Psychology of Success* (New York:
Ballantine, 2013), p. 204.

23. Jessica Lahey, *The Gift of Failure: How the Best Parents Learn to Let
Go So Their Children Can Succeed* (New York: Harper Collins,
2015), p. 183.

24. Diane Tavenner, *Prepared: What Kids Need for a Fulfilled Life*
(New York: Currency, 2019), p. 83.

25. Scott Jaschik, "Grade Inflation, Higher and Higher," *Inside Higher
Ed*, March 29, 2016, https://www.insidehighered.com/news/
2016/03/29/survey-finds-grade-inflation-continues-rise-four-
year-colleges-not-community-college.

26. "Student Experience: Providing Personalized Support Every Step
of the Way," WGU, https://www.wgu.edu/student-experience/
learning/faculty.html (accessed August 21, 2021).

27. Jon Marcus, "Competency-Based Education, Put to the Test,"
Education Next 21, no. 3 (Summer 2021), https://www.educationnext
.org/competency-based-education-put-to-the-test-western-governors-
university-learning-assessment/.

28. Tavenner, p. 83.

29. Schoolhouse, https://schoolhouse.world/ (accessed February 4, 2022).

30. The Graide Network, https://www.thegraidenetwork.com/ (accessed
February 4, 2022).

31. Frederick Herzberg, "One More Time: How Do You Motivate
Employees?" *Harvard Business Review* 81, no. 1 (1968): 87–96.

32. Thomas Arnett, Bob Moesta, and Michael B. Horn, "The Teacher's
Quest for Progress: How School Leaders Can Motivate Instructional
Innovation," Clayton Christensen Institute, September 12, 2018,
https://www.christenseninstitute.org/publications/teachers-jobs-
to-be-done/.

Chapter 7

The Parent Experience

When Dr. Ball had a minute to herself again, she finally texted Jeremy's mom. "How are you?"

Jeremy's mom responded right away. "I'm tired," it read, alongside a tired emoji for added measure.

Ball couldn't decide if it was a good or bad idea to use an emoji back. She passed and asked what else was going on.

Jeremy's mom's text back was short. "I'm fine," it said.

Ball asked if she could perhaps meet her for a walk in her neighborhood. After a couple minutes of no response, Ball texted again. "How's the year going for Jeremy?"

"I don't know," his mom replied.

What a contrast with Julia's parents. They knew everything and then some—or at least they had an opinion on everything.

A moment later, Ball received another text from Jeremy's mom. "How do you think he's doing?"

Ball paused. She had a sense he wasn't doing well, but she didn't want to start another problem today. She passed and instead asked how the after-school arrangement was working.

"Not enough hours," came the reply.

That's right, remembered Ball. Not a savvy question. A bunch of parents had pushed back on the school's attempt to allocate more resources toward providing more hours of care after school. Instead they wanted a space club or something because they were inspired by SpaceX or Blue Origin or something like that. What was the difference anyway?, Ball thought. She sighed.

Jeremy's mom needed more childcare and food. Mr. Owens wanted to make sure Julia didn't fall further behind the kids at the neighboring school. And Mrs. Owens wanted peace and tranquility. Or something like that.

Come to think it, peace and tranquility didn't sound so bad, Ball thought.

* * *

Parents are known for being resistant to big changes in education. They are seen as a conservative force for doing school like they did it. As for my mom or the subset of parents in a Massachusetts school district who were suspicious of a school leaving behind its A–F letter grading system, radical changes are often unwelcome.

Because most everyone went to school, most feel qualified as experts on what schools should do and look like. For those who were successful in school, like the parents of the Julias of the world, they often want the schooling experience to resemble significant parts of what they experienced. Nostalgia for certain aspects of the school experience—and a desire that the younger generation even experience some of the challenges they did—runs deep in many parental communities.

This conservative nature about schooling was present in the summer of 2021 as well, as most schools prepared for in-person schooling. According to a survey from *Education Next*, although a significant share of parents reported that their children had left public district schools to be homeschooled or attend private or public charter schools from the spring of 2020 to the fall of 2020 during the height of the pandemic, by June 2021, the percentages attending each of those different schooling categories were starting to return to what they were prior to the pandemic. Similarly, rather than hope for dramatic changes in education policy, the public's appetite for reforms on both the left and right had declined from prior to the pandemic—from falling support for higher teacher pay, higher school expenditures per pupil, and similar learning standards across states to a drop in backing vouchers, tax-credit scholarships, and charter schools.

Yet beneath these macro-level opinions, there's potentially more nuance within schools. On the heels of COVID-19, the federal government committed to an historic injection of federal dollars in schools. According to one poll, parents don't want schools just to use these funds on the status quo; they instead want schools doing more with digital learning, "work-based learning," and supporting students' emotional and mental health needs.[1] Parents would probably also be in favor of someone else grading their children's work rather than their child's teacher—if only for an improved relationship with the teacher. And, despite the *Education Next* survey, according to Tyton Partners, 1.5 million children were still enrolled in microschools and learning pods in the fall of 2021. Enrollment in many districts was still far below what it was before the pandemic.[2]

But many of these ideas don't dramatically change the schooling equation on their own. We also know that parents don't share the same priorities.[3] Given all these conflicting signals and rampant conservatism, how is a school or district to make significant changes—like implementing mastery-based learning or co-teaching models?

UNDERSTANDING PARENTS' QUEST FOR PROGRESS

Far more important than surveys and asking people what they want is watching what they do. What do they prioritize? What are the sets of events and forces that move them to act? People are rarely articulate about what they want. But you can learn a lot by watching their actions.

In watching parents, it's clear that they have divergent views and priorities. They don't all have the same definition of progress. They don't adhere to what others in their demographics believe or want. Their views are instead shaped based on their circumstances and the struggles they face. What's important to them changes over time as those circumstances shift.

In other words, parents have different Jobs to Be Done when it comes to children and their schooling. Given parents' conservatism, advocating for radical changes or innovations for other children can backfire. It's better to position the changes you want to make in terms of why they will help each individual parent make progress for *their* children, as that parent defines progress. Framing a change as an answer to a parent's quest for progress and leading with *why*—as opposed to the how or what—your proposal will help is crucial. But to do so well requires understanding what Jobs parents have as they approach schooling.

Although it's not a perfect proxy, colleagues of mine conducted research on why parents switch their child's school. What they learned is that parents select a given school to accomplish one of four Jobs to Be Done.[4] The research helps to understand the frustrations and desires that cause parents to take such a momentous and emotional action.

There are of course other actions that parents can take in a school. Having other researchers refine our understanding of the Jobs parents have when they take different actions would be valuable.

But what my colleagues uncovered provides a valuable framework for positioning change efforts as solutions to the progress that parents desire. By focusing on the extreme cases—the act of actually switching a child's school—they offer insight into parents' true underlying priorities that cause them to act, not just grumble. That switch occurred through a number of mechanisms—using any number of school choice policies in specific localities, applying to and then enrolling in a private school (and paying for it themselves or using financial aid), returning to the local district school, or even moving. What Job a parent found themselves in did not correlate to that parent's demographics.[5] Given that a core tenet of design thinking is to focus on the extreme users so that it's easier to capture the wide range of priorities all users have, this research can offer school leaders significant help in designing and positioning their change efforts.

Job 1: Help Our Child Overcome an Obstacle

The first Job that causes a parent to leave a school is to help their child overcome some sort of obstacle.

The belief that their current school is failing their child occurs when there is some mix of the following: parents believe their present school isn't addressing their child's specific learning needs or difficulties, their child is being bullied, they are worried that their child is falling behind, they have concerns their child doesn't enjoy learning anymore, and they are worried about what will happen to their child if they don't act now.

Parents make the switch so that their children can thrive in a school that caters to their specific needs, can have the attention they need, won't be teased or bullied by classmates, and won't fall further behind. This Job is more about leaving the current school because it isn't helping, believing that the new place will have what it takes to help their child thrive, and a sense of immediacy—that they need to help their child now. Parents with this Job care relatively less about the proximity of the school or even the cost to attend. They are often looking for a short-term fix rather than a longer-term solution where they will stay indefinitely.

Job 2: Help Us Be Part of a Values-Aligned Community

Parents with this Job are seeking to be part of a like-minded community in which their child can mature to be ready for the broader world. This is less about helping prepare their child to get into the best college possible or seeking relief from the challenges and troubles that their child may be dealing with in their current school. What the parents who experience this Job really want is to be part of a group that thinks like them. They are relatively less concerned about whether the school further develops their child's intelligence or ensures they are well-rounded.

Job 3: Help Us Develop a Well-Rounded Child

When parents switch schools for this set of reasons, they do so because they are seeking a school that will help their child develop socially and emotionally with life skills—and are less concerned about test scores and academics. Their paramount goal is a child who will be well-rounded and productive in society. Parents who experience this Job start looking for a new school when they feel the current one is not educating their whole child and is overly focused on academics. Concerns that lead to switching also mount when they feel that their child is living in a "bubble" with little diversity of people, thought, experiences, and so forth—in many ways the opposite of Job 2.

When they choose a new school, their motivations are for their child to not become arrogant. They want them to be well-rounded and understand how they fit into the world. These parents want to help their child learn how to interact with individuals who might be different from them, how to apply knowledge in real-world projects, and how to integrate into society.

Job 4: Help Us Realize Our Plan for Our Child

Some parents choose a school out of a desire for their child to get on the "right" track and have better opportunities than they had. In many but not all cases, the end destination for these parents is to see their child admitted to a top college. As a result, they want a school with excellent academics and a great reputation. These parents start to look for a new school when they believe they need to challenge their child and their current school doesn't have good data or a strong reputation around their students ultimately gaining acceptance to top schools—as the parents define "the top." These parents often have a clear plan for the type of college they want their child to attend, and they are laser focused on that goal.

These parents choose the new school to help their child build their resume and be ready for the rigors of college, and to ensure that their child will have the best opportunities available to them along the journey. This is less about the social and emotional well-being of the child—unless that's what's required to gain acceptance to school. And it's less about the child making their own choices or being in a diverse environment.

One Observation

Some readers may be surprised that none of these Jobs are "provide custodial care for our child" or "keep our child safe" or "help me with childcare." As the pandemic has revealed, brick-and-mortar schools play an important role in providing childcare for many families. I address this dynamic more later in this chapter, but for now, know that these sentiments are important for many families, but they aren't a full-fledged Job to Be Done because they aren't a full statement of the progress that a parent seeks in a struggling circumstance. Safe childcare may be an important feature or even a requirement for some families, but it's not the Job to Be Done itself.

IMPLEMENTING CHANGE

There are two implications worth highlighting from this research.

First, in our research on Jobs, we've learned that it's hard for any service or offering to be all things to all people. To successfully deliver on a parent's Job to Be Done, for example, you need to provide certain experiences—experiences that may be directly at odds with the ones that parents with different Jobs to Be Done have. One-size-fits-all offerings, in other words, often become one-size-fits-none and don't work. That means that schools need to make hard choices and identify which Job they should be serving—and by extension what they will choose to not do well. Or they need to offer distinct choices and options.

The second implication is that as schools seek to implement different innovations, they need to design and fit those initiatives into the progress that individual parents desire—not the progress that is important to the school, educator, or public education system writ large. And yes, that's the same lesson we learned about implementing changes with educators.

What follows is a deeper exploration of these two implications.

Focus: Be Good at One Thing, Not All Things

To see why it's hard to be all things to all people, consider how a parent would feel at a school that optimizes for a Job different from the one about which they care.

Imagine a parent who desires that their high school prioritizes developing their child into a well-rounded individual. But the school is laser focused on bolstering its academic reputation to increase the numbers of students it sends to Ivy League schools. It adds SAT and ACT prep classes alongside loads of Advanced Placement classes, and it pushes students to take AP classes starting freshman year. It offers constant college fairs and talks frequently about the test scores in the district. The stress around the college-choosing process starts as early as freshman year, if not earlier, toward the end of middle school. Students compete to participate in as many extracurricular and leadership activities as possible, which the school encourages. For the parent focusing on their child's life skills and social and emotional well-being and balance, these moves—or even a fraction of them—are at odds with what they care about. The reverse would likely be true as well.

Is there a middle ground? Certainly. Perhaps the school has a moderate number of AP classes, focuses on its test scores, offers a wide range of extracurricular activities that are appealing to colleges, and brings many college admissions officers to campus. At the same time, it offers after-school sessions on mental health and an extracurricular yoga club. It talks about maintaining balance in one's life, includes mindfulness practice as part of the school day, and holds frequent discussions on the importance of diversity. Will the parent who wants a school to help develop a well-rounded child be happy? There's a good chance that they will feel that the messages they care about—mental health, mindfulness, diversity, and balance—are undermined by the school's actions with regards to testing and college.

What about the parents who are focused primarily on a school helping them realize their plan for their child—with a highly ranked college being the goal? They'll probably wonder why their children are wasting their time with mindfulness—to say nothing of their dissatisfaction at the school's resource allocation choices.

Although it's possible that parents in either group won't be unhappy to the point of being ready to leave the school, moderation between the two won't make either excited or even satisfied. If excellence is the goal, choosing what to be excellent in—and, by definition, what you *intentionally* won't do or be good at is important.

From a change-management perspective, any initiative that moves the school one step in either direction will annoy or even anger one of the parents. It might even meet with outright resistance, which will create friction for the educator seeking to implement something new.

So what is an educator to do?

To be clear, you don't have to do *anything*. But coming out of the COVID environment where a subset of parents have become much more keenly aware of both their preferences, opinions, and priorities around schooling and education *and* the educations their children's schools are delivering, this may be an uncomfortable place to live.

Rather than remain stuck in the middle of an array of constituencies, as so often happens, schools and districts can create and run distinct options. This doesn't mean mashing different initiatives together as a set of options, but instead allowing people to opt in to thoughtfully crafted, differentiated experiences from the get-go.

What might this look like?

If you're leading a school district, a portfolio of schooling options can help. Different types of schools can offer different options to provide different experiences that meet the different parent, student, and even teacher expectations and desires. Those schools could be aligned around the different Jobs to Be Done parents have. They could also have different underlying educational philosophies. Perhaps you'd have a school that subscribes to the Waldorf philosophy and another that caters to those who prefer a Montessori education. Another might emphasize the classics, while still another might focus on college prep. To be clear, if you go this direction, you should be sure that doing so doesn't result in segregating populations by race or violating other educational norms in the United States. After all, one of the powerful things of the Jobs research is that parents don't fall in a particular Job because of their demographic—and there isn't a correlation between race and Job. What's more, parents can change Jobs multiple times as their children's circumstances shift. They can even experience different Jobs simultaneously for their different children who are in different situations. One of the most helpful things about having truly different educational options within a broader school community is that if a parent finds themselves in Job 1 multiple times needing to help their child overcome an obstacle, there are multiple options that might meet their needs.

If you're leading a school, choice and options can create the ability to innovate and better serve parents. Creating schools within schools, microschools, or learning pods can create subcommunities within a larger community to cater to different parental priorities—and create elements of the community center model for schooling described in Chapter 3.

Chapter 1's insights about the importance of creating a separate group to craft new initiatives and reframe threats as opportunities apply here. Chapter 11 offers further support for the power of separation. For now, bear in mind that different parents will have different priorities. That's just reality.

Innovating at the fringes rather than trying to overhaul an entire school or district from the get-go can aid your efforts. It will help you gain experience and improve a new innovation. If it's successful, more people will likely accept it as a viable way to do schooling. They won't see it as radically different. And they'll want to join. Because people can shift their own priorities and what progress means for them as their circumstances change, you can take advantage of this to expand important programs and ideas that can apply universally.

Fit Innovation into the Progress Parents Desire

Remember to fit new innovations or initiatives into the progress that individual parents desire—not the progress that is important to you.

Recall from Chapter 5 the story about the struggles of a suburban middle school principal in Massachusetts to implement standards-based grading. The principal's motivation was to create a more equitable grading system. But a subset of parents cared only about how it would impact their children's college prospects. They thought that what he was doing would hurt those prospects. The school's initiative, in other words, appeared to violate the progress that a subset of parents who were experiencing the fourth Job around fulfilling their plan for their child were attempting to make.

Would this dynamic have been different for parents of students from lower-income families or underrepresented minorities? Probably not. The narrative among the parents who were in Job 4 was that standards-based grading wouldn't allow students to be prepared for the traditional A–F letter grades that the high school gave. They believed colleges required those grades.

It was the parents who were in Job 3 for developing the whole child who likely felt differently.

If standards-based grading was the goal, how could the principal have worked to help the parents in Job 4 see the initiative as a way to make the progress they wanted?

After listening and showing that the school leader understood their concerns—and emphasizing their points of common ground[6]—perhaps the school leader could have told stories to show why this change would be in the students' interest and improve their college prospects and preparedness. Stories and showing rather than lecturing are often more valuable than data in persuading. The school leader could have told stories about students applying to college with significant holes in their learning because of the conventional grading policy, and how top colleges were able to see through that. He could have then brought up real case studies of how students who experienced mastery-based learning were better prepared because they hadn't been able to skate by key parts of the curriculum—and how top colleges recognized and valued that. He could have followed up with stories and evidence that colleges have long known how to evaluate students who come from educational backgrounds without traditional grades—from specific schools that have moved to standards-based grading to schools and homeschools without any grades at all. Sure, parents might say, but those are the exceptions. How do we know it will work for us? The principal might then have showed how more schools are adopting the Mastery Transcript Consortium. He could have brought in admissions officers from universities like Tufts, Wellesley, and USC that are working with the Consortium. Maybe he would have worked with parents to redesign parts of his solution to still use the familiar letter-grade nomenclature but within a standards-based grading architecture, as Chapter 5 discussed. By not talking about equity—something that the parents in Job 4 weren't prioritizing—and just focusing on the progress that these parents wanted to make, it might have been possible to gain significantly more support for the idea.

Iron County School District in the southwest corner of Utah is one of the many districts that has implemented standards-based grading. Its journey toward doing so wasn't straightforward, which makes it instructive. As Cory Henwood, the innovation coordinator for the district, said, "We knew this was going to be tough to grasp for people, [so we figured] let's just put it all together in a nice package, and here you go."

The district rolled out its initiative, but immediately faced resistance. The community found the new grade book complicated and confusing. The parents didn't understand it. The reaction, as Henwood said, was "a nightmare."

But it helped the district learn an important lesson. The district's struggles weren't just a communication problem. Rather than do innovation *to* the parents and broader community, it was important to innovate *with* them.

After the rocky reaction, the district stepped back. It framed why the traditional grading system wasn't meeting the needs of students, educators, or parents. Iron County's leaders focused on the areas of agreement with parents. They showed why the traditional system created uncertainty for students, parents, and educators. Expectations of what students were supposed to learn were unclear. The current system left gaping holes in students' preparedness. Iron County then marshaled evidence from the broader research base to show the problems with the traditional grading policies.

With agreement on the problem in place, they then listened to parents' concerns around changing the gradebook—and started to ask what the right path forward was that considered those perspectives. In other words, they framed the design of the new grading policy around the progress that the parents wanted.

Rather than adopt a new gradebook, the district ultimately took its existing gradebook and made modifications to it that met the new philosophy on which people agreed. They kept the letter grades, but instead of giving "a blanket B in chemistry," they gave letter grades on the specific outcomes that students were expected to master—such as understanding the elements in the periodic table or how to balance chemical equations—so that it was clear to parents, students, and teachers what a student knew and understood and what they didn't. Teachers could also more easily intervene and appropriately support students. As Henwood said, "Frankly the choice of whether to use a letter grade symbol at the end of the day to represent that body of learning, or to use another set of symbols, it really doesn't matter as long as you have these categories listed out and clear expectations for what is expected. That's the real key piece, and I think what propels things like standards-based grading towards our eventual goal, which is more personalized competency-based systems where [students] are more self-directed [and] students advance based on mastery of those listed standards."[7]

Iron County School District Grading:
https://www.youtube.com/watch?v=9u7U1ehrRbY

IS ANYTHING UNIVERSAL?

Many change efforts—like mastery-based learning—aren't inherently built for parents experiencing one Job or another. They can be the answer to many Jobs. What matters is how you present and shape them with the community.

Mastery-based learning, for example, can be a viable answer for the student who is having academic challenges, the first Job that can cause parents to switch a child's school. It allows teachers to understand clearly the child's struggles and have the time to assemble a range of supports for them.

It is a strong answer to those parents in the third Job who are interested in "whole-child education" with a focus on things like equity and social and emotional skills. Mastery-based learning can make sure we don't leave students with holes in their academic knowledge, skills, and habits of success. It is critical to building things like perseverance and growth mindset in children. It's also critical to creating a positive-sum education system, in which all students can "win," as opposed to the traditional zero-sum system in which there are winners and losers by definition.

For those interested in seeing their children be accepted to colleges with top reputations, it's ideal for offering a more rigorous education that also allows students to go deeper into areas that spark their interest.

If parents are in the second Job seeking a values-aligned education, mastery-based learning is perhaps most neutral. But even there, depending on what values parents are interested in, there could be ways to frame mastery-based learning as helpful. For example, if parents are interested in a more communitarian experience, using mastery-based learning could help reassure families that no one will be left behind. If specific values and ideas are important, mastery-based learning could guarantee to parents that children will learn and master those specific concepts.

When implementing something that can appeal to parents in a variety of the Jobs, it is important to make sure that parents don't feel like they are losing something, as discussed in Chapter 5. There is significant research that shows that most humans are paralyzed by what's called "loss aversion"—that the fear of loss is more powerful than the potential to gain. As a result, when considering a switch, individuals overweight the things that they will lose at the expense of an even surer-fire set of things they might gain.

Unpacking two other change efforts—altering the school calendar and the school day—that can have universal appeal across the four Jobs also illustrates the dangers of not eliminating parents' sense of loss when change is afoot. They also serve to introduce a framework about what motivates and impedes change.

The School Calendar

For some parents, few things feel as sacred as the school calendar. The notion of summer break and the nostalgia for summer memories—camps and trips—are embedded in their minds. They want the same for their children. At the same time, for many parents, the summer break is painful.

One parent, who joined our *Class Disrupted* podcast to discuss the anguish of summer break, said:

> We start planning for summer the preceding November when my girlfriends start emailing me about what my kids are going to do the following summer. The sign-ups start in early December here, and some of these camps are really popular and you have to sign up right away in order to get a spot for yourself. And that's just a crazy time of year already, with Thanksgiving and the holidays. And to be thinking, on top of that, about six-plus months in the future—it's crazy. And also you're not exactly

sure what your kid will be into or what you'll want your kid to do the following summer. So you're just making your best guess, and that just seems insanely early for me to be thinking ahead.

On top of that, she noted, each week of summer is different, which makes it really hard to create a rhythm. That's something you can at least do during the school year. She said:

> And when you have a whole team helping take care of the kids—my mother-in-law helps take care of the kids; we usually have a babysitter for the summer who helps take care of the kids on the days when my husband and I both work—that means each week conveying to at least three people—including the kids, five people—what that week's going to entail. So every Sunday during the summer, I have mild panic because I need to not only figure that information out for myself and print out maps of where the drop-off site is on this complicated campus, but now I've got to convey that information to three other people. So it's challenging.[8]

Challenging and stressful.

Even more astounding is that there's a solution to these challenges. It's known as a balanced school year—or year-round schooling. It can also create a stronger learning experience for students.

Many people mistakenly believe that the current school calendar with its long summer break—known in many circles as the "agrarian calendar"—began as a way to allow children to be home to help during the farming season when agriculture played a bigger role in the economy. Why you would want students in school, however, during the harvest in the fall seems never to have crossed many people's minds.

In actuality, children in rural farming communities who were enrolled in school in the nineteenth century typically spent five or six months in school—two to three months in the summer and two to three months in the winter.[9] They were home during the spring and fall for planting and harvesting.[10]

The children enrolled in urban areas in the nineteenth century went to school year-round with short breaks. In 1842, Detroit schools were open roughly 260 days. New York's were open 245 days, and Chicago's for 240.

School wasn't mandatory then, so many students didn't show—particularly in the hottest months in urban areas, given the lack of air conditioning. On top of that, many educators at the time worried that "too much schooling impaired a child's and a teacher's health." Others in the community were concerned that summer bred "epidemics, and [was] most fruitful of diseases generally," and said students would be better off at home or in the countryside.[11] To that end, wealthy families wanted to beat the summer heat, so they pulled their children out of school and took off to the countryside or beach where the weather was cooler. As mandatory public school expanded, legislators and labor unions consequently pushed for less school time and a more regulated summer break.[12]

Decades later, we now just treat this as the way school is done.

But there are public schools around the country that have been moving to year-round school, or what's often known as a balanced calendar. According to the Congressional Research Service, in 1985 there were "410 year-round public schools, serving about 350,000 students... During the 2011–2012 school year, there were 3,700 public schools" operating year-round school serving over 2 million students.[13]

These schools still offer breaks for students. In one model, for example, students attend school for roughly 12 weeks followed by three weeks of vacation year-round. In another popular model, students enroll for roughly nine weeks and have two weeks off in between—with the exception of summer, when they get roughly a month of vacation. From Charleston, West Virginia to Holt, Michigan and beyond, many schools that offer year-round schooling report improved parent satisfaction and teacher happiness.[14] Some also say they see improved student performance, but the consensus, according to the Congressional Research Service, is that studies on the practice show "no effect or a small positive effect on student performance"—and there have been questions raised about the methodologies behind the studies.[15]

The reason for the "happier teachers" may be that the schedules provide more frequent breaks that help them rejuvenate. That helps teachers avoid complete exhaustion at the end of the school year.

For students, some argue that it can eliminate the "summer slide," the idea that children lose their academic gains over the summer months. It can also address "summer melt," in which high school graduates choose not to enroll in colleges to which they've been accepted.

Although a debate among academics exists about whether the summer slide really exists, what's clear is that for some families, the summer is a time of vast enrichment that other families—particularly those from low-income backgrounds or those that lack the social capital to know which opportunities to seek out—don't have access to. It's true that these enrichment opportunities create amazing chances for individuals to build their passions.

But what if we rethought schooling to create more spaces for those sorts of activities at a more regular cadence throughout the year? Or by making projects a key part of schooling, what if the opportunities were embedded in the actual school experience itself? As students master material, in other words, rather than moving forward in the curriculum, they could also move deeper in the areas that they want to explore through school and community resources.

What about concerns that students will lose the opportunity to work during the summer? These work experiences are valuable, after all. Through them students can gain key skills and habits of success for the workforce, awareness of the various career pathways that exist, and connections that can benefit them in the future.

There are a few problems with this narrative, however.

First, fewer teenagers than at any time in our nation's history are working. Roughly 20 percent of teenagers worked prior to the pandemic, compared to 40 percent in 1990, for example.[16] There are a variety of reasons for this, including many families believing that their children are better served by loading up on impressive-sounding extracurricular activities in the pursuit of college than by holding a real job. But the bottom line is that most adolescents aren't taking advantage of summer to work. Second, as described in Chapter 5, by flipping the school day, we could create more opportunities for teenagers to experience the benefits of work as part of their schooling experience, rather than something that competes against it.

The School Day

Flipping the school day points to another use of time in school that creates childcare challenges and could have universal appeal across the four Jobs: the hours of the school day. The idea of school hours—Monday through Friday with high schoolers starting first and elementary last—with pickup times that often don't match a parent's work hours, feels stuck.

Countless communities have struggled to flip school times.[17] Creating later bell times for adolescent high schoolers that is more in line with the overwhelming research around the academic benefits of later school starts,[18] for example, has been hard because of at least two competing interests. Schools don't want high school extracurricular activities lasting too late. Nor do they want elementary school students waiting for buses in the dark. Although many schooling communities now offer a variety of extended-day programs to provide more coverage for families with parents who work later hours, in most cases, the politics of different parental factions combined with the complications of making the school bus schedule work for different bell times has prevented change.

How can schools create more childcare coverage for parents, while also recognizing that different families need different hours and even weeks of coverage? And how to do so while improving the student and teacher experience?

There are a few different pathways. In one, creating schools within schools, staggered starts within a school, microschools, or separate schools with different scheduling hours and calendars can come in handy. Some parents, students, and teachers will prefer one schedule perhaps, whereas another will prefer a different option. Rather than plan transportation logistics by age, perhaps the transportation schedule could sort students based on the coverage that different families need.

Another compelling option is to rethink of schools as community centers, as Chapter 3 described. In these centers, students would master academics using a mastery-based learning system, but they would also be given the space, time, and opportunity to pursue other topics that grab their interest—from filmmaking to athletics to astronomy. Within and around the school community, there would also be a range of supports available to help children depending on their needs and those of their family. This would include having hours that were both far more extensive year-round as well as flexible. For example, once in a mastery-based system, so long as students are making at least a certain amount of progress each year to stay on track for graduation, the amount of time they attend school can be flexible. That also means the 180 days of required school can be flexible as well. Some students will need far more time. Other students will require less. Some will be able to learn in other settings. If each individual makes adequate progress on what the schooling community says is most important—from academics to skills to habits of success—the time should matter less. "Whatever it takes" should be the mindset.

Many microschooling communities already do this. They allow students to move in and out as makes sense for their needs and family schedules. The schools are open almost fully year-round. The only exceptions are for major holidays.

As Chapter 3 discussed, Spring Grove Public Schools moved to staggered school starts during the pandemic, in which there were flexible times when students could show up. One of the unintended benefits? Each child was able to be personally greeted and receive far more individualized attention.

In schools like these, there is space for common activities. There are fixed times when students need to be in person and present as a community. Schedule is still helpful. But the point is that the schools are designed with significantly more flexibility and availability to better serve different family and student circumstances.

People are quick to point out why this might not work for teachers who have built their lives around a traditional schedule and need certain breaks. But in a co-teaching model, teachers would have far more flexibility to create the schedule that worked for them. They would have less pressure around the chaos that ensues by being sick and missing a day or wanting some extended time for themselves. When Saint Paul Public Schools in Minnesota changed school start times, it continued to offer at least one elementary option that began at 9:30 a.m. in each attendance zone so that both parents and teachers had an option that could work for them. The point is that these obstacles can be overcome.[19]

The key is first understanding what progress looks like for different families. Then understand what experiences you have to nail to provide that sense of progress. What must be prioritized as you navigate investing scarce resources?

From Loss Aversion to What Is Gained

If parents and students stand to gain from making changes to things like the school calendar and day, why would changing these things also give parents such a profound sense of loss? The short answer is that just like moving away from the traditional grading system creates a sense of loss aversion, any move is likely to have a similar dynamic.

There's nostalgia for the summer break—the vacations, time by the pool, summer camps, and more—that holds people back from embracing a balanced school year. I have a deep fondness for my own summers—from playing tennis to holding jobs. American culture has a deeply romanticized notion of summer break that's even cemented in pop songs devoted to the joys of summer. Not only that, but there are also entire industries that have sprung up around summer vacation, from camps to classes and resorts. In New England, where I live, there are towns that basically only exist for the summertime because their economy is so dependent on the vacation and tourist activity that takes place during those months of the year. As a result, there are vested interests in keeping summer break just the way it is.

Concerns around losing something aren't unique to summer break or grading. The status quo often has a big constituency behind it ready to push back on any significant change. Just as it's important to reframe the conversation from learning loss to one around mastery and success, it's important to focus on what parents will gain from any moves made so they can overcome their entrenched habits. But it's maybe more critical to find ways to address the inevitable anxiety that people will experience around proposed changes.[20] Switches only occur when the pain or challenges of a current situation plus the allure of the new overcomes existing habits and anxieties. The framework pictured in Figure 7.1 can help you think about what it will take to help people overcome the allure of the status quo.

Figure 7.1 Forces of progress equation

WHEN	Push of the current situation + Pull of the new > Current habits + Anxiety of the new
THEN	People Switch Behavior

This equation means leaders must work both to increase the excitement behind a change and to reduce the friction that impedes it. In many cases, that may mean helping lead the community to a solution over some period of time. Don't make an instant change, in other words. Nor should you start with the solution and work backward. Leading a community to a solution is a technique that has been used by some of America's greatest leaders, from President Abraham Lincoln to President Franklin Roosevelt.

In the case of Lincoln, he had felt for some time that freeing the slaves would be important. But he knew that many in the country, whose support he needed, weren't ready for such a bold stroke. He therefore carefully prepared the ground so that people would come to his conclusion. Lincoln knew from navigating rivers by flatboat that the straightest line to a destination wasn't always a straight line, but often zigging and zagging as the currents changed so that you would get to where you wanted to go.

Similarly, prior to the United States entering World War II, Roosevelt had gradually brought the country along to support the United Kingdom through a series of moves like the "Destroyers for Bases Act" and the "Lend-Lease Act." He also prodded the country through statements like saying that if your neighbor's house was on fire, of course you would lend them a garden hose and that while the United States would remain neutral, he could "not ask that every American remain neutral in thought." He made sure not to get too far ahead of the public.[21]

Chapter 11 introduces a comprehensive framework about which tools will work in what circumstances to help leaders drive change, but for now, know that the same principle that applied to Lincoln and Roosevelt applies in public education when there isn't clear consensus on goals. Don't start with the solution. Instead, make the case for why people should be uncomfortable with the status quo. Listen to the challenges they have. Help them realize that some of their current habits—the current priorities, processes, and structures of school—are exacerbating those challenges. Only then paint the picture that there are other possibilities. Above all else, as you do this, don't preach at or prosecute people for not seeing it your way. Doing so can be a recipe for failure.[22]

Boston Public Schools offers one such cautionary tale. The story is around changing bell times.

In 2017, the district announced a plan to move high school start times later and elementary ones earlier. The reaction from some parents was swift and furious. People believed that the move would hurt low-income parents because it would make it hard for them to work and hold their jobs. Or it would force them to pay more money for daycare because they didn't have flexibility in their schedules.

Only after the uproar did the district release an analysis showing that the current start times were disproportionately hurting minority families.[23] If the district had instead started with a conversation around the evidence of how the status quo was hurting low-income and minority families to amp up the problems with the current situation, it would have created more of a *push* to change the status quo. Parents would likely have grown angrier about how the schedule was impeding their ability to work and how it was hurting student learning. Then many in the community might have started looking for solutions on their own accord. At that point, the district could have showcased the stories of the 13 percent of school districts that offer high school start times after 8:30 a.m. That would have increased the *pull* of a new solution.[24] The parents would have then likely worked with the district to codesign a solution right for Boston—evidence that these change efforts aren't just about improving communications. Sharing stories from parents in the districts that had recently made the switch could have helped tackle people's *anxieties* as the district introduced solutions. Ultimately the idea would be to focus on what's gained, and reduce the sense that people were losing much if anything.

KANO MODEL

If you're reading closely, however, something might still be nagging at you. Would everyone really benefit from increased school hours? Although many families showed how much they valued childcare during the pandemic, others did not. They preferred to have their children safe at home. More broadly, how should a school make prioritization decisions around where they invest scarce resources given parents' different circumstances and quests for progress?

The Kano Model, developed in the 1980s by Tokyo University of Science Professor Noriaki Kano, offers some guidance on how to make these prioritization decisions.

The model essentially says that there are three kinds of experiences—basic, performance, and delighters—that are important to understand to serve a given stakeholder. As Figure 7.2 shows, the x-axis measures how fully something is implemented, and the y-axis measures the corresponding satisfaction someone does or doesn't feel as an experience feature is implemented.

The first set of "needs" or experiences are what we call "Basic." Basic experiences are things that need to be there, but the school gets little credit for improving them. Think of a car, for example. If there are no seat belts, people are highly dissatisfied. But

Figure 7.2 Kano model

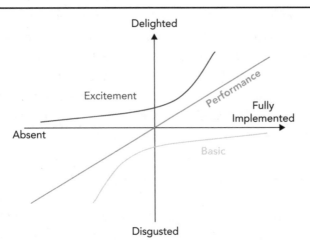

improving the seat belt doesn't make people satisfied. Similarly, in most schools, parents expect a certain level of safety and cleanliness, but the school arguably gets little credit for improving much beyond a baseline.

"Performance" experiences, however, are different. For every dollar invested in improving a performance experience, there is almost a one-to-one level of satisfaction improvement. This is where things like investing in more AP classes, for example, might be highly appealing to parents who are in Job 4 when they enroll their children in a school. Every extra AP class offered is likely to bring more satisfaction, and, conversely, the absence of any AP classes is likely to highly disappoint this group of families.

Finally, the last category of experiences are what is known as "Delighters." These are things that if they are absent, no one complains or is upset. But if they are present, they can delight someone. Things like amazing connections to a local community-based organization for after-school internships or projects that allow students to connect to leading professionals in a given field for feedback might fall under this category for certain families.

There are two important points to note about this model.

First, the model is dynamic. That means that what at one time is a Delighter experience can become a Performance feature. And those Performance features over time tend to become a Basic experience as more parents come to expect them as a fundamental feature of schooling. If that happens for parents in Job 4 with AP classes, for example, then a school won't get extra points for adding more AP classes—but they will meet with considerable resistance any time they try to cut them.

Second, these characteristics—Basic, Performance, and Delighters—are all relative to the Job to Be Done and one's circumstance. Not all families will feel the same about all experiences a school might provide. How they feel depends on how a particular experience fits into the progress they are trying to make in their lives.

AP classes matter for some but not all families, for instance.

To illustrate with another example, many schools have moved to a model where they are providing free lunches not just for students on the free and reduced lunch federal program, but also for all students, regardless of economic need. Is this a good use of funds? For families who don't need the lunches and may still be sending their children with homemade food, it probably seems like a waste of money. For those who come from lesser means, they might appreciate that school lunch is free for all because it doesn't stigmatize them and send a signal that they are different from others in the school. If these are the dynamics, what might a middle ground look like? Perhaps every student would be given an ID card or use biometrics with preloaded accounts for school lunch expenses. Families who didn't need the support could pay to put money on the cards in advance, and those who needed the support could receive funds in advance from the school so that no individual student or person working in a school cafeteria would know which students were from which families—but the school wouldn't be paying to subsidize individuals who didn't need the support.

These two points have important implications for schools relative to families' need for childcare. Earlier I said that custodial care wasn't a "Job to Be Done," but it was an important feature of school for many families. The Kano model can help individual schooling communities shed more light on this important topic and break apart the sets of issues for different families.

Here's one possible way to think about it. Until the pandemic hit, childcare was likely a Basic experience for many families. This was true of parents who enrolled their children in brick-and-mortar schools regardless of the Job to Be Done they were experiencing. A baseline of childcare was something they took for granted. That requirement became far clearer once many schools went remote and some families started searching for in-person options.

It's also possible that many families have realized that childcare coverage isn't just a basic feature. Now that parents have been forced to step back and not take school and childcare for granted, they've had the space to think about what they ideally need from a school. Many may now see childcare as a Performance feature in which more coverage that is more flexible will significantly improve satisfaction.

Still, some other families might view childcare as a Delighter. They don't need it, but they are thrilled when it's there. And other families have probably realized that childcare just isn't that important to them at all. They might even wonder why a school is "wasting money" on more childcare when it doesn't specifically help them. The school could be spending those dollars on something else, after all.

Regardless of where different families fall, it's also possible that as their circumstances shift, their view about childcare and schooling will also shift.[25]

Perhaps more importantly, this reinforces the importance of moving to a more flexible system capable of responding to the different circumstances and desires for progress that individual parents have at different times.

FLEXIBILITY AND UNBUNDLING

To create a more flexible, customized set of offerings, the interdependence and modularity theory introduced in Chapter 3 offers valuable insights. As discussed, the theory shows that schools must integrate further into services traditionally thought of as outside their realm in order to serve those students who need the most supports.

But as noted, the growth of digital learning has created other opportunities for those families where the traditional public school *overserves* them with offerings they don't need, as it allows schools to increasingly modularize parts of the school and classroom experience to customize a student's education. Because of the pandemic and the continued maturation of digital learning tools, some parents now don't just want a customized experience for their children. They increasingly want to *control* and customize that experience, just as we've seen in other sectors.

Although that may be a bridge too far for many schools, it's worth considering some of the efforts on the ground.

As Chapter 1 discussed, Edgecombe County Public Schools in North Carolina is creating a "spoke-and-hub" microschooling model. Several parents in Edgecombe have reported that they want their children to stay in these arrangements and not return to traditional in-person schooling. It's not hard to see why. Taking advantage of all the community resources in the "spokes" is a real draw. Digital learning enables this increased customization because it makes learning more personalized and changes the role of the educators. It also creates greater freedom around where and when students learn.

Prior to the pandemic in Florida, a subset of parents, particularly at the elementary school level, were beginning to manage their children's education and customize a mix of public brick-and-mortar school, online school, homeschool, and even some private education (such as private music lessons). A student might take core academics online at home, come in to the local elementary school for arts and physical education, and then enroll in a music academy for private piano lessons. Or the core classes could be at the public school and extracurricular activities could be delivered online. All of this is possible in Florida because of Florida Virtual School's (FLVS) Flex program, which allows students to attend part-time.[26]

The emergence of a wide variety of microschools points to a similar phenomenon. The families who send their children to microschools often want an option other than homeschooling that will personalize learning for their child's needs. They are often thrilled to have a stripped-down, small school that students attend a couple days a week so they can customize their children's experience around the edges in areas like music, the arts, science, engineering, and sports. To these parents, it's fine that the school has a limited offering because they will find other ways to provide their children with the other desired experiences.

Parents of homeschooled children have done this for years. Increasingly, some of them want some of the benefits of their local public school, for which they are paying with their tax dollars. As author Michael McShane documented in his book *Hybrid Homeschooling*, districts from Colorado to Michigan and Kentucky are able to take advantage of provisions that allow them to serve "hybrid homeschoolers" in a variety of part-time arrangements. Kentucky's superintendent of the year, Brian Creasman, from Fleming County Schools, for example, seized the opportunity to enroll hybrid homeschoolers in mastery-based programs and take advantage of the state regulations that waive the Carnegie Unit, a measure of seat time at odds with mastery-based learning. These regulations that enabled innovation, Creasman said, were "staring at us in the face."[27]

Many observers may worry that this trend will be expensive. Students could use a disproportionate number of state-funded services.

But according to FLVS's internal numbers from before the pandemic, that's not the case. By looking at students who were declared ineligible for its Flex program in the most recent academic year because they had not attended public school in the year prior, FLVS was able to follow where those students went. Some students returned to a homeschool or private school environment. Others attended FLVS full-time (a more affordable option from the state's perspective than a traditional public school). Some enrolled in a traditional public school. Had those students instead all enrolled in FLVS Flex, the net impact on public financing would have been positive to the tune of a roughly $400 to $500 savings per student. That's significant in a state where total per-pupil funding hovered around $8,500.

Although we see movements toward increased customization most vividly in microschools, districts can create schools that offer the benefits of a microschool but look like community centers. In these centers they could provide an array of professionals and offerings in the building to support learners who have different needs, as well as access to online-learning offerings from providers like FLVS, Outschool, Arizona State University's Prep Digital, Edmentum, Edgenuity, Pearson, Stride, and the New Hampshire Virtual Learning Academy Charter School. During the pandemic, Oakland Unified School District worked with Salesforce to keep connecting students to vital services. It became 36 percent faster at matching students from a referral to their actual service and ensured that 100 percent of teachers were connected to the student's referral-for-service for follow-up.

Digital learning can help unbundle schooling. It can help create modular offerings that leverage the greater community to create more choices. For those who don't take advantage of these choices, educators can support them to create the right structure for them to succeed and thrive.

THE STRESS OF SCHOOLING FOR PARENTS

Parents face many challenges with school as it exists currently. It doesn't provide the custodial care that they need in many cases. It doesn't fully support some students. Others feel overserved by the offerings and want something more customized. For the vast majority, their relationship with their children's teachers are often strained when those teachers aren't just teaching and supporting their child, but also grading and judging their child. And many today feel like they themselves are being measured and judged against some yardstick of how their child achieves—or doesn't.

Another parent, Mira Browne, who also served as the executive director of the nonprofit Prepared Parents, which helps support parents in raising successful children, spoke on our *Class Disrupted* podcast and further illuminated just how stressful all of this can feel. Her comments are worth quoting at length:

> There's an evening in January . . . that is so vivid in my mind. We were sitting at the kitchen table. It was probably close to midnight. We were exhausted. And we had spreadsheets in front of us. You would think we're doing financial planning, and in some ways we were, but no. We were literally carving out our summer week by week . . . and this is pre-COVID—trying to figure out: When am I traveling? When is he traveling? What camps are available? Where should we send our kid? How much does it cost? We had a spreadsheet minute by minute, basically week by week of summer, and then in that,

you're also putting, "Okay, when does this camp open registration?" and whatever it might be. It was like moving puzzle pieces around—that's essentially what you're trying to do to fill your summer. Not all camps are all day. So if you're a full-time working parent and a camp ends at 12 or 1, it's not really that helpful. And you just have to leave your job to go pick up your kid and bring them home or whatever it might be, and then figure out how to cover an afternoon. So which camps are all day? Or afterwards have extra for pay—afterschool programming, afterschool meaning after camp programming. And then how do you stay within your budget? What's too far away? There are some great camps that are 45 minutes away. As a working parent, how do you drive 45 minutes both directions to drop off one kid here, another kid here? And if you have multiple kids, you're thinking about all of their individual needs.

And so that night was so exhausting.

And at the same time, I felt this crazy pressure as a parent because we were new to Austin and some friends had sent us their spreadsheets because every parent has the summer spreadsheet—or so I've learned the last two summers. And again, it was all of these camps, from sports to nature, to robotics, to coding for young kids. And I was looking, and they had literally sliced and diced their kids' time into all of these passions and interests and camps and things. They had what was going to be enrichment versus fun.

They were sending it to me to be nice, and I still appreciated it, and yet I felt so much anxiety. I thought about my son, who had had an extremely tough school year, who doesn't do well with transitions, and going from, like, camp to camp to camp, every week learning new expectations and new rules, being with a new group and also commuting every day. I was like, "I can't. How am I going to do this?"

But then I felt this pressure. Am I leaving him behind? Which sounds so silly when you're thinking about summer; you're, like, thinking about eight weeks of the summer. But am I leaving my kid behind? If I don't give him the Legos and the exploration and the robotics and the nature and this and that.

There's so much as a parent wrapped into summer, because summer has essentially just become like this extension of this race you're on as a parent. You feel it all year round with what extracurricular your kids are in, or what you're exposing them to, what experiences they have.

It's starting younger and younger and younger, and parents are really stressed about how do I fill the time, and how do I make sure that my kids are getting the best of the best if they can afford it? And if you can't, you're trying to fill eight weeks or whatever it might be of the time with how am I going to patchwork family members and friends to watch my kids and make sure they're safe because I still have to work?

Mira's comments point to something much larger than the stress of navigating summer break: the rat race that many parents feel they must not only navigate, but also excel and win—if there is such a thing as winning.

The 1960s and 1970s saw the emergence of a segment of parents who had not been raised in the Great Depression, but rather in an environment of relative prosperity. Their definition of good parenting consequently expanded to encompass providing enriching experiences for their children. Whereas before, as Clayton Christensen had observed, children used to work for the parents to help accomplish household tasks and chores, in many households parents now work for the children. Mirroring this evolution, the term *parenting* first appeared in the Oxford English Dictionary in 1918, but it only became popular as a word starting in the 1970s, when "to parent" appears for the first time in 1970. Parenting has come to replace the phrases child rearing and child care. The word connotes a sense of the "science" of how to raise children, with a deep centeredness on the role of the parent. It thereby plays on parents' anxieties around their ability to parent well. As Britt Peterson summarized thoughts from George Mason professor Peter N. Stearns, who wrote *Anxious Parents: A History of Modern Childrearing in America* in a piece in the Boston Globe, "as the 20th century progressed, parents absorbed an increasingly broad range of responsibility for their children's well-being, happiness, and future" at the same time that parents were busier outside of the home than ever before in two-income households.[28]

The question of whether one is doing parenting "well," however, has often focused on achievements and the sense of opportunities that parents are "providing" for their children. Often there is an accompanying set of questions around what parents are missing out on providing.

Much of this has come not just from the changed circumstances of the country and family structures, but also because our schooling system has remained stuck in a zero-sum game, where for every winner there appears to be a loser. Many parents feel like they must keep up because it's all about getting ahead and being successful in an artificial rat race of accolades. But as individuals branch out into the real world, climbing a linear ladder becomes less relevant as our journeys and pathways and what's important to us twist, turn, and change. In the book *Choosing College* I coauthored, we learned that for many students, among the principal reasons they go to college is to get into their best school for its own sake or to do what others expected of them. In both cases, college was the next logical step on a journey that had been laid out for them. They rarely questioned that journey. The process was all about getting in, not about what they would do or how they would continue to develop once they were there.

If, however, we transform our schooling system into a positive-sum one—where the goal isn't for students to be the best relative to others, but for them to be their best and develop into their unique selves, whomever that might be and whatever that might entail as they build their passions and fulfill their human potential—then the equation for parents might shift as well. Perhaps the stresses of parenting—with a scarcity mindset in a world of abundance—might dissipate, too.

With that said, although people's behaviors can change rapidly, we've seen that it's hard for people's fundamental sense of progress to change quickly. Parents may hang on to their sense of what they are "supposed" to do for their children for some time. Friction can result. Rather than focusing on the habits of success they are helping to instill in their children—such that their children are capable individuals able to navigate life, contribute to society, and learn new things as they choose—parents may remain locked on *what* their children know and can do and their achievements as a signal of accomplishment for themselves as parents. As a result, they may resist changes that cut against the grain and attempt to change that dynamic. But if educators can help parents navigate that shift in the move to a positive-sum education system—minimizing the loss and emphasizing the gains that can result like sanity and calm—perhaps the definition of parenting can change in a positive way as well. This isn't to say it will be easy, but it is to say the change is worthwhile. There are ways to innovate with parents on this journey, not impose it on them.

KEY TAKEAWAYS

- When parents switch schools, they are looking to help their child overcome an obstacle or be part of a values-aligned community, develop a well-rounded child, or realize their plan for their child.

- It's difficult for any school to be a one-size-fits-all solution for all the circumstances and forms of progress parents desire. Focus on being good at one set of things, not all.

- As educators seek to make changes, it's important to design those solutions to support the progress that parents desire.

- Changing the school calendar and school hours would seem to be things that could help many parents, but it needs to be done in a way that matches the progress that parents are prioritizing.

- Reframing changes around what is gained, not what is lost, is an important step in gaining buy-in. Don't lead with the solution or impose innovation on parents. Innovate with them.

- Kano's model can help a school understand which experiences and investments to prioritize as they make changes.

- Being a parent in this day and age is stressful. Moving to a positive-sum education system can help tackle these causes of stress.

NOTES

1. Robin Lake, "Building Public Education Back Better: Could Learning Hubs and Micro-Schools Be the Foundation?," Center on Reinventing Public Education (CRPE), May 2021, https://www.crpe.org/thelens/building-public-education-back-better-could-learning-hubs-and-micro-schools-be-foundation.

2. Howard Blume, "L.A. Unified Enrollment Drops by More than 27,000 Students, Steepest Decline in Years," *Los Angeles Times*, September 28, 2021, https://www.latimes.com/california/story/2021-09-28/lausd-enrollment-drops-by-30000-students-amid-covid-19.

3. At the height of the Omicron variant, parents expressed starkly different priorities about education and health. According to an NBC News poll, 30 percent were more concerned about COVID while 65 percent were more concerned about children falling behind in their education. "220027 NBC News January Poll," NBC News, Hart Research Associates/Public Opinion Strategies, https://www.documentcloud.org/documents/21184709-220027-nbc-news-january-poll, p. 18.

4. This section summarizes much of the following article: Amada Torres, "Research Insights: Why Parents Choose Independent Schools," National Association of Independent Schools (NAIS), Winter 2019, https://www.nais.org/magazine/independent-school/winter-2019/research-insights-why-parents-choose-independent-schools/.

    Although this summary focuses on independent schools, we have conducted further research to verify that this framework applies for other schooling switches as well.

5. The families in this research spanned a range of demographics in terms of race with children who were a range of ages, from elementary school to high school. They enrolled in private schools, public district schools, and public charter schools.

6. For more on how to change people's minds, see Adam Grant, *Think Again: The Power of Knowing What You Don't Know* (New York: Viking, 2021).

7. Michael B. Horn, "Inside Iron County's Reinvention of Its Schools," *The Future of Education*, September 29, 2021, https://michaelbhorn.substack.com/p/inside-iron-countys-reinvention-of?s=w.

8. "Should School Be Year-Round?" *Class Disrupted*, Season 1, Episode 9, July 20, 2020, https://www.the74million.org/article/listen-class-disrupted-episode-9-should-school-be-year-round/.

9. Juliet Lapidos, "Do Kids Need a Summer Vacation?," *Slate*, July 11, 2007, https://slate.com/news-and-politics/2007/07/why-do-school children-get-a-three-month-summer-vacation.html#targetText= In%201842%2C%20Detroit's%20academic%20year,the%20 1870s%2C%20attendance%20was%20low.

10. Lucas Reilly, "Why Do Students Get Summers Off?," *Mental Floss*, August 21, 2019, https://www.mentalfloss.com/article/56901/ why-do-students-get-summers.

11. Frederick Hess quotes historian Kenneth Gold in this article. See Frederick Hess, "Summer Vacation Is No Longer Necessary," in *Year-Round Schools*, edited by Adriane Ruggiero (New York: Greenhaven Press, 2008), https://www.cbsd.org/cms/lib07/ PA01916442/Centricity/Domain/338/Summer%20Vacation% 20is%20no%20longer%20necessary.pdf.

12. Reilly, "Why Do Students Get Summers Off?"

13. Rebecca R. Skinner, "Year-Round Schools: In Brief," Congressional Research Service, June 9, 2014, https://sgp.fas.org/crs/misc/ R43588.pdf, p. 2.

14. Alayna Fuller, "Piedmont Elementary Teachers Say Year-Round School Benefits Students," *Charleston Gazette-Mail*, July 10, 2019, https://www.wvgazettemail.com/news/piedmont-elementary-teachers-say-year-round-school-benefits-students/article_31ea492a-9b7a-594b-a10d-9980c8ec1cee.html.

15. Skinner, "Year-Round Schools," p. 2.

16. Jeffrey J. Selingo, *There Is Life after College: What Parents and Students Should Know about Navigating School to Prepare for the Jobs of Tomorrow* (New York: HarperCollins, 2017), p. 160.

17. Danielle Dreilinger, "How to Make School Start Later: Early-Morning High School Clashes with Teenage Biology, But Change Is Hard," *Education Next* 19, no. 3 (May 21, 2019), https://www .educationnext.org/how-to-make-school-start-later-early-morning-high-school-clashes-teenage-biology-change-hard/.

18. Jennifer Heissel and Samuel Norris, "Rise and Shine: How School Start Times Affect Academic Performance," *Education Next* 19, no. 3 (May 21, 2019), https://www.educationnext.org/rise-shine-how-school-start-times-affect-academic-performance/.

19. To this end, we're also seeing a wave of innovation in school transportation. Arizona, "through the non-profit A for Arizona, awarded $20 million in grants to a group of charter school operators, school operators, school districts, cities, and other districts" to promote "innovation in student transportation." Mike McShane, "Arizona Is Modernizing School Transportation," *Forbes*, November 11, 2021, https://www.forbes.com/sites/mikemcshane/2021/11/11/arizona-is-modernizing-school-transportation/?sh=20b59f3a9c98.

See also Matthew Ladner, "The Case for Improving Equity Through the Modernization of Arizona K–12 Transportation," Arizona Charter Schools Foundation, November 4, 2021, https://azcharters.org/2021/11/04/oh-the-places-well-go/.

Phillip Burgoyne-Allen, Katrina Boone, Juliet Squire, and Jennifer O'Neal Schiess, "The Challenges and Opportunities in School Transportation Today," Bellwether Education, July 23, 2019, https://bellwethereducation.org/publication/challenges-and-opportunities-school-transportation-today.

20. To be clear, people won't lose many of the things they fear losing. For example, those New England towns and summer camps can continue to exist, as students will still have time off during the summer. And with increased breaks in the fall and spring, the changes will create new opportunities. For people who loved their summer work, that work could still occur but it could be part of everyone's experience as part of a flipped school day, a micro-school, or community school that creates time off-campus. It could also take place in the expeditions structure that Summit Public Schools offers. Or it could occur during the more frequent breaks that exist in a balanced school calendar.

21. Doris Kearns Goodwin does a great job of portraying this dynamic in her book *No Ordinary Time: Franklin and Eleanor Roosevelt: The Home Front in World War II* (New York: Simon & Schuster, 1995).

22. Grant, *Think Again*, Ch. 1.

23. Dreilinger, "How to Make School Start Later."

24. Heissel and Norris, "Rise and Shine."

25. In a *Class Disrupted* episode, Diane Tavenner also made the case that it's possible that the pandemic caused some teachers to realize

they have a different view of their responsibilities—that they seem themselves primarily as educators, not people responsible for childcare, and they realized they could now educate remotely. This may have contributed to a deeper split between how some teachers and parents view the role of school. "What Is Driving Parent Frustration With Schools?" *Class Disrupted*, Season 3, Episode 11, February 8, 2022.

26. FLVS Flex, https://www.flvs.net/flex.
27. Michael McShane, *Hybrid Homeschooling* (Lanham, MD: Rowman & Littlefield, 2021), Ch. 5.
28. Britt Peterson, "The Effects of 'Parenting' on Child-Rearing," *Boston Globe*, May 10, 2015, https://www.bostonglobe.com/ideas/2015/05/09/the-effects-parenting-child-rearing/2V1W0g4g YGcouAGki40ScL/story.html.

Chapter 8

The Technology

Thirty minutes later, Julia was rolling her eyes again. Mrs. Alvera passed out worksheets to the students at the end of each row of desks, who in turn handed the sheets to the other students to work on a science assignment about matter and energy in ecosystems.

Why all the worksheets?!? Julia wanted to scream.

She kept her mouth shut, of course, but she knew she wasn't the only one feeling frustrated.

Mrs. Alvera could sense something was up as well. This time she quietly approached Julia.

"Hey Julia, is everything okay?" she said.

"Yeah, kinda, I mean, I dunno," Julia answered softly.

"Julia," Mrs. Alvera began. And then she paused. Five seconds later Julia filled the silence.

"It's just, during the pandemic we like used a lot of edtech for these sorts of things," she said. "Why can't we do that now?"

"You liked learning on the computer, huh?"

"Yeah, I did," Julia said. "I mean, not for everything. But I liked how I could go as fast as I wanted, it told me how I was doing, like, right away. And I already know this stuff that we're doing right now anyway."

"Oh?" Mrs. Alvera's interest piqued.

"Yeah, I watched a bunch of videos on YouTube last week about ecosystems and matter and energy because I was curious. Then my dad and I did a couple experiments with some plants in our house just to check it out ourselves," Julia said. She was feeling more relaxed and confident. She could see Mrs. Alvera was genuinely interested. "Yeah, and like, all that stuff on indentured servitude before, I had learned about that from YouTube also. Plus, all this other stuff we didn't cover."

Julia paused and then chuckled. "And, yeah, I probably saw a few other things I wasn't supposed to see. But . . ." She trailed off. She hadn't meant to say that last part. But it was true.

Mrs. Alvera nodded. "I understand, Julia. I do. I sometimes wish we were still doing more with the technology as well. I'll look into what's possible starting this afternoon. But maybe, for now, you can walk around and see if any of the other students could use your help?"

Julia's eyes lit up as she bounded out of her chair. Mrs. Alvera watched her and smiled, too. Maybe some positive social energy would take Julia's mind off the lack of technology—and whatever inappropriate stuff she had watched online—for now. But there must be a better blend going forward, she thought.

* * *

In the wake of COVID-19, education technology became ubiquitous for most educators, students, and parents. Zoom, Google Classroom, educational software and digital content, and various digital tools like PearDeck, Flipgrid, EdPuzzle, Nearpod, and Outschool became household names.[1]

Yet despite the hype, technology isn't a panacea for all that ails education. Many frustrated students, parents, and educators can attest to that based on their experiences over the past few years.

A central argument in my first book, *Disrupting Class*, was that technology couldn't be a silver bullet. Instead, the model in which technology is used is far more important. In *Disrupting Class*, our conclusions supported education historian Larry Cuban's research about how technology had had a limited impact in schools to that point[2] by providing the academic theory to undergird his assertions and documentation.

A central reason why technology isn't a silver bullet is that when it's crammed into an existing model, at its best it can only serve as an additional resource to bolster that model's existing processes and priorities. That means it can make an operation more efficient or allow it to take on additional tasks, but it can't reinvent the model in and of itself. It also means that in many cases it will conflict with the organization's processes and priorities and therefore go largely unused.

If today's school system optimized everyone's ability to build their passions and fulfill their human potential, then technology could be quite useful. But that's not the case.

Today's school system wasn't built to optimize everyone's potential. It was designed to deliver instruction for the masses in the most economical way then known and to sort students along the way. It was built as a zero-sum system, not a positive-sum one. The results it does deliver are exactly what the system was built to achieve. Implementing technology within that system will only perpetuate and marginally improve it.

This isn't to say that making something more efficient or slightly better or allowing it to take on more things isn't valuable. Witness the good implementations of technology to help build individual students' ability to read or do math, for example. But the value is limited in the sense that it will not be transformational. What's more, it's an outright waste when technology directly contradicts a school's processes and priorities and there-fore goes unused.

With that said, it's clear that digital technology is increasingly a requisite for navigating today's society and knowledge-based economy. Trying to function in society without digital technol-ogy and access to the Internet is hard. That means using digital technology in education is now critical. This goes particularly for older students, but also as educators seek to reinvent the learning model to prioritize mastery for each and every student.

This chapter isn't a recitation of the vast potential of technol-ogy to aid in that reinvention of the learning model. My past books, *Disrupting Class* and *Blended*, have done that. *Blended* remains a useful guide to help design a better learning model to take advantage of technology. Nor is this chapter a comprehen-sive guide to implementing 1-to-1 computers or other such edu-cation technology initiatives. Instead, this chapter offers a few practical ideas about how to think about its adoption. What are the baseline must-haves? What should schooling communities look for, and what should they avoid as they adopt education technology?

THE BARE MINIMUM

For many families in the United States, the Internet is a utility like water or electricity. Having a dedicated device on which to work and navigate our lives seems like a requirement. Prior to the pandemic, 90 percent of American adults regularly used the Internet, and roughly three-quarters of the country had broad-band Internet access at home.[3]

But as COVID-19 showed vividly, that means many didn't have that access. Prior to the pandemic, more than 16.9 million U.S. students lacked high-speed Internet access at home. 7.3 mil-lion students did not have a dedicated device at home.[4] Roughly 2.9 million students didn't have *any* home Internet access.[5] For many, this meant that it was nearly impossible to participate in remote learning. This phenomenon disproportionately and significantly impacted low-income students.

Remote learning is not the future for most students. When writing *Disrupting Class,* we calculated that homeschool or full-time virtual schools were an unlikely option for at least 90 percent of students. Although the pandemic and the resulting innovations may change that somewhat, the reality is that most students will learn in person. That's a good thing. For most students (although not all), in-person learning works better than remote learning, for a variety of reasons.

But the lack of technology access was not a problem just because schools needed a disaster-preparedness system to enable remote learning.

The lack of access to digital technology to do meaningful schoolwork is a problem for older students in particular if a key goal of school is preparing students to lead a life filled with choice and purpose. If 90 percent of adults regularly use the Internet, how will students be ready to use technology in the world upon graduation without regular access to it?

To think about why this is important, imagine this scenario.

An 18-year-old is in a school where the students are not allowed to bring in their own devices. The total ratio of computers to students is 1-to-4. Those computers are stored on a laptop cart that is shared by classrooms such that each student has limited time on a device. Couple that with the possibility that this student does not have access to an Internet-connected device at home. They have a smartphone perhaps, but not a computer. That is relevant because the use cases and type of work done on these devices are different. Imagine what happens when that student arrives at college or shows up to work after high school. The college or employer will likely expect her to be fluent with devices on a variety of platforms. Two-thirds of the jobs created in the past decade require at least moderate computer skills.[6]

On top of that, how is this student supposed to do even limited projects in school, let alone the type of experience described in Chapter 5 in which projects become more central? Think about simple projects, like researching and writing a paper. A computer is table stakes for this sort of work today. Mobile consumption—learning knowledge via a phone through videos, mobile learning like Duolingo, or even digital textbooks—isn't enough for a project like this. The act of creating and applying knowledge in deep ways to develop skills requires more. The library has its perks, but today's world is created through regular access to online technology, regardless of whether we like it.

A recent whitepaper identifying 56 foundational skills that workers need to succeed homed in on digital skills as one of the key ones. It also found, however, that adult proficiency was lowest in this category—namely in using and developing software and understanding digital systems. That said, individuals from high-income households were much more likely to be proficient in these areas. Those who were proficient across all digital skills, for example, were 41 percent more likely to earn a top-quintile income than others.[7]

It may sound ridiculous when so many books talk about students being digital natives, but being able to swipe left and type with your thumbs is different from learning how to use technology in a professional environment. According to the Pew Research Center, in 2018, 95 percent of teenagers reported having a smartphone, but fewer had access to a desktop or laptop computer—including just 75 percent of teenagers from households earning less than $30,000 a year.[8]

Where will students who don't have access learn if schools don't intentionally foster that environment? As Diane Tavenner said, "What happens when that student starts trying to type on a keyboard with two thumbs? I know that sounds ridiculous, but I've actually seen that happen. . . . You learn tech tools when you practice them. We're definitely not encouraging typing class. . . .

But the best way for all kids to develop employable skills with computers and software is to regularly use computers and software to learn and do their work."[9]

Just how challenging this could be in the future for students who haven't worked with technology was laid bare during the pandemic. A student outside Houston, Texas, Kacy Huerta, who attended Dobie High School—located in the Pasadena School District, which issued devices to all 56,000 of its students prior to the pandemic—said about her friends in other districts who hadn't used technology much, "My friends do struggle sometimes because they don't know how to submit a document. They don't know how to . . . turn things in online or learn it themselves because they're so used to having a teacher in a classroom teach it for them. So it has been a challenge for some of my friends."[10]

Dobie High School:
https://www.youtube.com/watch?v=OQ1jzfnWEWc
https://www.youtube.com/watch?v=bdcq7ogB8I8

HOW TO ENSURE ADEQUATE TECHNOLOGY FOR ALL STUDENTS

EducationSuperHighway was founded as a nonprofit to ensure that all of America's classrooms, not just the schools, had high-speed Internet. That way all students and educators could take advantage of robust digital learning experiences. Just before the pandemic, the organization had announced its intention to shut down, as it had accomplished its goal of making sure every classroom had meaningful Internet access at an affordable price.

Once the pandemic began, however, calls emerged for EducationSuperHighway to remain operational to make sure every student had adequate access to the Internet and a device for learning *at home*—which it decided to do as EducationSuperHighway 2.0. Evan Marwell, the founder, joined our *Class Disrupted* podcast. He outlined the challenge as having three parts:

1. Knowing which students have access, which ones don't, and why they don't, because good data have not existed historically.

2. Then figuring out which Internet service providers can help and which offer the best deals.

3. Then putting the vast number of devices that schools already own into the hands of those who need them, rather than stored away in laptop carts or storage closets—or figuring out ways to procure the needed devices.

To help schools tackle the challenge, EducationSuperHighway started a new website, DigitalBridgeK–12.

To understand who has access, the site offers a questionnaire, which the Council for Chief State School Officers has adopted, to help schools collect the right data to understand:

-   What devices students have access to;
-   Whether those devices are shared with others;
-   Who provided the devices to the students;
-   Whether the students have Internet access at home;
-   If not, why not?;
-   Or if yes, what type of service they have; and
-   Whether students can complete critical learning activities at home without interruption because of poor service.[11]

As of this writing, this remains a critical set of questions. As an *EdWeek* Research Center survey revealed in April 2021, a year into the pandemic teachers estimated that there were still millions of students who didn't have access to Internet at home or a device. A CommonSense Media report found that although the access gap had shrunk, 9 to 12 million students still lacked adequate Internet access at home. EducationSuperHighway suggests 28 million households lack Internet access as of November 2021. Many of these households have school-age children, Marwell said. This is an ongoing problem that needs attention and clarity.[12]

To understand how to help, once a school system has the data, DigitalBridgeK–12 offers a connectivity toolkit. The toolkit helps find the right solution for each student—whether that's low-cost residential broadband, a super hotspot on a school bus, or a personal hotspot. It also identifies ways to remove the financial burden from the family and create alternative learning spaces or solutions for rural areas.[13]

Finally, the site offers a variety of resources to help schools figure out if they can lend existing devices or if they should buy new ones for students. It then helps schools determine what policies to put in place around lending devices—from privacy policies, expectations for use, and fees and insurance to how the devices will be managed, supported as they break, and returned at the end of the year. It also addresses the core question of how to make sure the devices are used well and appropriately and how to build the notion of digital citizenship into the curriculum.[14]

Loaning existing devices should be able to solve much of the device gap. To see why, let's assume that districts don't have to provide devices for everyone. That's a commonsensical assumption that would save districts scarce dollars given that millions of students have the means and ample access to devices, such that a computer to them is equivalent to the Trapper Keeper of the 1980s and the accompanying pencil pack. Having a Bring Your Own Device policy in place would mean that districts can use their existing resources to buy or loan devices for those who don't have the means to access a machine. According to Marwell, U.S. schools purchased 50 million devices in the three years prior to the pandemic. With roughly 50 to 55 million students enrolled in K–12 schools,[15] that means there should be enough devices for students. Attention should instead focus on how to loan them in a responsible fashion for the safety of the students and the devices, how to maintain them, and how to manage a variety of devices on the network.

It's also the case that younger students are in a different circumstance from older students. For younger children, a 1-to-1 device-to-student policy may be unnecessary. As we documented in *Blended*, many schools have set up Station Rotation models in which students rotate among centers in the classroom, where only one of them offers digital learning. This allows the school to have a 1-to-3 or 1-to-4 device-to-student ratio. The results from many of these models have been sterling in helping students build mathematics and reading skills. They also help mitigate concerns of excessive screen time.

For younger elementary school students—certainly under third grade—let the model guide how many devices are needed. Although having a disaster preparedness plan in place lest the school or individual student must unexpectedly move to a remote-learning situation once again is important, most students at this age don't need to be lugging a relative heavy device back and forth from school, as it's unlikely they will need to do much online work from home.

HOW TO USE DIGITAL LEARNING WELL

How to use the devices so that they add value and so that schools don't go overboard in their use is also important.

Although concerns around screen time run rampant in many circles, the reality is that more important than *how much* screen time a child has—particularly as students get older—is *how* that time is being used and *for what*.[16] Most agree that balance in all things is critical, which means making sure that children have enough time to exercise, to be outdoors in nature, and to have fun with family and friendships in person. But after that balance is satisfied, the question of how to use time online becomes more important. For younger children, the more social and active that time is on a screen, the better. For teenagers, there are productive and counterproductive ways to use technology, as many others have documented.[17] Teenagers are prolific at using devices for social media and gaming—but less so for educational reasons.[18]

How do we change the script and wisely use technology in school? One heartening trend is that despite the many teachers who initially struggled to adopt technology in the wake of the pandemic, many are increasingly reporting that their ability to effectively use technology has improved.[19] Whether this will usher in a greater use of technology not for its own sake but to help create more active, tailored learning experiences that engage learners remains an open question.

Three Baseline Imperatives

To start, however, any technology tool should do at least one of three things, according to Larry Berger, who is a longtime observer of the digital learning landscape and the CEO of Amplify, an education curriculum and assessment company.[20] Technology must:

1. Save teachers time;
2. Extend the reach of teachers; and
3. Deepen teachers' understanding of their students.

That list implies that education technology must help teachers with something that they are already prioritizing or doing on a regular basis. In line with the thinking from Chapter 6, it cannot layer "just one more thing" on top of a teacher's already busy workday.

When Berger speaks of extending the reach of teachers, he means that technology can't be "some field trip to somewhere else where they're not going." That means that as educators and school committees adopt technology tools, they can't fall prey to companies' pitches that their products or services will improve student learning—if only teachers would use them correctly. The tools must help teachers accomplish something they are already trying to do at least as efficiently, if not more so. If they aren't designed for that but what they *are* designed to do is a goal that is more important than other existing priorities, then the school must first revisit and redesign its schooling or classroom model to make sure that goal becomes a priority for a teacher. If it isn't really as important a goal as other priorities on educators' already full plates, then schools shouldn't adopt the tool.

Berger and his team did all three things with the first offering they created when their company was called Wireless Generation. Wireless Generation offered a mobile education assessment solution to help teachers understand their students' reading abilities, something the teachers were already trying to do. The solution allowed teachers to accomplish this with greater ease such that it improved and simplified their lives, rather than further complicated them.

If the education technology you're considering will save teachers time, extend their reach, and deepen their understanding of their students, then it's worth going one step deeper. There are three more value propositions that digital technology offers to improve student learning, which schools should use to evaluate their choices: enabling more robust feedback; creating hard-to-offer experiences in the immediate physical environment; and automating manual, laborious processes.

Feedback

Digital learning tools can enable both quicker and greater feedback to enhance student learning in the same way a tutor can. As Chapter 5 highlighted, feedback is critical for learning. In our *Class Disrupted* podcast, we explained how the traditional education system of worksheets and textbooks ignores the importance of feedback.

As Tavenner shared, think about how people improve at a sport. Imagine a basketball player who wants to get better at making free throw shots. To do so, they engage in deliberate practice. They stand at the free throw line, set their body in a particular way, position their elbows, and focus on their wrist and follow-through. After shooting the ball, they see what happens and receive immediate feedback. If the ball went in, then they will likely try to do the same thing again. And if it didn't go through the net, then they will try to adjust or sharpen their technique on their next attempt.

This is a far cry from a worksheet. If the goal is immediate feedback, the only natural way students receive that is by searching the answer key, which often feels artificial and like a way to "cheat"—to get the answer before they've put in any effort. For learning to take place, effort is always required.

This hints at a larger observation, which is the importance of active learning. Significant amounts of research show that passive learning—which is often learning through lectures—is far from the ideal. The contrast to passive learning is active learning, in which, according to the book *Building the Intentional University*, in its ideal students are engaging in activities, answering questions, or partaking in discussions as they learn 75 percent of the time while they are in class, and the experience engages their skills of comprehension, reasoning, memory, and pattern perception.[21]

The results of this type of learning versus passive learning are clear. In a meta-analysis of 225 studies of how well students learn from lectures versus active-learning seminars, the authors found that active learning would raise average grades by half a letter and that failure rates under lecturing increase by 55 percent over the rates observed under active learning.[22]

Much of the teaching that occurred during the pandemic through online video was passive. Learners sat back and watched without truly engaging in the material. They also received little feedback when they worked through problems. These sessions replicated many of the passive learning environments that don't work well for students but placed them in an environment where students were effectively isolated and estranged from their fellow classmates and teachers. Of course it wasn't going to work well.

Yet there are all kinds of digital tools that don't replicate the worst of worksheets, but instead create active learning cycles and opportunities for feedback. To go back to the free-throw basketball analogy, these sorts of tools act as the hoop and the video of a student's performance so they can reflect—and allow the student to continue to adjust and engage in deliberate practice.

To take the basketball analogy further, the learning doesn't just occur as a product of the deliberate practice—the effort and natural feedback—but also thanks to coaching. When a player is practicing basketball, there are ideally times where they will work with a coach. That coach will watch them—sometimes live and synchronously and other times by reviewing video—to offer guidance and feedback based on their expertise. The player can also receive feedback from their teammates or peers or parents. The player can take all this feedback to reflect and figure out the right path for them and keep practicing. Not because they have 25 more free throws left on the proverbial worksheet, but because it's what they need to reach their goals. Their pathway will likely be different from others' on their team, which points to the power of technology to help personalize learning and create opportunities for more self-direction.

There are of course reasons to be cautious about personalization. Teachers can give students choices that lack the proper scaffolding and structure that students need to succeed. Or educators might customize in ways that are unhelpful to unlocking student learning by tailoring to "learning styles" or outdated notions of how students learn.

But when a good digital tool enables the sort of feedback outlined in the free-throw example, big gains are possible. This feedback doesn't need to be from some magical adaptive engine. Indeed, the feedback ideally won't be just from the tool itself. The tool should instead help bring the teacher, peers, and other experts and trusted sources into the learning process to support the learner in obtaining her goals. This is one of the benefits of a tool like MasteryTrack that enables mastery-based learning. It should allow teachers to better work with individual students or in small groups and create a more active and engaging experience where students are part of the process of setting a goal, interacting with the material, applying their knowledge, receiving feedback, reflecting—and then repeating that process.

The rapid feedback will allow for more personalization that will keep students engaged—as opposed to bored because the class is moving too slowly or quickly for them.

As Huerta, the twelfth grader from outside Houston, said:

> I always worked faster than other students. So being in a regular classroom, I'd have to wait for everyone to get done with a subject or whatever and then it would just take forever. [With self-pacing,] I was able to work ahead and work at my own pace so I didn't have to wait for everyone else. . . I saw a lot of kids that are really slow too, and there's not a problem with that. People just learn [at] different paces, but with kids learning a little bit slower, they're able to take more time. To learn that subject and master it well, and they would just be able to continue going through what they need to so they can understand it better, rather than in a traditional classroom, you just learn it, take a test, fail, oh, well. You just keep moving on.

She further explained that the feedback the technology provided also allowed the students to support each other. "Since some of us did fall behind," she said, "other students would help out. The teacher is always there no matter what [as well]."[23]

Experiences Hard to Offer in the Immediate Physical Environment

Technology can create experiences that are hard or impossible to do in a traditional environment. For example, "If a science teacher said, 'I have an idea. Let's dump 100 million tons of methane into the atmosphere and see if it warms up,'" Berger said, "that would be frowned upon by the principal. But in a simulation, you can do that, and you can see what happens."

Similarly, technology allows students to experience things that they wouldn't otherwise be able to by bringing content alive with dynamic images and bringing in real people and knowledge from other parts of the world.

Virtual reality and simulations are hot topics in this vein, but simple video-based stories can also give life to topics and help students build background knowledge with which they might otherwise struggle. There is considerable evidence about the power of good stories to teach—as opposed to a simple recitation or showing of facts and images. As Bror Saxberg, vice president of learning science at the Chan Zuckerberg Initiative, said, "Five thousand years ago, story lines and learning were totally tied together. They were inseparable. Myths are all about learning. They are full of rich, evocative material that happens to carry with it a lot of information at the same time."[24]

Given the emerging evidence around the benefits of field trips,[25] one of the big areas of excitement is the potential to provide students with virtual field trips to places they would never otherwise be able to visit. There are other potentially worthwhile applications as well. Wayee Chu, a partner at Reach Capital, a venture-capital firm focused on education technology, cited several, including empathy and diversity training, supporting students with psychological and cognitive disorders, and vocational training in "real" workplaces. For empathy and diversity training, teachers could be prepared to better understand the situations from which their students come, and students could experience life as a member of another culture, race, or gender, for example. Students with certain phobias could work on overcoming them through encounters in virtual reality. And with a growing emphasis on workforce training, students could be "placed" in real situations where they experience what the workplace might be like, from emergency-room settings to rescue situations for firefighters.

Berger and Amplify offer students an "engineering internship" in different units, for example. In it, the students are part of a fictional team at a fictional science and engineering company. According to Berger,

> In the unit where we're learning about changing climate, we've been tasked with designing rooftops for a city, and we are trying to use the science we've learned, but in an applied way, working with our team, designing rooftops, and we've set it up so most of the time, the really good idea that your team has fails for an interesting scientific reason and you've got to go back to the drawing board, like real engineers. It's also the case that in every unit there is the hands-on experimentation that good science programs have been doing for awhile, and then there's the moment where that transitions to a digital simulation that lets you do things that you can't do in a normal science classroom. A great example would be natural selection, one of the really hard concepts to get. And the misconception that the population changes, like each animal wants to learn to swim

because otherwise it can't survive, is one of the hardest ones to unroot. But . . . we put you on a little island that has trees and carnivores and herbivores. And then we let you adjust the temperature of that island. And if you move it down towards freezing, you start to watch how over a thousand generations, the herbivores with fur survive and the ones that don't have it, don't. But you also see that if there is no mutation that generates for it, they just die. And so kids have that ability to essentially accelerate time to run thousands or millions of years of evolution in 10 seconds in their classroom to watch what happens to the population.

That ability to move from reading and writing about a topic to making it hands-on through technology has significant potential to increase students' active engagement and understanding of topics that have traditionally been challenging. The opportunity to simulate experiments and lab environments that would never otherwise be possible in a K–12 school through tools like Labster holds promise. And the ability to provide access to courses and expert teachers that students in certain locales would never otherwise have access to continues to be a virtue that online learning holds.

Automation of Manual, Laborious Processes

Finally, when technology is used well, it can enable greater productivity—not only in making learning more efficient and engaging for students, but also because it can automate certain manual and laborious processes that take up a lot of a teacher's time but don't add a lot of learning value in and of themselves. When processes are rules based, technology should be able to step in and do them better and more reliably. That's a good thing because it leaves more room for where technology can't help, which is in all the areas where helping a child isn't rules based and an educator's expertise, judgment, and intuition are valuable and necessary.[26]

* * *

The big takeaway is that just because something is digital doesn't inherently make it good or bad. But digital learning has arrived, and it's only going to grow. The choices educators and schooling communities make around what they adopt is critical. They should seek to not only arm students with the tools, but also create a more active, engaging, and feedback-rich set of experiences that otherwise would not be possible.

KEY TAKEAWAYS

- There's a new baseline for older K–12 students in particular. Given the nature of the world and how work is done today, they need a digital device that is more than a smartphone, and they need high-speed Internet access.

- EducationSuperHighway offers a tool to help schools and districts make sure every student has what they need.

- Digital technology isn't a silver bullet for education. It isn't inherently good or bad. How it's used is what matters. If it's used in today's dominant factory-model system, it will not produce the desired outcomes.

- At a minimum, education technology must save teachers time, extend the reach of teachers, and deepen teachers' understanding of their students.

- From there, digital technology should do at least one of three things: enable quicker and greater feedback; create hard-to-offer experiences in the immediate physical environment; and automate manual, laborious processes.

NOTES

1. Thomas Arnett, "Breaking the Mold: How a Global Pandemic Unlocks Innovation in K–12 Instruction," Christensen Institute, January 2021, https://www.christenseninstitute.org/wp-content/uploads/2021/01/BL-Survey-1.07.21.pdf.

2. Larry Cuban, *Oversold and Underused: Computers in the Classroom* (Cambridge, MA: Harvard University Press, 2001).

3. "Internet/Broadband Fact Sheet," Pew Research Center, https://www.pewresearch.org/internet/fact-sheet/internet-broadband/ (accessed February 5, 2022).

4. Christine Pitts, Travis Pillow, Bree Dusseault, and Robin Lake, "Virtual Learning, Now and Beyond," The Center on Reinventing Public Education, January 2022, https://www.covidcollaborative.us/assets/uploads/img/final2-Virtual-learning-post-COVID-report.pdf, p. 9.

5. "A Digital Divide Haunts Schools Adapting to Virus Hurdles," The Associated Press, January 18, 2022, https://www.edweek.org/technology/a-digital-divide-haunts-schools-adapting-to-virus-hurdles/2022/01.

6. Ryan Craig, "America's Skills Gap: Why It's Real, and Why It Matters," PPI, March 2019, https://www.progressivepolicy.org/wp-content/uploads/2019/03/SkillsGapFinal.pdf.

7. Marco Dondi, Julia Klier, Frederic Panier, and Jorg Schubert, "Defining the Skills Citizens Will Need in the Future World of Work," McKinsey & Company, June 25, 2021, https://www.mckinsey.com/industries/public-and-social-sector/our-insights/defining-the-skills-citizens-will-need-in-the-future-world-of-work.

8. Monica Anderson and JingJing Jiang, "Teens, Social Media and Technology 2018," Pew Research Center, May 31, 2018, https://www.pewresearch.org/internet/2018/05/31/teens-social-media-technology-2018/.

9. "Why Doesn't Every Student Have a Device and the Internet? How One Texas School District Is Leading the Way for Virtual Learning," *Class Disrupted*, Season 1, Episode 1, May 18, 2020, https://www

.the74million.org/article/listen-class-disrupted-podcast-why-doesnt-every-student-have-a-device-and-the-internet-how-one-texas-district-is-leading-the-way-for-virtual-learning/.

10. "Why Doesn't Every Student Have a Device and the Internet?" *Class Disrupted.*

11. "For School Districts: Question Bank," EducationSuperHighway, https://docs.google.com/document/d/1h_6vHmqTECDJqlA32JYa BdRJnWvg68J6NXqgXrhPysk/edit (accessed March 4, 2022).

12. Mark Lieberman, "Most Students Now Have Home Internet Access. But What About the Ones Who Don't?," *Education Week*, April 20, 2021, https://www.edweek.org/technology/most-students-now-have-home-internet-access-but-what-about-the-ones-who-dont/2021/04.

13. "Explore Home Connectivity Solutions," DigitalBridgeK–12, https://digitalbridgek12.org/toolkit/ (accessed February 5, 2022).

14. "How to Set Up a Successful Device Lending Program," DigitalBridgeK–12, https://digitalbridgek12.org/toolkit/research-options/device-lending-program/ (accessed February 5, 2022).

15. "Back-to-School Statistics," National Center for Education Statistics, https://nces.ed.gov/fastfacts/display.asp?id=372#PK12-enrollment (accessed February 5, 2022).

16. For some of the great books about the use of digital technology at home and screen time, check out:

    Anya Kamenetz, *The Art of Screen Time: How Your Family Can Balance Digital Media and Real Life* (New York: Public Affairs, 2018).

    Richard Culatta, *Digital for Good: Raising Kids to Thrive in an Online World* (Boston, MA: Harvard Business School Publishing, 2021).

    Jon M. Garon, *Parenting for the Digital Generation: A Guide to Digital Education and the Online Environment* (New York: Rowan & Littlefield, 2022).

17. See, for example, several of Sherry Turkle's books, including *Life on the Screen* (New York: Simon & Schuster, 1995), *Reclaiming Conversation* (New York: Penguin Books, 2015), and *Alone Together* (New York: Basic Books, 2017).

18. Anderson and Jiang, "Teens, Social Media and Technology 2018."

19. Kevin Bushweller, "How COVID-19 Is Shaping Tech Use. What That Means When Schools Reopen," *Education Week*, June 2, 2020, https://www.edweek.org/technology/how-covid-19-is-shaping-tech-use-what-that-means-when-schools-reopen/2020/06.

20. "Why Is My Child Doing So Many Worksheets Right Now?," *Class Disrupted*, Season 1, Episode 2, May 25, 2020, https://www.the74million.org/article/listen-class-disrupted-podcast-why-is-my-child-doing-so-many-worksheets-right-now/.

21. Stephen M. Kosslyn and Ben Nelson, eds., *Building the Intentional University: Minerva and the Future of Higher Education* (Cambridge, MA: MIT Press, 2017), p. 11.

22. Scott Freeman, Sarah L. Eddy, Miles McDonough, and Mary Pat Wenderoth, "Active Learning Increases Student Performance in Science, Engineering, and Mathematics," *Psychological and Cognitive Sciences*, May 12, 2014.

23. "Why Doesn't Every Student Have a Device and the Internet?," *Class Disrupted*.

24. Michael B. Horn, "Online Learning Goes Hollywood," *Education Next* 19, no. 2 (2019), https://www.educationnext.org/online-learning-goes-hollywood-using-video-storytelling-motivate-learning/.

25. Jay P. Greene, Brian Kisida, and Daniel H. Bowen, "The Educational Value of Field Trips," *Education Next* 14, no. 1 (Winter 2014), https://www.educationnext.org/the-educational-value-of-field-trips/.

26. Thomas Arnett, "Teaching in the Machine Age: How Innovation Can Make Bad Teachers Good and Good Teachers Better," Christensen Institute, December 7, 2016, https://www.christenseninstitute.org/publications/teaching-machine-age/.

Chapter 9

Culture

After her exchange with Jeremy's mom, Dr. Ball turned to her next task: planning for tonight's PTA meeting.

The PTA Boosters Club was conducting its annual drive to raise money for the school. They wanted Ball to speak at tonight's meeting to tell them about some of the school's priorities so they could pick a few projects to fund.

As she outlined her remarks, she couldn't help but wonder if the laundry list of things the school could use reflected any priorities at all.

And then she wondered if the drive was maybe excluding families like Jeremy's. She hadn't thought of that before.

The fundraising drive was in its 31st year. The focus was on participation. "Any gift of any size counts," Ball murmured. "It's the thought that counts."

The winning class—the one that had the highest percentage of parents give money—got a prize. This year that prize was free pizza during family star-gazing night—another longstanding tradition at the school.

But could Jeremy's mom really spare even a dollar to give to the funding drive? Ball didn't think so. Nor did she think making Jeremy or his mom feel badly about that was okay.

It wasn't that Ball didn't appreciate what the school's PTA Booster Club was trying to do. She did. But this wasn't some participation drive for alums at the small, selective liberal arts college from which Ball had graduated; most of the alums there now held better-paying jobs than Ball did.

And come to think of it—was the family star-gazing night unintentionally excluding kids like Jeremy, too? His mom, after all, worked the night shift.

Canceling the night, though, didn't feel like the right answer either. But what was? And what signal was the school sending with these longstanding traditions?

* * *

Culture matters.

Before nodding in agreement, it's worth considering: What exactly is culture? And how do we build a strong one that prioritizes the value and success of each child?

WHAT IS CULTURE?

It's tempting to talk about culture by using adjectives like "casual" or "formal" and to note the "vibe" of a place or talk about a school's chants and "attitude." But there's a more precise definition that can aid educators in creating an environment conducive to each child's success.

Edgar Schein is a professor emeritus at MIT and expert in organizational behavior. In his book *Organizational Culture and*

Leadership, he defines culture as "a pattern of shared basic assumptions that was learned by a group as it solved its problems . . . that has worked well enough to be considered valid and, therefore, to be taught to new members as the correct way to perceive, think, and feel in relation to those problems." He further wrote that culture is "a way of working together toward common goals that have been followed so frequently and so successfully that people don't even think about trying to do things another way. If a culture has formed, people will autonomously do what they need to do to be successful."[1]

In other words, as a group works together to make progress, if it is successful then it tends to use that same solution—or process—the next time it confronts a similar problem. If what it tries is unsuccessful, however, then the group will likely search for a new solution.

Over time, an organization's *priorities* around *what* matters and *processes* for *how* to operate become so internalized that they become a matter of habit—or culture.

People automatically follow these routines, traditions, and steps. Sometimes these processes are explicitly codified, but more often than not, much of culture is implicit. It's just the "way things work here" as a group tackles repeated tasks and solves similar problems.

In schools, that means that culture forms as educators do everything from creating student schedules to celebrating student success and from disciplining students to delivering lessons. That each teacher and classroom might have different processes because they aren't co-teaching can be a sign that there are many different cultures in a school and that the culture across the school isn't strong and unified.

HOW TO CREATE A STRONG CULTURE

As Diane Tavenner shared with me on *Class Disrupted*, "One of my board members has always said so thoughtfully—a culture will develop and exist, the only question is if it's the one you want."[2] In other words, all organizations develop de facto cultures, but how do you intentionally shape a culture that fits with what your school is trying to accomplish?

Culture fortunately doesn't have to emerge from happenstance or luck. But it does take effort.

It starts with doing much of what we talked about in Chapter 2 of this book: being clear about the end and values of an organization: its purpose, goals, priorities, and how you would measure if it has been successful. What are you really trying to accomplish? As we have highlighted, this is often hard work once you dig below the surface, grapple with trade-offs, and move beyond the easy-to-agree-upon platitudes. When an organization doesn't have clarity around its goals and priorities, it can be tricky to define that culture. Chapter 11 speaks more to this dynamic and what you as a leader can do about it. But know that, consistent with the message from Chapter 1, one critical tool can be to create a separate team that has unity around its priorities so that it can intentionally build a strong and consistent culture internally. Educating and framing challenges with a common language and theory of action comprise another valuable tool. Bringing in outside groups to convene individuals with divergent views to build trust and identify and build areas of common ground can also help.[3]

The second piece of intentionally building culture is making sure that processes in an organization are consistent with the organization's goals and priorities. Are they truly accomplishing what you want them to in a way that is consistent with the organization's values? If you have a group that has agreement on values and goals and a shared sense of what actions will lead to what results, then leaders can deliberately build the strong culture they need by following six steps:

1. Define a problem or task that recurs again and again.

2. Appoint a group to solve the problem.

3. If the group fails, ask it to try again with a different process.

4. If it succeeds, ask the same group to repeat the process every time the problem recurs. Culture forms through repetition.

5. Write down and talk about the culture.

6. Live in a way that is consistent with the culture. Communication is important, but actions speak louder. In the same way that we can talk about the importance of growth mindset and perseverance to children but it doesn't stick when we systematically don't reward them for those habits, the same is true for all individuals with regard to the processes and priorities that we say are important but don't always model as such. You can discern the health of an organization's culture by asking, "When faced with a choice on how to do something, do members of the organization make the decision that the culture 'wanted' them to make? And was the feedback they received consistent with that?"

Reading this list may sound simple on the surface, but it's not. If you are comprehensive about following these steps for every single problem or task a school might tackle and are intentional about leaving nothing to chance, you will quickly realize how deep this six-step process can cut. The process is as complex as you want to make it. Even though I've described processes as following priorities, you will quickly realize that that's not always how things work. Your stated priorities might be different from your actual priorities when you start realizing the outcomes of the processes themselves—and which problems, tasks, and processes you choose to undertake. You may find that people disagree on what processes will lead to what results. If this is the case, Chapter 11 will offer you tools to navigate the challenges. Either way, as you think about how exhaustive you want to be in following this six-step process and how many details you want to sweat, remember that every organization will have a culture. The question is whether it's the one you want.

THE POWER OF GREAT CULTURE

District leaders often complain to me that they cannot replicate charter school models that have coherent cultures across all their classrooms because in a district school, each teacher has significant autonomy to create their own classroom environment. Regulations and work rules, leaders say, inhibit their ability to create a school with one strong culture as opposed to, say, 20 distinct ones in each classroom.

A visit I made several years ago to the Enlarged City School District of Middletown, New York, blew that notion to shreds. The Middletown district is a small-city district with seven schools serving roughly 7,000 students—37 percent of whom are White, 19 percent Black, and 38 percent LatinX.[4] A longtime partner of Education Elements, an education consultancy of which I was formerly a board member, the district had implemented blended learning across its schools in a thoughtful and deliberate way. But what stood out wasn't the technology in the buildings. It was the consistent culture in every single classroom I visited.

As I walked into multiple classrooms in Maple Hill Elementary School in Middletown and strolled the halls, the practices and models were the same everywhere. The culture was strong, tight, and consistent. Routines were crisp. Students understood expectations and, at all ages, could articulate not just what they were working on, but often why. I could never tell whether I was in a classroom with struggling or accelerated students. Every student had a plan personalized to their needs with teachers who were working hard in small-group settings.

Then-principal Amy Creeden (she's now the Assistant Superintendent for Instruction) spent large parts of her day in the classrooms supporting her teachers. Support was a key facet of the culture in Middletown—for all stakeholders, from students to teachers and staff. That the district sweated each of these details ahead of time was clear.

Enlarged City School District of Middletown:
https://www.youtube.com/watch?v=-Cfm2gKpGB4

THE RISKS OF GETTING CULTURE WRONG

Culture is too important to leave to chance. In profiling Anacostia High School, a 697-student Title I school in Washington, DC, that has long been one of the district's most underperforming schools, a report by the American Enterprise Institute a few years ago highlighted the school's efforts to move to a blended-learning environment. The authors wrote about how the students used netbooks with an online portal that gave them access to both an array of multimedia tools for learning and on-demand assessments that provided immediate feedback. The report talked about how students could log in with unique passwords so that teachers could track each student's individual progress.[5]

And yet, the authors wrote, as they were observing a class, they saw that students logged in not with their unique ID but with a generic one. Some students struggled even with that, and it took them up to five minutes to enter the password. Rather than use the online assessment capabilities, the teacher used paper worksheets. And when one student struggled to understand a word, rather than use the computer's dictionary or Google, she walked over to a bookshelf and took her time flipping through a dictionary for help.

This represents a classic example of a program where leaders have left culture to chance, rather than aggressively shaping it. Middletown, on the other hand, helps illustrate the power of creating a crisp culture that pervades the school.

REINVENTING CULTURE

As schools seek to reinvent themselves, caring about culture is critical. The following are three observations about what that means right now.

First, in the current zero-sum education system, it's impossible to create a culture where every single child is valued. The current time-based system that focuses on sorting students compels teachers to not only judge students, but also judge them relative to others, rather than focusing solely on how to support each child so that all can be successful. Until schools move to a positive-sum system where schools center around a mastery-guarantee rather than time, it won't be possible to create a true culture that prioritizes every child. That is a sobering thought. Some educators in schools that sweat the small stuff for every child will undoubtedly protest its validity, but writ large across the system, it's true.

Second, as schools try to build—and rebuild—relationships with every child and family in the wake of the pandemic, establishing trust will be critical. Far too many families and children don't trust institutions and experts right now. As Annette Anderson, a professor in the School of Education at Johns Hopkins University, said to me, "There [were] so many conflicting reports that I think a lot of people began to start saying, 'Okay, I'm not getting help from my school, I'm not getting help from the media, I'm not getting help from our government officials, I need to figure this out for my family,' and so it became a personal thing. Every single parent had to have conversations about their personal risk assessment." On top of the pandemic causing a lack of trust, families of color in particular, Anderson said, lack even more trust because of the racial pandemic. Layer on top of that a history of being poorly served by schools and what many of them saw firsthand in schools' response after the pandemic— either in virtual classrooms or in the lack of a response—and there are whole swathes of families that have a significant lack of faith right now in schools.

What will it take to build trust? Time, Anderson said. But not just that. To build trust, schools must create personal connections with each and every child and family as a matter of routine. This can't just be a one-hour meeting, but instead must be a rhythm of deep connections that occur over time. Students and families should feel and see through the actions of the school on a day-to-day basis that they belong in the community—and that the school and the educators with whom they work have a vested stake in their success, which must transcend their academic scores to also include their health, wellbeing, and habits of success.

That means that schooling communities must do many of the things that we have discussed in this book—clearly identifying the priorities, values, beliefs, and ultimate outcomes they want for students; focusing on using the evidence around human development and learning to inform how they support children; paying attention not just to academic knowledge, skills, and habits of success, but also to the health, wellbeing, and social connections of students; fixating on mastery, not learning loss; and more. In other words, this isn't the work of a simple slogan or a few meetings, but it must permeate all of a school's actions, from how schools greet someone who comes into the building to how they listen to them to the first time they ask a question or register a complaint.

Third, implicit in all this is a revisiting of a school's existing relics of its culture, namely its traditions, rituals, and historical practices. It's important to remember that traditions that exist in a community were not created from on-high. They are an outgrowth of tackling certain problems and circumstances that made sense for a certain era when they were put in place. They are reflections of a culture and a process that someone decided was important.

Many, if not most, schools are now in a different circumstance. They have different students from when these traditions were established. There are different concerns.

In some cases, schools and educators will realize that the spirit of what a tradition is designed to accomplish—say, unifying the school community—is still important, but that the tradition itself needs updating because it no longer accomplishes that objective. For example, a certain tradition may alienate unnecessarily members of the community—look at pep rallies or fundraisers or even the traditional school calendar with its long summer break that we discussed in Chapter 7. When this is the case, follow the six-step process outlined earlier, as it can help you to not just shape a culture, but also change one. The challenge becomes how do you replace a tradition with something more inclusive, but also through a process so that those who are happy with the present tradition don't get upset when it changes because they feel they are losing something? How do you make sure, in other words, that they view any change as a gain?

Chapter 11 addresses managing change in more depth, but for right now, here's the takeaway: don't just stick with a practice for tradition's sake. Think about why that tradition exists—what its purpose is—and see if the tradition or its purpose need a rethink.

KEY TAKEAWAYS

- Culture is critical and is comprised of the shared priorities and processes of a group.

- To create a strong culture, you need to have agreement on the values or priorities of a group.

- With that in place, then there is a six-step process that you can follow repeatedly to build the proper processes in service of those stated priorities.

- Today's zero-sum education system makes it impossible to create a culture where every single child is valued.

- To build and rebuild trust with every student and family, time and intentionality in all priorities and processes is important.

- Don't take traditions for granted; revisit them if they are no longer serving the purpose for which they were originally created—or if the purpose itself is outdated.

NOTES

1. Edgar Schein, *Organizational Culture and Leadership* (San Francisco, CA: Jossey-Bass, 1988), as summarized Clayton M. Christensen and Kirstin Shu, "What Is an Organization's Culture?" Harvard Business School Background Note 399-104, February 1999 (revised August 2, 2006).
2. "What Schools Must Do Before the Fall," *Class Disrupted*, Season 2, Episode 14, March 15, 2021, https://classdisrupted.wordpress.com/2021/03/15/season-2-episode-14-what-schools-must-do-before-the-fall/.
3. Convergence used this process to take a group of unlikely bedfellows and develop the inspiring vision for a learner-centered education called Education Reimagined. See "About Convergence," Convergence, https://convergencepolicy.org/about-convergence/ and Education Reimagined, https://education-reimagined.org/.
4. Middletown Schools Validated Study, https://www.middletown-cityschools.org/Page/251, accessed October 7, 2021.

   Middletown City School District, National Center for Education Statistics, Education Demographic and Geographic Estimates, https://nces.ed.gov/Programs/Edge/ACSDashboard/3619320, accessed October 7, 2021.
5. Daniel K. Lautzenheiser and Taryn Hochleitner, "Blended Learning in DC Public Schools: How One District Is Reinventing Its Classrooms," American Enterprise Institute, January 30, 2014, https://www.aei.org/research-products/report/blended-learning-in-dc-public-schools-how-one-district-is-reinventing-its-classrooms/.

Chapter 10

Test Your Assumptions and Learn

Dr. Ball's musings about culture were interrupted by her calendar beeping. Ten minutes till dismissal. After that she had a meeting with all the fifth-grade teachers.

She stood up, smiled, and marched out to check in with her staff and then say goodbye to all the students.

After the buses departed, she went back to the main office. The fifth-grade teachers assembled soon thereafter.

There was the usual chit-chat. Then, before Ball had a chance to set up the meeting, Mrs. Alvera dove in.

"I think we need to do something bigger to turn things around for these students," she said.

Ball raised an eyebrow. She could sense Mrs. Alvera's frustrations.

Another of the teachers, Mrs. Vincent, asked, "What did you have in mind?"

"I dunno," Mrs. Alvera said. "I just know that something isn't working right. Julia was complaining to me about better ways to learn—and I agreed with her on almost every item. Jeremy looks totally lost in class, and it isn't just him. And I've been missing how during remote schooling—you know, just a few years ago—we were all co-teaching. That was hard playing off each other, but it also became kinda magical. I miss that."

Mrs. Vincent jumped right in. "I'm having the same experience in my class, but you know we can't just do something big and change everything. I'm at my wit's end as it is."

Ball nodded sympathetically.

"And you remember the last time we tried something big?" Mrs. Vincent said. "That ended real well, right?" The sarcasm dripped from her voice.

Mrs. Alvera did remember. In 2012, before Ball was around, the school had decided to flip all the classrooms—at once.

It was a disaster. They bought computers for every student, sent them home with them, and then watched in horror as every nightmare scenario took place, from stolen computers to students not having Internet access at home to teachers abandoning the experiment within weeks.

The community was upset afterward. The effort wasted a lot of the money from the prior year's fundraising participation drive. A year later the principal was out.

"Yeah, we can't do that again," Mrs. Alvera agreed. It felt like the air was seeping out of the room.

Ball piped in. "But there's gotta be another option, right?"

The teachers stared at her. Did she want to lose her job, too?

"I mean, in retrospect, a lot of the things that went wrong were predictable, right? Like, they rested on some big assumptions that we could have tested first."

"Like what?" Mrs. Alvera said.

"Well, for starters, like every student having good Internet at home. That's an easy one. The school could have figured that out beforehand."

Another thought dawned on Ball. "I actually read something about this once. Something called discovery-driven planning. After you come up with a plan that's pretty different from anything you've done before—like, it's kinda radical—rather than just putting it into action if you think it'll work, you test the key assumptions first. What if we did something like that for just the fifth grade? Could we try that maybe? I'm not committing to do anything, but . . ." Her voice trailed off.

All the fifth-grade teachers nodded.

"I'll get us started," Mrs. Alvera said.

* * *

We've discussed the purpose of schooling and the scope of schools. I've offered ideas on how to reinvent the student, teacher, and parent experience, as well as the use of technology and the culture in a schooling community. I've talked about the importance of creating a separate group from the schooling community so that, armed with the proper resources, educators can frame the challenges they are facing as an opportunity.

And now, hopefully, you're inspired to create a new group and make some changes. But, like Mrs. Vincent, perhaps there's something in you that says this is risky. Maybe too risky.

WILL YOUR PLANS TO REINVENT SCHOOLING "WORK"?

If your ideas are bold and brand-new enough to your schooling community that they require a new group, then there's no question that the plan won't be entirely correct. Even as you are hopeful about your ideas, there are risks. We can say with certainty that your ratio of knowledge to assumptions (or hypotheses) about how your plan will work is low right now.

But which parts are incorrect? Will the plan help achieve the results for all children to prepare them for their futures? Where will the community be supportive? Where might people push back in ways that could shuttle the whole concept? And how do you get the space to try things out, learn, and adjust your plan accordingly? Another reason to create a separate group, after all, is to avoid the reduced experimentation that stems from top-down control. You want and need a spirit of flexibility and innovation to try new ideas.

Educators may be asking another question. Given that we haven't done this before and we are certain about so little of what we're dreaming up, isn't it risky to innovate when children are involved and the odds are uncertain?

The answer can be yes. But not innovating in our schools also carries huge known risks for the Jeremys and Julias and the future of our society.

A LESS RISKY PATH THAT EMBRACES INNOVATION

Educators fortunately don't have to choose between two risky endeavors. There is a proven way to de-risk the innovation process: discovery-driven planning.

First introduced by Rita Gunther McGrath, a professor at Columbia Business School, and Ian C. MacMillan, a professor at the Wharton School of the University of Pennsylvania,[1] discovery-driven planning bears a resemblance to the newer design methodology that people love to talk about called "lean start-up." Lean start-up is an approach that Steve Blank conceptualized in 2003 based on the concept of discovery-driven planning. Discovery-driven planning also includes concepts that resemble the popular notion of a "minimum viable product" or MVP, of which you may also have heard (and if the MVP is a concept that's new to you, know that it also stems from the lean-startup movement, and it refers to the simplest possible product one can build to get feedback from prospective customers).

What all these processes share is a focus on testing and learning before launching something new and uncertain. The basic idea is to acknowledge that your solution and strategy aren't correct or even fully formed at the outset. They must emerge over time.

The question is how to structure a process that allows for learning but also mitigates outsized risk.[2] The answer is to mirror the scientific method and the process of learning. That's what discovery-driven planning is all about. It provides a process for testing hypotheses and embedding the opportunity for lots of fast failures—and reframing those fast failures as learnings. Fast failures reframed as learnings help teams avoid spectacular failures that waste significant time, money, and political capital on something that wasn't vetted and could not have worked—as happened in the fictional vignette during the flipped-classroom experiment in 2012.

One clarification first. MVPs are not the only way to test assumptions in the discovery-driven planning process. In education, MVPs can also leave students exposed unnecessarily.

As Gagan Biyani, the founder of two education startups, wrote, an MVP "is a basic early version of a product that looks and feels like a simplified version of the eventual vision."[3]

But if educators start with something akin to an MVP—a prototype of their plan or solution—they may be overlooking several critical assumptions about how the world works and the progress individuals are trying to make. By embedding some of those assumptions in that first minimal solution, they may be missing the opportunity to test them.

A better path is to conduct what Biyani calls "minimum viable tests," or MVTs, that test specific assumptions that must be true for a plan to succeed. It's prudent to test these assumptions early and at a small enough grain size before getting too locked into a clear vision. The subtle shift is from the "build, measure, learn" ethos of the lean startup to "test, measure, learn."

MVTs have one more potential advantage over MVPs in education. Because most schools are already working with students, parents, and teachers who have existing expectations for their school, MVTs create fast, cheap ways for schools to learn without creating a full-blown prototype to use with their existing stakeholders. If the assumptions you're making start to prove true when conducting MVTs, those MVTs will eventually encompass MVPs before launching something new and bold. But starting with tests that are short of a full-fledged MVP poses less risk for students and greatly increases the odds of success.

THE STANDARD PLANNING PROCESS

Discovery-driven planning flips the conventional planning process on its head. In the standard planning process, you make a plan, look at the projected outcomes from the plan, and then, assuming those outcomes look desirable, you implement it.

This approach works well when you have tried something similar before or the innovation is familiar and proven—think a new lesson plan in a class that's been taught for years. Just to be sure, check to see if three conditions have been met before taking this path:

1. You have a plan that addresses all of the important details required for success, with a high degree of confidence that the assumptions being made are correct, and those responsible for the implementation understand each important detail.

2. The plan makes as much sense to all members of the organization as they view the world from their own context as it does to the person making the plan, so that everyone will act appropriately and consistently.

3. Outside forces—such as the reaction of the community and students or the impact of other schools, programs, or technology—are reasonably stable and predictable.

If all three of these are true, then the typical planning process can work well. Just implement away.

When doing something that's novel for the community, however, and the only thing you can say with certainty is that unforeseen things will occur, following a different planning and implementation process is key.

WHAT IS DISCOVERY-DRIVEN PLANNING?

When launching something that is unfamiliar and unpredictable, with a low ratio of knowledge to hypotheses, educators need to change the planning and design process. Note that we're not talking about plans as a noun, but instead planning as a verb.[4] The standard planning process of making "one plan" that everyone will then implement won't work because the assumptions, both implicit and explicit, on which the outcomes rest are often wrong.

The key to success will instead often be the ability to test hypotheses and continue to iterate on plans as you gain more information. Therefore, when educators are creating something new that is different from what they have always done previously, they need a different way to create a plan—particularly if the tolerance for failure is low and the need for caution is high, as is so often the case when innovating in education with children.

In a discovery-driven planning process, start with the desired outcomes in mind. From there, the crucial next step is to list all the assumptions that must prove true to realize the desired outcomes. With the assumptions in hand, the next step is to implement a plan to learn, which means testing, as quickly and cheaply as possible, whether the critical assumptions are reasonable. This is what Biyani is referring to when he wrote about the MVT or minimum viable test.

If the assumptions prove true, then your schooling community can continue to invest in executing the strategy. If assumptions prove false or uncertain, then organizations can change accordingly or continue to test before they have gone too far.

Discovery-Driven Planning Process

1. List desired outcomes.

2. Determine what assumptions must prove true for outcomes to be realized.

3. Implement a plan to learn whether the critical assumptions are reasonable.

4. Implement the strategy when key assumptions prove true.

Let's dig deeper into each of the steps.

Start with the Outcomes

The first step in a discovery-driven planning process is to identify the outcomes that you want to achieve as a result of the innovation. If everybody knows what the outcomes must look like for the innovation to be worthwhile in the first place, then there is no sense in playing a game of Texas Hold 'Em. Just lay the cards out on the table at the outset. What does the final state of the innovation need to do? What are you trying to accomplish? And how will you know you have been successful?

This is why it's so critical to start with the end in mind and then plan backward. Understanding the purpose of your schooling community, as we discussed in Chapter 2, but also the specific purpose of any innovation you put in place is vital. Being able to codify that purpose into a SMART goal—meaning one that is specific, measurable, attainable, realistic, and time-bound—upon which everyone can agree is tricky. But it is important to make sure there's clarity and agreement on the desired outcomes. If you have doubters—a SMART goal feels too broad or simplistic, for example—then you probably need to do more work to nail why you're undertaking something and what you hope to achieve out of it.

Create an Assumptions Checklist

With the desired goals and outcomes identified, the second step is to compile an assumptions checklist. Take the draft plan around the student, teacher, and parent experience and list all the assumptions being made that must prove true in order for the desired outcomes defined in step 1 to materialize.

In this step, you want to focus on the efficacy and sustainability of an idea. Be exhaustive. All the assumptions that schools make implicitly should be on the table, including the use of time and school schedules, space, and staffing. Lay out all the design elements you plan on putting in place, including the type of team implementing the innovation and who is on the team; the student experience; the teacher experience; the parent experience; the software, hardware, infrastructure, and facilities; the curriculum; the learning model and where it is being implemented; the culture; the implementation plan; and the budget. By cataloging all these assumptions—and their implicit underlying components— you will assemble a comprehensive list of assumptions. That means everything from "This math software will be rigorous enough" to "Our teachers will have the data they need to intervene in the right ways" to "The time we give students to learn is enough for them to master the curriculum."

As you write the assumptions down, state them as a hypothesis— an affirmative statement that the assumption you're making is correct—so that when it comes to test it, an affirmation of the hypothesis will give more confidence in your plan, whereas something that disproves the hypothesis will lead to a change in plan.

When Summit Public Schools, for example, moved to implement blended learning in its schools, it didn't start by just implementing its plan across all of its schools. It instead followed a rigorous cycle of building, measuring, and learning—a process it has continued to do as it continually innovates. Summit started by prototyping a Station Rotation model in which students moved between different centers of online learning, projects, and so forth at discrete times during the day. The school's goal in innovating at that time was to boost the percentage of students ready to succeed in college. For that to occur, Summit assumed it had to better support students developing agency—meaning that students would be capable of making their own choices. Implicit in trying a Station Rotation plan was that it would give students better opportunities to build their agency. After watching the experiment unfold, however, Summit soon concluded that a Station Rotation model wouldn't provide enough opportunities for students to make daily choices to help them develop this habit of success. As a result, Summit altered its plan.

The process of listing assumptions could take a day or two, and it is time spent well. Sometimes the list of assumptions at this stage will number more than 100! For each initial assumption you identify, it's often the case that there are at least two to five more embedded assumptions that you're also making. To capture the full set of assumptions, it is ideal to have a diverse array of people at the table in this brainstorming exercise who represent a variety of departments and perspectives so that the assumptions list will be exhaustive and will help the leader understand what assumptions are on different people's minds.

This step can sound intimidating. There are two other ways to proceed. Having an outside facilitator or consultant assist in this process can provide the capacity a school or district needs to do this process. Alternatively, educators can run a stripped-down version of this step by focusing on what they see as the most critical assumptions underlying two key domains of their plan: its *efficacy* and its *sustainability*.

Either way, to assist in the brainstorming process and give a sense of the range of assumptions that you may be making—either implicitly or explicitly—in a plan, Figure 10.1 offers a set of

Figure 10.1 Be expansive about assumptions

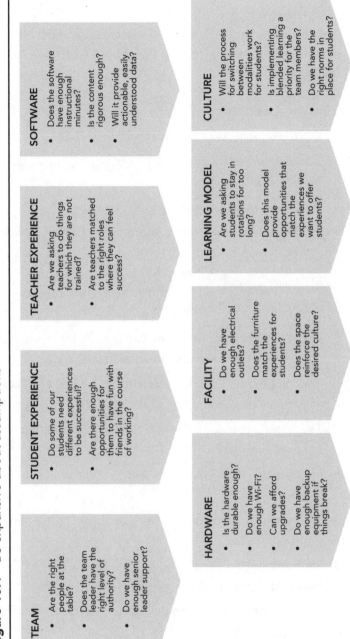

TEAM

- Are the right people at the table?
- Does the team leader have the right level of authority?
- Do we have enough senior leader support?

STUDENT EXPERIENCE

- Do some of our students need different experiences to be successful?
- Are there enough opportunities for them to have fun with friends in the course of working?

TEACHER EXPERIENCE

- Are we asking teachers to do things for which they are not trained?
- Are teachers matched to the right roles where they can feel success?

SOFTWARE

- Does the software have enough instructional minutes?
- Is the content rigorous enough?
- Will it provide actionable, easily understood data?

HARDWARE

- Is the hardware durable enough?
- Do we have enough Wi-Fi?
- Can we afford upgrades?
- Do we have enough backup equipment if things break?

FACILITY

- Do we have enough electrical outlets?
- Does the furniture match the experiences for students?
- Does the space reinforce the desired culture?

LEARNING MODEL

- Are we asking students to stay in rotations for too long?
- Does this model provide opportunities that match the experiences we want to offer students?

CULTURE

- Will the process for switching between modalities work for students?
- Is implementing blended learning a priority for the team members?
- Do we have the right norms in place for students?

categories from which you should think through the assumptions in your plan.

Here is a real list of 25 assumptions that other school leaders have brainstormed to help give an idea of what these might look like:

25 Sample Assumptions

1. The master schedule includes a special ed teacher.

2. Teachers buy in (want to do this) and want to work together to teach all kids together.

3. Teachers have the capacity to do this type of work.

4. I will convince the district to fully fund my project, meaning:

    a. Computers

    b. Math software

    c. Aide

5. Professional development time will work within 64 minutes after-school, site-based collaboration time.

6. The collaborative learning environment will lead to sustainability (point person, training, cross training).

7. The 70-minute block will work: tier 1 instruction, intervention, and acceleration.

8. My team and I can make this happen by the start of next school year.

9. The computer schedule will work for fifth graders and for their podmates.

10. Math software will work on different devices under a Bring Your Own Device policy.

11. Math software will work on the district's old computers.

12. Existing technology will last the school year.

13. We have enough headphones to last the year.

14. We have enough students willing to bring their own headphones.

15. We have enough computer mice to last the year.

16. We have enough students able to bring their own devices.

17. Substitutes will understand the plan.

18. Substitutes will be able to execute the plan.

19. We will be able to train teachers to read and use reports by the start of the year.

20. Kids will be fairly independent on the new program from the start (with minimal aide support).

21. The technology will work daily (lead to a backup plan).

22. A staff member is available and has capacity to handle student provisioning.

23. Parents will be comfortable with their children concurrently doing middle school work in elementary school.

24. The math software is robust enough to serve as my only intervention tool.

25. The number of fifth graders we are serving will stay the same.

26. There is sufficient monitoring to help with the transition to other fifth-grade rooms.

Rank Your Assumptions

When you are finished compiling the assumptions, the next job is to rank the assumptions from the most to the least crucial. Here's where those assumptions around efficacy and sustainability will really matter. Innosight consulting, which regularly uses discovery-driven planning, has found that having the same group of individuals ask two questions about each assumption is the best way to systematically accomplish this step with some rigor behind it.[5]

First, ask what could happen if you are wrong about an assumption. In other words, which of these assumptions, if proved untrue, would most seriously derail the success of the project? If the assumption is wrong, will it be catastrophic to the project? Will it require a major overhaul of the plan? Is the impact just minor, and does it require only a few tweaks? Or is being wrong no big deal, as it will have no impact on the plan? If being wrong will be catastrophic to the project, assign it a priority value of 1; if it's no big deal, assign it a 3. A rank of 2 is in between.

Second, ask how confident you are that each assumption is correct. A fun test of how confident people are is to see if they are willing to give up one year's salary if they are wrong—meaning they have a high degree of confidence that they know the answer. Perhaps they are willing to give up only one week's salary if they are wrong? Or one day's worth? Or maybe they aren't willing to bet any of their salary because they have no sense of whether the assumption is correct. Assign a value based on confidence. A rank of 1 signals no confidence that the assumption is correct, whereas a rank of 3 suggests high confidence that it is correct.

After rating all the assumptions, take the two scores, average them, and then rank-order the averages. Those assumptions with a rank close to 1.0—because they are the most crucial to the project's success and yet you have the least confidence in whether they are right—are the most important assumptions to pay attention to in the next step. Those closer to a 3.0 are not as critical for the project's success. You can therefore afford to test them later.

To illustrate, imagine you had assumed that the cost of a particular math software program for a new plan you wanted to implement would be roughly $10 per student, and you planned to purchase 30 licenses. This assumption might rank closer to a 3.0 than a 1.0. Why? If you're wrong about the cost of the software—it's more than $10 per student—it's probably not much more than that, so it is unlikely to change your plan much. And when it comes to the confidence rating, you are likely to have some certainty around the cost figure, or at least know the ballpark range.

On the other hand, if there is an outlier—that is, someone vehemently disagrees and has this assumption at a 1.0—then this is a great way for a leader to surface where there is disagreement about the plan and where there is a lack of unanimity without making those disagreements personal. That's one reason why it's helpful to have each person do this ranking by themselves before coming together as a group to create a consensus view of the riskiness and confidence in the assumptions.

After rank ordering them, bucket the assumptions in three zones. Zone 1 will be those with scores ranging from 1.0 to 1.6; these assumptions are the most critical and urgent to test. Zone 2 will be those with scores ranging from 1.7 to 2.3. Zone 3, those with scores ranging from 2.4 to 3.0, are the least urgent to test. (See Figure 10.2.)

Figure 10.2 Prioritizing assumptions

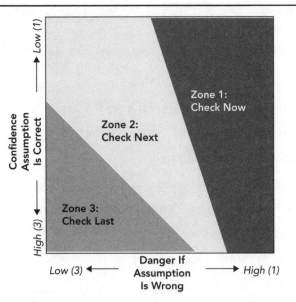

Implement a Plan—to Learn More

With the prioritized assumptions checklist in hand, the next step is to implement a plan to test the validity of the hypotheses. Plan to check the most important assumptions—those in Zone 1—first. That's because those are the hypotheses with the least confidence behind them that are also the most crucial to the project's success.

In the initial stages of planning, the tests should be as simple, inexpensive, and quick as possible. Remember, as Biyani described, these tests should literally be the minimum viable test! They should simply provide a sense—not a clear answer—about whether the most critical assumptions are reasonable.

For example, it is a good idea to look at other schools to see whether the assumptions hold water before going too far down a road. Make time to read the existing research and have early conversations to see if ideas hold water rather than rely on what you think is common sense. You could also create an MVP, like a quick mock-up or prototype. A prototype is anything that helps communicate the idea of what you are doing, which can mean everything from mock-ups and models to simulations and role-playing experiences.

Here are some ways to creatively and quickly test your assumptions.

Test Creatively: Keep It Simple, Keep It Cheap

- Quickly create a "good enough" prototype.
- Talk to students and parents.
- Talk to internal resources.
- Talk to other schools doing something similar.
- Visit other schools.
- Look to your history.
- Read the research.

- Identify early milestones.

- Talk to the business manager to make sure it is sustainable.

- Talk to experts in the field.

- Conduct a focus group.

- Launch a pilot, perhaps in the summer or after school.

Here are some further sample tests that are smaller than an MVP for some specific assumptions just to give an idea of what this might look like.

- **Assumption:** Our weekly schedule for second-grade students creates enough flexibility for teachers to truly personalize for each student—as in, students won't get locked into groupings inappropriate for their learning needs—such that we will see student achievement soar.

  Early test: Talk to other schools that have implemented a similar weekly schedule to see how they have balanced the need for structure with the need for flexibility and how they have evolved, as well as what student achievement has been.

- **Assumption:** Stakeholders—students, parents, teachers, administrators, and community leaders—will support the transition to and implementation of mastery-based learning.

  Early tests:

  - Talk with students about their current and hoped-for school experiences.

  - Invite teachers who are excited about leading a school-wide change to lead reflective teachers' meetings.

  - Hold individual meetings with parents to surface concerns they may have about their children's schooling experience today and probe whether mastery-based learning could help answer those challenges.

- **Assumption:** Our plan for how we're incorporating projects as the centerpiece of our curriculum won't overburden (create too much cognitive load on) our novice learners in specific subject areas (based on the research that novice learners do better with active forms of direct instruction).

  Early test: Visit other schools that have implemented similar plans to observe students and collect data to see if you have created the proper scaffolding and mix of activities for novice learners.

- **Assumption:** Our administrators will take on the challenge of leading transformative change and supporting teachers at all times.

  Early tests:

  - Look to past examples in your school's history of major change to learn how administrators handled those instances.

- **Assumption:** Our school Wi-Fi network will support a large number of devices used at once throughout the campus.

  Early tests:

  - Ask IT administrators at other blended-learning schools about their experience.

  - Run a summer practice test with teachers simulating the number of students using computers at once.

Decide On Next Steps

The last step is to decide whether to continue implementing the strategy.

Set a checkpoint—a specific date when the tests of several of the assumptions should be completed—so that the team can come together and evaluate what it has learned. The period leading up to the first checkpoint could last one month and be designed to give team members time to test some of the most critical assumptions at a high level. These checkpoints could coincide with existing meetings to make sure that they don't fall through the cracks and that they don't overburden your team. You could, for example, use a regular planning meeting or scheduled professional development days for these checkpoints. Having an outside facilitator help run the process and hold the team to the checkpoints can also help.

At each checkpoint, you have a decision to make.

If the assumptions are proving true, then keep moving forward to the next checkpoint.

If they are not—as will more than likely be the case—there are a few options. Perhaps you can tweak the plan to keep moving forward; for example, maybe the math software an educator had planned to use will be good for only 20 minutes of instruction a day rather than the 30 minutes your team was thinking. This in turn means the daily and weekly schedules will have to be adjusted.

Alternatively, there may need to be bigger adjustments. Perhaps you need a different team to implement your plan. You've realized that your current plan won't work in an individual grade, so you instead need to start it as a new school within your existing school because that will give you more time to fine-tune the innovation before scaling it.

Or finally, perhaps the assumptions underlying the success of the plan are wildly unrealistic, and the plan won't work. Perhaps you had assumed that math software alone could somehow ensure that all students met a certain level of academic achievement that you now see won't happen. If this is the case, then there is an opportunity to shelve the plan before too much time and money have been invested and the stakes have become too high to abandon the idea.

If you do decide to move forward, don't just move to implement the whole plan right away.

Look at your assumptions again and brainstorm tests that are more comprehensive, precise, and perhaps more costly than the previous ones. The key is to keep your tests as low-cost and quick as possible, but precise enough that you will gain more knowledge than you had before. That means the tests will both be bigger and, as you move through different checkpoints, will move into the MVP territory. Assumptions that you didn't test before might now be tested. The important thing is not to invest a lot of time and resources early before knowing whether the assumptions are proving true—or at least are in the right ballpark.

More concretely, perhaps a key assumption your team might be making concerns the rigor of a math program. A school or district could, as an initial test, read about the program and talk to others who use it. For a second test, the school or district could then ask for one license for the math program so that its teachers can poke around and see if it passes their own smell test for being rigorous enough. If it passes, the school or district might then implement a third test by finding a place—such as in summer school or after school—to pilot the math program for a couple of weeks before buying it and using it for all of its students for an entire year. And it might do this for a couple of other programs as well.

Establish a rhythm for your tests with more checkpoints. Perhaps the second checkpoint will occur in another month and a third will be a month after that. The tests during the second checkpoint might include an analysis of the software market. Further down the line, a checkpoint might include a working prototype and then the launch of a new learning model itself.

At each checkpoint, the team will gain new information. An assumption that seemed correct at a previous checkpoint may be revealed to be more complex than it was originally thought to be. That's okay. And if the team learns that ultimately the assumptions are unrealistic and that it won't be able to pull off the program, that is not a reason for despair.

Fast failure, as we discussed, is a success: the team learned that the idea would not work before wasting a lot of time and money. The key is to celebrate each time a decision is made. People should not feel that they must defend a pet idea. The victory is in *learning* more about an assumption, not in proving that someone is right or wrong.

As the team makes adjustments and iterates, it may find that it is going down a path with assumptions that are proving true. Even though the design and plan that is emerging and gradually being implemented is different from the one that was foreseen originally, if it will be successful in realizing the desired outcomes, then that's a resounding success—and the ultimate value of the discovery-driven process. What's more, you've done it without putting any students in harm's way—and hopefully dodged and parried all the social and emotional challenges that come with innovating in schools.

That process—of how to manage change when there is disagreement in your school community, as there almost always is, is what the next and final chapter discusses.

KEY TAKEAWAYS

- Although implementing new and uncertain innovations in schools can be risky, not innovating also carries huge known risks.

- Discovery-driven planning is a process that de-risks innovation. It's a better planning process when undertaking something new and uncertain where your ratio of knowledge to assumptions (or hypotheses) is low.

- The basic idea is to identify assumptions and then test, learn, and adjust. The process is all about learning.

- Step 1 is to begin with the end—the desired outcomes. Codify them into a SMART goal, meaning one that is specific, measurable, attainable, realistic, and time-bound.

- Step 2 is to create an assumptions checklist—or a list of hypotheses—that must prove true in a plan to realize the desired outcomes.

- Step 3 is to rank the assumptions based on how risky they are and how uncertain they are.

- Step 4 is to test the most critical assumptions with the lowest cost, fastest test possible that will yield new learning.

- Assemble the team at predetermined checkpoints to go through the results of the tests and then decide whether to proceed as planned, adjust the plan, or shelve it.

NOTES

1. Rita Gunther McGrath and Ian C. MacMillan, *Discovery-Driven Growth: A Breakthrough Process to Reduce Risk and Seize Opportunity* (Boston, MA: Harvard Business Press, 2009).
2. In his book *The Lean Startup*, Eric Ries talks about the importance of "validated learning" as the central unit of progress for any organization doing something uncertain and new. Eric Ries, *The Lean Startup: How Today's Entrepreneurs Use Continuous Innovation to Create Radically Successful Businesses* (New York: Currency, 2011).
3. Gagan Biyani, "The Minimum Viable Testing Process for Evaluating Startup Ideas," *First Round Review*, https://review.firstround.com/the-minimum-viable-testing-process-for-evaluating-startup-ideas (accessed October 12, 2021).
4. This insight stems from Anthony Kim and Alexis Gonzalez-Black, *The New School Rules: 6 Vital Practices for Thriving and Responsive Schools* (New York: Corwin, 2018).
5. Scott D. Anthony, Mark W. Johnson, Joseph V. Sinfield, and Elizabeth J. Altman, *The Innovator's Guide to Growth: Putting Disruptive Innovation to Work* (Boston, MA: Harvard Business Press, 2008), pp. 177–178.

Chapter 11

Implementing Change When People Don't Always Agree

Later that evening, Dr. Ball strode into the PTA meeting. After her breakthrough with the fifth-grade teachers, she felt more hopeful about implementing some changes that might create some forward momentum in the school.

But she still wasn't sure how to rally the parents and teachers— nor how she could shift them away from doing their participation- based fundraiser. She had a sense that tonight might not be the time or place to make that stand, though. But when was?

She expertly wound her way around the room to greet everyone in attendance. She knew most of the parents by now, but she also knew the politics of the moment. Don't slight anyone. Make them all feel special—and give them something special to share with their child when they saw them the next morning.

After 20 minutes of socializing, Patty Burkins, a parent and the head of the PTA, bounded to the microphone. "Welcome, everyone, to another exciting year of our annual fundraiser!"

Ball couldn't help but laugh at Burkins' enthusiasm. Despite the well-worn nature of her act, the energy in it was genuine, and it lit up the room. Too bad Ball felt a lot less excited about the campaign than everyone else in the room did.

"Here to inspire us with all the things Spruce Park Elementary might do with those dollars we're going to raise is our principal, Dr. Ball!"

The assembled group clapped politely. Ball slow-jogged to the microphone to try and maintain the energy in the room.

Before diving into her list of projects for the school, she looked out into the sea of faces and thought about who wasn't in the room. Jeremy's mom, for one. How is her voice represented in these meetings and among the school's priorities? Ball already knew the answer to that question. Her stomach dropped.

She thought about the complaining and bickering from the Owens family earlier in the day. She saw them in the audience and forced a smile.

She then thought about the meeting she had had earlier with the fifth-grade teachers and frowned. Even if they came up with a feasible plan to test, how was there any hope of getting the school to agree on a path forward?, she wondered. Better to stay with the incremental for now, she thought.

Looking down at her notecards, she started in on the school's list of possible projects.

* * *

One of the most challenging things school leaders face is making changes in a community when people don't agree on what they want or on what actions will lead to what results—which some days feels like . . . always.

As we've gone through this book, we've talked about the importance of beginning with the end by clarifying the purpose and goals of a schooling community. We've spent time on thinking about what might help a schooling community achieve those goals—from the proper scope of schooling to mastery-based learning, co-teaching, and specific technologies. We've also talked about the importance of building a strong culture in which there is clarity and consistency around priorities and processes.

But people in a schooling community often won't agree on any number of these and other items. As we've also discussed, although people might agree at a high level on some things, when it gets into the nitty-gritty of implementation and parents consider the progress they are trying to make in their lives, how resources are allocated and which programs are prioritized can fall into hot dispute. Oftentimes parents aren't all that empathetic either when they disagree about a hot-button issue or a specific initiative that they don't think is wise or is promoting something for their children with which they disagree. Public education in America ultimately happens within a representative democracy in which there are many voices that compete to be listened to and followed.

Given these dynamics, it's tough to manage change in a school or school system.

So what to do?

UNDERSTANDING THE LEVEL OF AGREEMENT

For the past seven years, I've taught a seminar to roughly 40 school leaders in Nevada. Of all the theories and frameworks on how to successfully manage innovation, the one that has consistently been among the most well received has been a theory about what tools to use when there are varying levels of agreement within an organization or community.[1]

Once a school leader has clarity around what they want to change, they still need to convince other individuals who will play a role in the change—teachers, administrators, students, staff, parents, district officials, and potentially more—to work with them. That can be true even if they have designed and tested it with significant parts of the community.

How to convince individuals to cooperate and work together? There are a variety of tools, ranging from motivational, visionary speeches to command-and-control orders that an individual can use to elicit cooperative behavior. We call these the "tools of cooperation."

The first important thing to know is that *most of these tools don't work most of the time.* As a result, leaders often fail when trying to manage change, as the tools they use waste credibility, energy, and resources. Therefore, the most important thing to do up-front is to figure out the level of agreement people in a community or organization have on *what* the organization's goals should be and *how* it can achieve them relative to any specific plan.

Figure 11.1 depicts these two variables. The vertical axis in the figure measures the extent to which the people involved agree on

Figure 11.1 Tools of cooperation

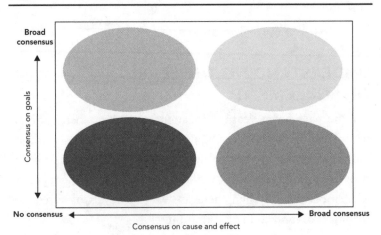

the goals. In other words, what do they want? This incorporates the results they seek from being part of the schooling community to what their values and priorities are to which trade-offs they are willing to make to achieve those results. The extent of agreement can range from none at the bottom to complete agreement at the top.

The second dimension is plotted on the horizontal axis. It measures the extent to which the people involved agree on *cause and effect*—which actions, or processes, will lead to the desired results. In other words, how will we achieve our goals? Little agreement on cause and effect places an organization on the left-hand side of the diagram, whereas strong agreement places an organization on the right-hand side.

Individuals in organizations in the upper-left domain of Figure 11.1 share common hopes for what they will gain from being part of the organization, even though they have different views of what actions will realize those hopes. Think of a school that is highly aligned on the importance of boosting graduation rates and test scores, but there are a range of views of how to get there. Some favor whole-class, direct-instruction methods with lots of test-prep practice. Others are interested in a coherent, interdisciplinary learning experience that emphasizes project-based learning. The majority may not have a strong opinion on what's done but believe it needs to be different from what's currently taking place.

In contrast are schools in the lower-right corner. These schools might be filled with parents who are sending their children to accomplish very different Jobs to Be Done in their lives and with teachers who have very different ideas for what school should prioritize. But both agree on which methodologies produce which results.

Schools in the upper-right quadrant have individuals who agree both on what they want and how to get there. There's a deep meld of goals and culture. What's the challenge? Clear consensus on both dimensions makes these organizations' cultures resistant to change. People are satisfied with what they get out of being in the organization and agree about how to maintain that status quo. When something has fundamentally changed in the world, however, it's difficult for the organization to change as well.

Finally, schools in the lower-left quadrant are made up of individuals who agree neither on what they want nor on how the world works. This is the school where individuals have a wide range of goals—Test scores? College admission? An emphasis on culture, connectivity, and diversity?—and disagree on methods, such as whether school discipline should follow a zero-tolerance attitude or a restorative justice mindset.

To be clear, there is no "best" situation for leaders. The key is recognizing which situation corresponds most closely to the situation they are in and then selecting the cooperation tools that will work effectively in that situation. This simple model applies to units that range from families, business units, and schools to corporations, school districts, and nations.

LEADERSHIP TOOLS

In the upper-left quadrant (Figure 11.2), tools that are focused on results—as opposed to those that are focused on process—are more effective because there is a high existing consensus about what individuals want from being part of the organization. Charismatic leaders who command respect, for example, often do not address how to get things done. They instead motivate people to just do what needs doing.

Think of the visionary and charismatic school superintendent or principal. Lofty statements and speeches are effective here because members of the school community are in agreement around what they want. They will follow a leader who appropriately rallies them to go get it. So long as the leader doesn't overly focus on the "how" up-front—where there may be plenty of

Figure 11.2 Tools of cooperation (leadership tools)

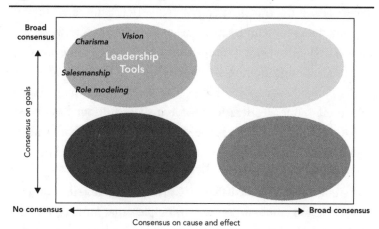

disagreements or lack of firm conviction—and just lays out the plan with a focus on the goals, they will rally individuals to the cause and help them overlook where they might disagree on what actions will lead to the results they all want.

This was where Lindsay Unified School District, which we discussed in Chapter 5, found itself in 2007. There was broad consensus among everyone that something had to change. The metrics along every dimension were poor. The district was failing its students. To illustrate just how bad things were, Lindsay's superintendent Tom Rooney often tells the story of how a new principal at Lindsay Unified High School, Virgel Hammonds, was settling into his role when "in walked a father and his son who had graduated the week before. The father took a newspaper off the desk and gave it to his son, asking him to read it. After a few minutes of silence, the young man looked up with tears in his eyes. 'Dad, you know I don't know how to read.'"[2]

Although there wasn't agreement on what to do, everyone wanted to do something. Rooney swung into action.

As Thomas Arnett of the Clayton Christensen Institute wrote, "Over the course of eight months, he and the school board worked with a consultant to develop the rough outlines of a shared vision for transforming their district. They then invited 150 stakeholders to an intensive, two-day community work session to articulate their shared values and goals in the form of a strategic design document[3] that would be their compass for guiding all subsequent decisions. The district staff then worked with their school leaders to reinforce shared understanding of the strategic design while at the same time giving school leaders both autonomy and support to develop new practices in line with the district's vision."[4]

As competency-based expert Chris Sturgis noted, although there is some unity in certain principles that undergird how Lindsay Unified now operates—from mastery-based learning to blended learning and a deep sense of accountability—the actual day-to-day practices at Lindsay Unified differ depending on what individual educators and students believe they need to make progress. As she wrote, "Outcomes are clearly defined, with empowered students working alongside empowered teachers to figure out how students will learn and demonstrate their learning. . . Teachers often raised the fact that they had permission to take risks and be more creative, as long as there were clear reasons why it would be helping students."[5]

In other words, the district rallied people around a vision and then allowed individuals to figure out how they would go realize that vision. Rooney did not sell the details up-front, but instead stayed focused on the big picture and empowering communities to chase the shared vision.

There is a cautionary note here, however. You need to be honest about where your community is in the matrix because the same actions that individuals view as inspiring and visionary when they're in the upper-left corner are often regarded with indifference or disdain when they are in the lower quadrants. For example, when people agree on what they want to achieve, vision statements can be energizing. But if people do not agree among themselves about what they want, vision statements typically do little more than induce a lot of eye-rolling.

MANAGEMENT TOOLS

In contrast to Lindsay Unified School District would lie a schooling community in the lower-right quadrant of the matrix (Figure 11.3). Here the tools that will work are coordinative and process-oriented in nature. These management tools include training or professional development, standard operating procedures, and measurement systems. For such tools to work, group members need to agree on cause and effect but not necessarily on what they want from their participation in the organization. In these cases, a school leader can introduce a new program with a methodology other members agree will contribute to better outcomes, so long as it doesn't violate their sense of what they want the school to focus on.

What might this look like in practice? Imagine an elementary school principal leading a school that doesn't follow the current evidence around how to teach reading. With many in the community having wildly divergent views of why they are in the

Figure 11.3 Tools of cooperation (management tools)

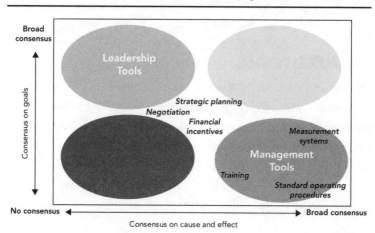

school in the first place, momentum has built through education and news reports around how the school should be teaching reading, which gives the principal the ability to introduce a new reading program and use professional development and other training support to make sure that it's implemented well.

Conversely, if there is no consensus among concerned people that following the new methods will lead to the specified results any better than what they've been doing, they are unlikely to behave differently after professional development. The effectiveness of the training, in other words, is more dependent on the level of agreement about how the world works than on the training itself. That means that if you're in a school where teachers, for example, have other beliefs about how to teach reading, then it will be hard to implement a plan by simply offering professional development.

Public schools rarely sit in this quadrant. Most of the work of a teacher can't be boiled down to predictable rules such that educators with diverse goals will simply follow what others tell them to do. This is one of the reasons that many remedies with which reformers have experimented in the past have seldom worked. The model also asserts, for example, that financial incentives, like pay-for-performance schemes for teachers, won't work unless a school sits in this quadrant or nearby with a modicum of agreement on what is wanted and how to get there.

CULTURE TOOLS

In organizations that lie in the upper-right quadrant (Figure 11.4), individuals will cooperate almost automatically to continue in the same direction. They have a deep consensus on priorities as well as what actions they need to take to achieve these priorities, which is the essence of a strong culture that we discussed in Chapter 9. In other words, in organizations with strong cultures, people instinctively prioritize similar options. Their common

Figure 11.4 Tools of cooperation (culture tools)

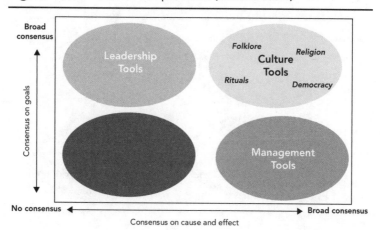

view of how the world works means that little debate is necessary about the best way to achieve those priorities.

But this very strength can make such organizations highly resistant to change. The tools of cooperation in the culture quadrant—like ritual, folklore, and democracy—facilitate cooperation only to preserve the status quo. They are not tools to cause change. Managers can also use leadership and management tools here, but only to reinforce the existing culture. For example, if a manager were to use a vision statement here that was at odds with what employees wanted, it would not work. Hewlett-Packard's Carly Fiorina learned this the hard way when she tried to challenge the "HP Way." Her public clashes with HP's employees and board resulted in her ouster.

POWER TOOLS

When an organization's members share little consensus on either agreement dimension, the only tools that will elicit cooperation in pursuit of a new course are power tools, such as fiat, force, coercion, and threats.

Figure 11.5 Tools of cooperation (power tools)

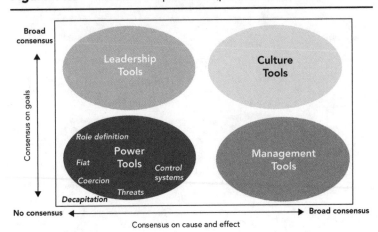

This quadrant (Figure 11.5) arguably captures where many public schools sit today, with occasional traces in the upper-left quadrant. Teachers, taxpayers, administrators, parents, students, and politicians have divergent priorities and disagree strongly about how to improve—from more money to more computers; from fewer computers to fewer group projects; from better teachers to smaller class sizes; from more autonomy to less autonomy; and many more.

Although power tools may work well in autocratic governments, they are normally—and typically rightly—unavailable to school leaders in a democracy.

Consequently, when leaders try to wield power tools in America's public schools, they often struggle to remain in charge or to see their changes endure unless they deliver clear, quick wins. Michelle Rhee's stewardship of the DC Public Schools may be the most prominent example. Her tenure was marked with tension and fights as she sought to shock the district schools into changing their culture. Although she arguably succeeded in changing the culture within the district organization itself, many of the traditional public schools resisted the cultural shifts she attempted. Similarly, in inner-city Chattanooga, Tennessee, the elementary schools were failing. Superintendent Jesse Register turned to power tools and replaced all but one of the schools' principals. He made all the teachers in the schools reapply for their jobs and pass a test. Although he could not actually fire the 100 teachers who did not make the cut, he managed to shift them out of the inner-city schools into the suburban Chattanooga schools where the infrastructure offered them more support. The schools did improve, as test scores rose in every grade, sometimes dramatically.[6] But a few years after he left, the system remained mired with some of the same fundamental challenges as when he entered, with few students performing at grade level.

The scary thing about this situation is that democracy—the primary, although certainly not only, tool that the law allows—is effective only in the upper-right circumstance, when there is already broad, preexisting consensus on what is wanted and how the world works. Democracy is not an effective tool for radical change. School districts typically are governed by elected school boards, whose members generally decide by majority vote what must be done and how to do it. Not surprisingly, few such boards are capable of mounting a decisive change in school strategy. The democracy tool wasn't designed to deliver consensus in the face of the fractious debates that characterize many school board meetings. Over the past 20 years or so, some states have placed certain low-performing districts in receivership to get around the mechanics of school boards. Some mayors of large cities have moved to disband school boards and take direct control of their school districts. The mayors then appointed a superintendent who shared their vision, such that the superintendent didn't need to worry about pleasing disparate school board members who had competing visions for reform. Of course, this strategy only worked as long as the mayor remained in office. It didn't free the superintendent from the rules of a democracy. And although federal and state policies gave more power to state and local leaders to take over, close, and replace schools, they still operate within a democracy where it is difficult to wield power tools over an extended period of time.

Where does this leave most school leaders? There are three other paths forward they can take.

TOOL OF SEPARATION

There are instances in which there is such fundamental disagreement among the parties in an organization that it is simply impossible to reach consensus on a course of action—and yet no one has amassed the power to compel cooperation. In these instances, there is another tool that a leader can use that does not reside within the agreement matrix. We call it separation— dividing the conflicted parties into separate groups with a set of teachers, parents, and administrators who are in strong agreement with others inside their own group, and yet they don't need to agree with those on other teams. To create a separate group, a leader may have to use the power tool of fiat, but after that, the separation tool creates other options for school leaders.

This is part of the logic behind creating a separate, autonomous unit as a solution to the threat-rigidity that Chapter 1 detailed. Such a team can have resources aligned on processes (cause and effect) and priorities (goals).

In business, the only instances where an industry's leading company also became the leader in the ensuing disruptive innovation* was when the leaders wielded the separation tool. They established an independent business unit under the corporate

---

*A disruptive innovation is one that transforms a market characterized by offerings that are complicated, expensive, and relatively inaccessible to one where the services are simpler, more affordable, and more convenient. The leading organizations typically struggle to succeed when a disruptive innovation in their field emerges. You can learn more about the theory of disruptive innovation by reading Clayton Christensen, Michael B. Horn, and Curtis W. Johnson, *Disrupting Class: How Disruptive Innovation Will Change the Way the World Learns Expanded Edition* (New York: McGraw-Hill, 2010).

umbrella and gave it unfettered freedom to pursue the disruptive opportunity with a new business model.

This is the logic that caused SNHU's President Paul LeBlanc to separate its online division from its brick-and-mortar campus. It's why Kettle Moraine succeeded by creating microschools and district-run charter schools within its schools. And it's why a central recommendation throughout this book has been to create different zones where schooling communities can innovate together.

This doesn't have to be so dramatic. If a school isn't looking to overthrow everything about its existing priorities, the separation can occur within a school with its existing structures by rounding up a coalition of the willing who want to make a dramatic change. This is in many ways what the Enlarged City School District of Middletown did. In the fall of 2013, 33 teachers opted to implement a blended-learning program that used i-Ready for both reading and math, alongside Dreambox Learning, Lexia Learning, Achieve3000, and myON—depending on students' specific needs. Students in the blended-learning classrooms outperformed students in nonblended classrooms, as they gained 35 percent more in reading and 47 percent more in math on benchmark exams from NWEA, a nonprofit assessment organization. Over 70 percent of students using i-Ready progressed through more than one grade level in one year in math, and over 50 percent of students progressed through more than one grade level in reading. With that record of success, the following year 120 classrooms across its three elementary schools and two middle schools were using blended learning.

The Los Altos school district in California similarly implemented a Station Rotation model of blended learning with Khan Academy with a couple of fifth-grade teachers who raised their hands before expanding after they experienced success.

Anthony Kim, an education consultant and author, recommends building with this coalition of the willing or starting in a certain grade span and then expanding gradually—say grade by grade or subject by subject over a set period of time, perhaps three to five years. The time frame and milestones for the rollout should be defined in advance. Those milestones should correspond to the checkpoints within the discovery-driven planning process so an initiative won't get stuck as a small pilot and can scale as assumptions prove true.

That means that success with the coalition of the willing is what allows a leader to expand from a pilot to a school- or district-wide initiative. And that bleeds into the other two mechanisms a school leader has at their disposal.

MECHANISMS OF MOVEMENT

The other mechanisms that leaders have are the power of success and the work of common framing to move an organization to different places in the matrix.

Success

For groups in the matrix's lower-left quadrant (Figure 11.6), if their members succeed repeatedly in doing their work, the

Figure 11.6 Tools of cooperation

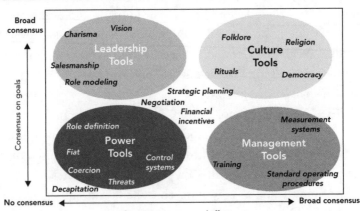

success tends to build consensus on both goals and cause-and-effect until a strong culture ultimately emerges within the group. Eventually, if the formula that led to success stops working and the organization drifts into crisis, then consensus weakens. Success moves an organization toward the upper right; failure and crisis shift it toward the lower left.

The point is that success can breed agreement in a broader group, but also excitement about joining a group's efforts. When there is at least a modicum of agreement on the goals of an organization but less agreement on how to achieve them, success can be a powerful way to move a whole organization to agreement on a new set of actions.

Common Language

The second mechanism of movement is when people are given a common language and a common way to frame a problem, which can occur if there is a sound theory that people broadly understand. In most meetings where the participants are plotting change, they talk past each other. For example, in a school setting, one person sees class size as the problem. Another targets the teachers union. A third contends that better management is the answer. And so on. They talk past each other with their solutions—and they can't agree on solutions because they don't share a common definition of the problem.

A prerequisite for getting agreement is having a common language and a shared framing of the problem. We see what happens when this isn't in place playing out right now in debates over grading in schools. One side suggests making grading more equitable. Another hears that as code for being less rigorous. The former group talks about decoupling the grading of content knowledge from behaviors and habits like meeting deadlines. The latter groups hears this as no longer caring about deadlines. And it goes on and on.[7]

To illustrate how to solve this, in the mid-1990s, Intel was being disrupted at the low end of its market by the much cheaper microprocessors that Cyrix and AMD sold. Intel chairman Andy Grove established an educational seminar at which Intel's top 2,000 managers (this was not a small undertaking!) studied the disruption model from Clayton Christensen's book *The Innovator's Dilemma*. As a result, Intel launched its Celeron chip at the bottom of its market—a disruptive strategy that was counterintuitive to the common logic of how to make money at Intel but was *very* successful in fending off the would-be disruptors.

Reflecting back on that history, Grove later told Christensen, "The disruption model didn't give us any answers. But it gave us a common language and a common way to frame the problem so that we could reach consensus around a counterintuitive course of action." In other words, a shared and sound model of causality, which brings with it a common language and a common framing of the problem, can shift an organization toward the upper-right quadrant. The success of this technique is of course contingent on people being ready to learn; it's not nearly as powerful a mechanism of movement as success is. But it works faster. One observation is that it often helps if an outside group, rather than the leader, introduces the common framing. It's hard to be a prophet in your own land. But it doesn't need to occur this way.

Iron County presents an interesting case study of how this mechanism can work. On the heels of a series of successful changes and with some momentum at their backs, when the school leaders decided to introduce a new competency-based grading system that disbanded the traditional A–F letter grades, they used leadership tools by selling the new policy in a nice package to the parents, as we discussed in Chapter 7. In effect, they were implicitly assuming the district sat in the top half of the agreement diagram, but in reality the district leaders were out of step with the parents on grading. A firestorm ensued.

The leaders stepped back and introduced a new framing for why they wanted to replace the grading system by focusing on the areas of agreement with students, educators, and parents. They showed why the traditional system created a lot of uncertainty. The parents and other stakeholders bought in to the point. With that common framing in place, they then worked with parents to design a new grading policy that everyone could get behind—which was a modification of the existing gradebook. That allowed the district to innovate *with* the parents, rather than impose an innovation on the parents when there wasn't the agreement they thought existed. Having a common language and a common framing of the problem was critical.

THE POWER OF EDUCATION

The story from Iron County offers a bigger lesson for educators. Educators are ultimately in the business of educating—helping to lead forth by building language, framing challenges, and facilitating discussions with disparate points of view. Doing this work not just with a school system's students, but also its parents and stakeholders, represents an opportunity to deepen understanding, create agreement, build consensus for change, and co-design new solutions. Given that this is the work educators do for a living, it presents a natural opportunity that many other organizations lack. It's an opportunity on which educators can capitalize to create more progress in the pursuit of building a positive-sum education system that serves all students and families well.

KEY TAKEAWAYS

- There are a variety of tools, ranging from motivational, visionary speeches to command-and-control orders that an individual can use to elicit cooperative behavior. We call these the "tools of cooperation." Most of these tools don't work most of the time.

- The first step is to diagnose the level of agreement people in a community or organization have on the organization's *goals* and how it can achieve them—do they have agreement on *cause and effect*—relative to any specific plan.

- There is no "best" situation for leaders. Accurate diagnosis is what's important.

- Depending on the quadrant an organization is in, leaders can choose from among leadership, management, culture, and power tools.

- There are three other paths forward to create change: the tool of separation, success, and a common language or education.

NOTES

1. Much of what follows is adapted from Clayton M. Christensen, Michael B. Horn, and Curtis W. Johnson, *Disrupting Class: How Disruptive Innovation Will Change the Way the World Learns* (New York: McGraw-Hill, 2008), first edition. That book in turn drew from Clayton M. Christensen, Matt Marx, and Howard H. Stevenson, "The Tools of Cooperation and Change," *Harvard Business Review*, October 2006, https://hbr.org/2006/10/the-tools-of-cooperation-and-change.

2. Chris Sturgis, "Six Trends at Lindsay Unified School District," *CompetencyWorks* blog, March 2, 2015, https://aurora-institute .org/cw_post/six-trends-at-lindsay-unified-school-district/.

3. Lindsay Unified School District Strategic Design, https://www.lindsay.k12.ca.us/filelibrary/LUSD%20Strategic%20Design%201.pdf (accessed October 4, 2021).

4. Thomas Arnett, "Catching Education's White Whale: School Improvement," Clayton Christensen Institute, November 15, 2017, https://www.christenseninstitute.org/blog/catching-educations-white-whale-school-improvement/.

5. Sturgis, "Six Trends at Lindsay Unified School District."

6. John Merrow, "Chatanooga [sic] Elementary Schools Struggle to Improve Low Test Scores: The NewsHour's Special Correspondent for Education John Merrow Reports on Efforts to Fix a Group of Troubled Elementary Schools in Tennessee," The NewsHour, June 20, 2006, http://www.pbs.org/newshour/show/chatanooga-elementary-schools-struggle-to-improve-low-test-scores.

7. Paloma Esquivel, "As Ds and Fs Soar, Schools Ditch Inequitable Grade Systems," *Los Angeles Times*, November 8, 2021, https://www.latimes.com/california/story/2021-11-08/as-ds-and-fs-soar-schools-ditch-inequitable-grade-systems.

Chapter 12

Conclusion

The next day was a beautiful one. Dr. Ball floated through her morning and into recess. It was her day to serve as playground monitor. She saw Jeremy and Julia chatting on the side of the kick-ball game and snuck over so she could eavesdrop.

As it turned out, Jeremy was telling Julia a story.[1]

"I'm just so confused in class right now, and, like, I don't know why," he said. "I remember when I was in kindergarten in a different school. The teacher asked all of us if any of us had ever hurt our knees. Like we basically all raised our hands.

"She then said, 'Jeremy, I'm sorry to hear you hurt your knee. Here's a Band-Aid for your knee.'

"Then she said, 'Okay, has anyone ever skinned your elbow?' A bunch of us say yeah, so she calls on another kid and says, 'I'm so sorry to hear that. Here's a Band-Aid for your knee.'"

Julia raised her eyebrows. Ball did, too.

"Exactly, right?," Jeremy said. "We're all like totally confused. But then the teacher keeps going. She says, 'Has anyone ever hit their head?' A few people raise their hands, and she calls on one of them and says, 'Here's a Band-Aid for your knee.'

"And then we start laughing. And the teacher says, get this, 'Look, you all hurt yourself, but what's crazy is if I say you all need the same thing to help you feel better. The same is true to help you learn. Sometimes you will need the same lesson. And sometimes you don't all need a Band-Aid for your knee.'

"I just feel like we're all getting Band-Aids for our knee right now," Jeremy finished.

Ball shot straight up. That was it, she thought. Not everyone in the school needed the same thing. Not the students. Not the parents. Not the teachers.

Then she thought some more. Maybe Jeremy needed some extra tutoring and longer afterschool hours. She couldn't afford everything through the school's budget, but what if she somehow shared resources with other schools? If she did that, then maybe she could get Jeremy and several other students the support they needed.

Different strokes for different folks.

And then she had an even better idea. Maybe Jeremy's mom couldn't take him to the family star-gazing night because of her work, but maybe Julia's parents could. Ball wouldn't be overt, of course, but perhaps a little nudge in the background might help set up a play date that day for Jeremy and Julia to work on a project in Mrs. Alvera's class.

And that brought a smile to Ball's face.

* * *

With so many recommendations in this book pointing to the importance of carving out separate, autonomous, and initially smaller spaces for educators to work with students and parents to reinvent schooling, readers may have some concerns about whether this approach will bifurcate and personalize schooling too much. Might this detract from the communal aspect of schooling and the importance of students and communities wrestling intentionally with the wonderful messiness of disagreements and the inherent diversity across America?

I worry about this, too. I believe that a core purpose of schooling is to help individuals learn that people can see things differently—and that those differences merit respect rather than persecution. School is also about learning to be a part of something larger than self. It should help individuals ask how they can best contribute to the world, from the civic to economic realms.

This work seems vital. Disagreements about schooling run deep. Many educators feel that questions around how schooling is done have never been more contentious. There are a wide range of views. Some fraction of people seem to believe that those differences merit persecution. From arguments around mask mandates to what schools are teaching, many educators feel they are in a constant tug of war with the public that impedes their ability to best serve students. Many parents and members of the public feel similarly.

Yet these current dynamics only strengthen the importance of the insights from our research on how to successfully transform enterprises. These insights draw on sound and tested theories of leadership and innovation.

Pulling from the successful experience of other sectors, what we see is that creating separate, autonomous spaces where the relevant stakeholders can come together to reinvent schooling is a vital part of the toolkit. The Jeremys and Julias of the world—as well as society more broadly—need that progress.

In Chapter 1 we reviewed the challenge that threat rigidity poses. To escape that rigidity, after framing something as a threat, an organization must reframe it as an opportunity by creating a separate team unencumbered by the organization's existing processes and priorities.

In reviewing the theory of interdependence and modularity, Chapter 3 shows how many students may need a different set of integrated supports to help them be academically successful and prepared for life after K–12 schooling. If we're serious about ensuring that all students have a fair shot at opportunity, these supports may require different schooling structures.

In Chapter 7, understanding the progress parents seek—their different Jobs to Be Done—illustrates that what parents prioritize from schooling may sometimes be in fundamental conflict with what other parents are seeking. Organizations that strive to be all things to all people by being good at many different Jobs tend to become one-size-fits-none organizations. These organizations make suboptimal decisions for any given group. Having separate organizational structures that have the freedom to optimize on any given Job to Be Done is critical.

The last chapter illustrates the importance of wielding the tool of separation to bring together the parties that *do* agree so that they can make progress, demonstrate success, and bring more people along over time.

RESOLVING THE PARADOX

How do we resolve the apparent paradox of needing separation to make progress in schools yet needing school to help people learn to respect those with different viewpoints?

Part of the answer is that people who are concerned that creating separate teams will lead to an overbifurcation and overpersonalization of schooling don't fully recognize both the challenge of the current conditions in American society and the role of community in the potential paths forward that this book suggests for schools.

Today's Existing Separation

People already segregate in American schooling.

The oldest form of school choice is where you buy your house. As Harvard Professor Paul Peterson wrote, "Choice is an inherent feature of the American education system. The right to a private education is guaranteed by the Constitution. And public schools allow families to choose their school when selecting the neighborhood in which to live."[2]

One notable result of the present system, however, is that individuals don't have the same set of choices of where to live because of differences in wealth. Families with money, the luck to have access to scholarships, or the fortune to benefit from certain public policies are also able to make choices that others can't. They can choose to enroll in school options that include Montessori, Waldorf, classical, Reggio Emilia, Quaker (Friends), Catholic, Jewish, Muslim, Christian, or even unschooling.

If school should be a place where the magic of the melting pot occurs in American society, one look at our fragmented country would suggest that it's not working.

In addition to the oft-noted racial and wealth segregation that occurs in society and ripples into schools, "98 to 99 percent of Americans live in areas segregated by partisanship."[3] That means that the vast majority of people in America live in areas where Republicans and Democrats don't mix. That segregation appears to be increasing—a trend that is, broadly speaking, the opposite of what society has experienced in racial segregation.[4] This means that people are choosing to live in places apart from people who think and vote differently from them.[5] That has an impact on schools, where students are less likely to mix with others who vote differently from their parents.

Cohesion and Community

Solutions that support all students don't have to mean the creation of a fragmented and deeply individualized education system. Far from it.

First, as discussed in Chapter 7, Jobs to Be Done do not segment based on demographics. Nor are a person's Jobs to Be Done fixed. They are fluid and change based on one's circumstances and priorities. Knowing a particular individual's demographic—which is a relatively static, unchanging set of descriptive characteristics—doesn't provide a window into what Job they hope school does. Given that a parent's Job to Be Done isn't based on race or wealth or political party, sorting by Job should allow students to learn alongside other learners from different backgrounds.

Even more promising, moving to a model of mastery-based learning where personalization and technology enable students to learn at the path and pace right for them can allow for an even greater mixing of students from a variety of backgrounds and at a variety of academic levels. Moving to this model breaks the traditional trade-off between learning and social promotion.

Instead, students can continue to learn whatever they need to do next while still having social experiences with a diverse group of other individuals. Mastery-based learning with personalization and technology also solves a few other problems, including that:

- Any individual's academic progress is likely to be uneven. A student may be ahead of what their "grade level" standards say they should be doing in math but behind in English Language Arts. Under this new system, educators don't have to promote or hold someone back across all material.

- A mix of students of different ages are able to learn more seamlessly together.

- Students can learn online with a mix of other students from around the world in synchronous and asynchronous environments. That means students do not have to be confined by their physical environment.

Having students learning at different levels and working on different concepts in a mastery-based model can be a perk because it creates the opportunity for students to serve as teachers and coaches for their peers. This is a wonderful way for students to solidify their mastery. Teaching something helps you learn it better. It can also help students further develop their academic skills, some of the habits of success, and leadership skills. For those worried about America's disinvestment in its gifted-and-talented programs and students, this system is a wonderful way to tackle that challenge without creating rigid categories that exclude those who may blossom later and unevenly. It allows all individuals to go deeper in areas of interest to them and to build their passions.

When we move from a zero-sum education system that pits people in competition against each other to a positive-sum world of schooling in which all individuals can learn from and support each other, it's easier to create a more cohesive, social experience that transcends some of the preference to segregate.

And given that a core Job to Be Done for most children is to have fun with their friends, any innovation that is isolating and too individualized *will not work*.

The recommendations in this book will often amount to the creation of schools within schools—places where students, families, and educators can work together to innovate and make progress, but remain part of a larger, permeable schooling community that represents something bigger and more diverse. Separating a team to innovate and make progress doesn't represent a permanent divider line. Recall how success and engagement in the Enlarged City School District of Middletown, New York caused more educators, students, and families to want to gravitate toward the exciting new models in action. Over time, blended learning became the way all schooling was done in Middletown, not just the way a portion of each school operated.

Significant success could ultimately move schools of the future to look more like community centers with a range of academic, health, and support services. In this new system, services and academics alike could be doled out in a flexible manner, with different resources, schedules, and supports for different students. Sometimes students would learn on-campus; often they might not. Their learning would not need to be confined by the four walls of a classroom. Schools could act as hubs to bring an array of people—both directly connected to schools and not—together around something larger that was designed to help all students make progress.

The road to that vision starts with small steps. Rather than impose a big vision of systems change that doesn't help individuals with their specific challenges, helping each child, teacher, and parent make progress as they define it will ameliorate their struggles, improve morale, ensure mastery for each child, and move us to a positive-sum school system over time. In this system, the measure would not be time, but progress, as each individual child chases their most daring dreams.

NOTES

1. I first heard a variation of this story from one of my children's teachers, Pamela Vernick. She heard it first from a third-grade teacher named Aimee here: https://www.upworthy.com/teaching-fairness (accessed November 16, 2021).
2. Paul Peterson, "Toward Equitable School Choice," Hoover Institution, December 1, 2020, https://www.hoover.org/research/toward-equitable-school-choice.
3. Christina Pazzanese, "Democrats and Republicans Do Live in Different Worlds," *Harvard Gazette*, March 16, 2021, https://news.harvard.edu/gazette/story/2021/03/democrats-and-republicans-live-in-partisan-bubbles-study-finds/.

4. See William H. Frey, "Black-White Segregation Edges Downward since 2000, Census Shows," Brookings Institution, December 17, 2018, https://www.brookings.edu/blog/the-avenue/2018/12/17/black-white-segregation-edges-downward-since-2000-census-shows/ and

5. Emily Badger, Kevin Quealy, and Josh Katz, "A Close-Up Picture of Partisan Segregation, Among 180 Million Voters," *New York Times*, March 17, 2021, https://www.nytimes.com/interactive/2021/03/17/upshot/partisan-segregation-maps.html.

Index

Page numbers followed by *f* refer to figures.